Medieval English and its Heritage

STUDIES IN ENGLISH MEDIEVAL LANGUAGE AND LITERATURE

Edited by Jacek Fisiak

Advisory Board:
John Anderson (Methoni, Greece), Norman Blake (Sheffield),
Ulrich Busse (Halle), Olga Fischer (Amsterdam),
Richard Hogg (Manchester), Dieter Kastovsky (Vienna),
Marcin Krygier (Poznań), Roger Lass (Cape Town),
Peter Lucas (Cambridge), Donka Minkova (Los Angeles),
Ruta Nagucka (Cracow), Akio Oizumi (Kyoto),
Katherine O'Brien O'Keeffe (Notre Dame, USA),
Matti Rissanen (Helsinki), Hans Sauer (Munich),
Liliana Sikorska (Poznań), Jeremy Smith (Glasgow)

Vol. 16

Frankfurt am Main · Berlin · Bern · Bruxelles · New York · Oxford · Wien

Nikolaus Ritt
Herbert Schendl
Christiane Dalton-Puffer
Dieter Kastovsky
(eds.)

Medieval English and its Heritage

Structure, Meaning
and Mechanisms of Change

PETER LANG
Europäischer Verlag der Wissenschaften

Bibliographic Information published by Die Deutsche Bibliothek
Die Deutsche Bibliothek lists this publication in the Deutsche Nationalbibliografie; detailed bibliographic data is available in the internet at <http://dnb.ddb.de>.

Gedruckt mit Unterstützung des Bundesministeriums
für Bildung, Wissenschaft und Kultur in Wien.

ISSN 1436-7521
ISBN 3-631-55006-5
US-ISBN 0-8204-9869-6

© Peter Lang GmbH
Europäischer Verlag der Wissenschaften
Frankfurt am Main 2006
All rights reserved.

All parts of this publication are protected by copyright. Any utilisation outside the strict limits of the copyright law, without the permission of the publisher, is forbidden and liable to prosecution. This applies in particular to reproductions, translations, microfilming, and storage and processing in electronic retrieval systems.

Printed in Germany 1 2 4 5 6 7

www.peterlang.de

Contents

Introduction vii
List of abbreviations xi

A. Phonology and morphology

Jeremy J. Smith
    Phonaesthesia, *Ablaut* and the history of the English
    demonstratives 1

Christian Liebl
    The A and O of a medieval English sound change:
    prolegomena to a study of the origins and early
    geographical diffusion of /ɑː/ > /ɔː/ 19

Julia Schlüter
    A small word of great interest:
    the allomorphy of the indefinite article as a diagnostic of
    sound change from the sixteenth to nineteenth centuries 37

B. Vocabulary

Philip Durkin
    Loanword etymologies in the third edition of the *OED*:
    the benefits of the application of a consistent
    methodology for the scholarly user 61

Michael Bilynsky
    Getting a diachronic view on synonymy:
    verbs and deverbatives 77

Ewa Ciszek
    -dōm in medieval English 105

Ferdinand von Mengden
    The peculiarities of the OE numeral system 125

Letizia Vezzosi
    From *agen* to *own* 147

C. Syntax and pragmatics

Ilse Wischer
    Grammaticalisation and language contact in the
    history of English: the evolution of the progressive form........165

W. Garrett Mitchener
    A mathematical model of the loss of verb-second in
    Middle English........189

Päivi Pahta and Arja Nurmi
    Code-switching in the *Helsinki Corpus*:
    a thousand years of multilingual practices........203

Tamás Eitler
    Audience rules: interspeaker accommodation and
    intraspeaker syntactic variation in Late Middle English........221

Index........237

Introduction

This volume offers linguistic contributions to the study of Early Englishes and their diachronic development. They originate in papers given at the 13th International Conference on English Historical Linguistics (ICEHL), which took place at the University of Vienna from 24-28 August 2004. Together with a second volume – published as *Syntax, style and grammatical norms: English from 1500-2000* in another Peter Lang series – they provide a good survey of issues that are currently discussed in English historical linguistics.

While the temporal focus of this volume is on Old and Middle English with occasional excursions into the Early Modern period, its coverage in terms of linguistic phenomena is fairly comprehensive. It discusses phonological and morphological issues, problems in lexicology, as well as syntactic and pragmatic topics. Some papers address long established questions from new perspectives, while others report new empirical findings, point out new directions for research, demonstrate how new technologies and research methods can be made relevant for the historical study of English, and/or manage to revise established scholarly views. All papers, however, represent original and innovative contributions to the discipline.

The volume is divided into three parts. The first contains three articles on phonological and morphological questions. Jeremy Smith focuses on the history of the English demonstratives and discusses the role which phonaesthesia may have played in it. He thus re-opens the discussion of an old, but still unresolved question: is the relationship between the phonological signifiers and the morpho-semantic signifieds that make up morphological and/or lexical signs really as arbitrary as post-Saussurean dogma suggests? Smith adduces both data and arguments to suggest that it is not, and that the enquiry into the role which sound symbolism may play in the evolution of stable sound-meaning pairings still represents a worthwhile endeavour.

Christian Liebl undertakes a detailed empirical investigation into the early geographical diffusion of the phonemic shift of OE /ɑː/ > /ɔː/. He shows that the *o*-spellings in both medieval manuscripts and place-names seem to confirm an 11th-century date for the change, but that traditional views as to the early stages of the spread of this innovation are not entirely borne out by the evidence. He suggests that the change, rather than spreading from the South to the North, might have started more or less simultaneously in several counties of the South and Midlands.

Julia Schlüter charts the historical development of word initial /h/ in the Early Modern period. She demonstrates how this phoneme, which had all but disappeared from English at the end of the middle ages, managed to re-establish itself firmly in English phonotactics. Empirically, her investigation is based on a number of digital text corpora, in which she traces the changing distribution of *a* and *an* before words with potential /h/-onsets. Theoretically, she relates the reestablishment of /h/ in onsets to the emergence of new word initial /j/-glides and attributes both developments to a tendency to (re-) introduce or strengthen consonantal onsets in formerly V-initial lexemes.

Section two, which focuses on lexical issues is opened by Philip Durkin's contribution, which provides information which will be of use to the *OED*'s readership. It explains the principles on which loan word etymologies have been established by the editorial team of the dictionary, and discusses, in particular, the extent to which the histories of loan words in their respective source languages need to be pursued for what is still essentially a dictionary of English.

Michael Bilynsky's paper is also concerned with the *OED*, but from the point of view of a linguist mining it as a source of evidence on the historical emergence and the development of (near-)synonymic relationships. He describes how a diachronic thesaurus can be built from *OED* entries, and illustrates what kind of questions can be addressed to it. In particular, he reports on a computer aided method for comparing the historical expansion of sets of near-synonyms to that of sets of (predictably also synonymous) words derived from them, and for quantifying the observable similarities and differences.

Ewa Ciszek shows how data from historical dictionaries and digital corpora can be used in order to revise established wisdom concerning the development of the suffix *–dom*, its productivity in word formation, and the senses which it could take during the OE and ME periods.

Ferdinand von Mengden takes a new look at the widespread notion that oddities in the OE system of cardinal numbers (such as *hund-teon-tig* 'ten-ty' for 100, *hund-endlef-tig* 'eleven-ty' for 110, or *hund-twelf-tig* 'twelve-ty' for 120) may reflect a duo-decimal rather than a decimal counting system. Discussing the relation between numerical systems and their linguistic expressions in great depth, he shows that this view is wrong.

Letizia Vezzosi's contribution closes the lexical section of this volume and provides a smooth transition to the final part. On the basis of extensive evidence from a number of historical corpora, Vezzosi describes how and when the lineage established by OE *agen*, ME *awen/agen* and ModE *own* began to develop a branch that could be used as a functional word, that is to say, an identity or phoric marker, whose function and occurrence is closely linked to the focussed identity marker or intensifier *himself*. She sees the development as a grammaticalisation process with strong pragmatic motivations.

The final group of papers deals with syntactic as well as social and pragmatic phenomena. Ilse Wischer's paper surveys current grammaticalisation research, and argues for considering the grammaticalisation framework as a theory in its own right. Wischer applies the theory to the evolution of the English progressive form, charts its grammaticalisation path, suggests a double scenario for the establishment of a periphrastic construction and the subsequent emergence of a new grammatical category, and discusses the role of language contact in the process.

Garret Mitchener presents a mathematical model of David Lightfoot's hypothesis that the loss of the verb-second rule in Middle English resulted from contact between a northern dialect with such a rule, and a southern dialect with a slightly different word order, as northern children would cease to hear enough cue sentences for the acquisition of verb-second, so that their dialect would become extinct. The model demonstrates how dynamical systems theory can be used to study language change.

Päivi Pahta and Arja Nurmi examine code-switching between English and other languages in a long diachronic perspective. Their study provides a quantitative and qualitative analysis of code-switching in the entire *Helsinki Corpus*, and focuses on the relationship of switching practices with the language-external background information coded into the corpus in the form of textual parameters. They demonstrate that switching was most strongly favoured in religious and scientific texts.

Tamás Eitler investigates word order in four late ME prose texts by John Capgrave and discusses the role which accommodation to target audiences may play for syntactic variation within an individual speaker's usage. He argues that it is likely to be the strongest determining factor underlying such variation, and shows that Capgrave's usage reflects a grammar internal competition between a local and a delocalised type of syntactic order.

The variety and the quality of all contributions to this volume show how vital the discipline of English historical linguistics is, and we would like to express our gratitude to all authors. We also owe thanks to a number of other people and institutions, however. Thus, we gratefully acknowledge the substantial financial support this book has received from the Austrian Ministry of Education, Science and Culture. We thank the numerous colleagues who acted as reviewers on the submitted manuscripts and who, naturally, have to remain anonymous here. We thank Jacek Fisiak, for offering to publish this volume in his *Studies in English Medieval Language and Literature*, and Norbert Willenpart from Peter Lang Publishers for his competent support. Julia Hüttner and Ursula Lutzky helped in the first stages of the editorial process. Theresa Illés competently supervised the copy-editing process and efficiently saw to it that the manuscripts turned into camera-ready copy. Any remaining imperfections are our own responsibility.

NIKOLAUS RITT
HERBERT SCHENDL
CHRISTIANE DALTON-PUFFER
DIETER KASTOVSKY

List of abbreviations

AF	Anglo-French
CF	Central French
EME	Early Middle English
EModE	Early Modern English
Goth.	Gothic
Lat.	Latin
LME	Late Middle English
LModE	Late Modern English
LOE	Late Old English
ME	Middle English
ModE	Modern English
OE	Old English
OF	Old French
OHG	Old High German
ON	Old Norse
PDE	Present-Day English
proto-Gmc.	proto-Germanic
WS	West Saxon

Jeremy J. Smith
Phonaesthesia, *Ablaut* and the history of the English demonstratives

1. THESE and THOSE

A classic problem in the history of English is the emergence of the modern standard English demonstrative determiners, proximal THESE and distal THOSE, distinguished formally by *Ablaut*. From a broad historical perspective these are 'false' forms, a point easily demonstrated. Table 1 displays the West Saxon (WS) and present-day standard English paradigms, and two Middle English (ME) sets, Early ME (represented by the two hands, A and B, in the Caligula text of *The Owl and the Nightingale*), and Late ME (represented by the Ellesmere manuscript of the *Canterbury Tales*). It should be noted that this table does not imply a linear progression; WS is hardly the ancestor of present-day standard English, and there is no linear dialect-relationship between the Caligula text (copied in the South-West Midlands) and the London English represented by the Ellesmere manuscript.

Table 1

WS	PDE	O&N A	O&N B	LME
þā	those	þo	þeo	tho
þās	these	þos	þeos	thise
Cf. *stān* > 'stone', *hām* > 'home'				

The Present-Day English (PDE) standard usage seems to have emerged through the operation of analogy, and the usual narrative explanation for the development may be summed up as follows. During the ME period, analogous forms arose. *þā* developed in the south and Midlands as *þo*, but this form began, towards the end of the ME period, to clash with *though* etc., as the final *gh* ceased to be pronounced. An alternative form was available, since *þās* (with reflexes such as *þos*) had arisen for THOSE as the *-s* marker for plurality spread across the demonstrative system. However, *þās* in turn clashed with *þās* for THESE. This latter clash encouraged the selection, from the pool of available variants, of an alternative analogous formation for THESE of the *thise-/these*-type whereby plurality was signalled by the addition of final *-e*, most probably an extension of the adjectival paradigm available in southern English dialects. Final *-e* was lost earlier in northern dialects, but alternative variants, derived from Norse, were available there, and thus an alternative path was followed in those areas. Selection of variables would then follow. Such a process of functional selection, of course, fits with an evolutionary model of linguistic development, whereby systemically-governed, therapeutically-driven selection is made from a pool of available variant forms. (See Millar 2000:288-289, and references there cited.)

Of course there were many alternative paths that could have been taken, and new sources of data give us a much fuller picture. The *Survey of English Dialects* (*SED*), for instance, gives us information about a wide range of twentieth-century systems, some of which take account of an extra, 'more distal' distinction *yonder*. This material appears in Table 2.

Table 2

Area	THESE	THOSE	YONDER
Essex	*theys*	*they*	--
Gloucestershire	*thick*	*they*	*they over there, thick over there*
Shropshire	*thesen*	*thosen*	*thosen yonder*
Wiltshire	*theasum*	*thick, they*	*they over there, thick (over) there*
Yorkshire	*these here thir*	*thore*	*yon*

We might also note the Yorkshire adjectival distinction between proximal *these here small whippletrees* on the one hand and distal *yon turnips, them baulks* on the other.

We can also now add, as an historical comparison, some evidence from the *Linguistic Atlas of Late Mediaeval English* (*LALME*). The range of recorded variation in late ME is very wide in comparison with that recorded in *SED*, whose *Grammar* is largely drawn from the *Incidental Material*; *LALME* records no fewer than forty-seven separate variants for THESE alone, ranging from widespread *þese* to very local *dese* (found in Kent and Sussex). In some areas, the system was fairly stable, e.g. Norfolk/Cambridgeshire/Ely, where the dominant system was as appears in Table 3.

Table 3

THOSE:	*tho, yo, þo*
THESE:	*these, yese, þes, þese*

However, there were areas of greater complexity, notably in border regions between varieties. (Of course, in a sense every region is a border region, for the ME evidence demonstrates – just as in PDE dialects – a pattern of overlapping distributions; however, some regions are more 'borderish' than others.) A good example of a complex border area is the West Riding of Yorkshire, where we find a wide range of variation. These variants appear in Table 4. The numbers in brackets refer to the number of texts in which the form survives. As a crude indicator of frequency, those forms which survive in ten or more texts have been underlined.[1]

Table 4

THESE
theis (1), ther (1), thes (8), these (9), theyse (1), thies (1), thir (2), this (3), thise (6), thyr (1), thys (3), thyse (3), yair (1), yees (4), yeir (2), yeis (1), yeise (1), yer (8), yer (2), yere (4), y^{es} (5), yese (19), ye3 (1), yhese (4), yier (1), yies (4), y^{i}es (1), yiese (1), yir (11), yis (14), yise (16), þes (6), þese (8), þe3 (1), þir (2), þis (4), þise (5), þuse (1), þyse (1), 3es (1)
THOSE
tha (1), thai (1), thaise (1), thas (1), tho (4), thoo (1), thos (1), those (3), ya (14), yaa (3), yai (1), yais (2), yaise (1), yas (7), yase (7), yay (1), yho (1), yo (22), y^o (1), yoo (5), yos (7), yo^s (1), yose (11), þa (2), þaa (1), þaas (1), þai (1), þar (1), þas (1), þase (1), þo (8), þoo (4), þoos (1), þos (6), þose (6)

---

[1] The 'more distal' form *yon*, which is cited by *The Middle English Dictionary* (*MED*) as "chiefly Northern" (s.v. *yon*), has not been included in Table 4. Citations for *yon*-type forms are given in the *MED* for a number of northern texts, including the Vespasian text of the *Cursor Mundi*, the Thornton manuscript and *The Wars of Alexander*. The operation of such systems beyond the twofold one is of course commonplace in the Indo-European languages, and has been discussed at least as far back as Karl Brugmann (cf. Szemerenyi 1996:204 and references there cited).

4   Jeremy J. Smith

There is obviously a good deal of what might be termed 'noise' in Table 4, i.e. sporadically-occurring forms found only in a few texts. But if forms only rarely recorded, or recorded as less common variables, are set aside, then a more coherent picture may be discerned, and this coherent pattern is offered in Table 5. Of course, such a strategy has the potential to be distorting; this noise is an important part of the story, and there are some intermediate forms (e.g. *yase* for THOSE) which are of considerable interest.[2]

It will be observed from Table 5 that the most commonly recorded form for THESE is *yese*, with *yise* and *yir* following in frequency, and the most commonly recorded form for THOSE is *yo*, with *ya* and *yose* following.

Table 5

THESE	
Form	Texts (by *LALME* Linguistic Profile number)
yese	(27) (53) (175) 191 200 ((358)) 364 373 398 406 ((473)) 496 526 589 601 603 604 (614) 1102
yise	(53) 175 204 234 (364) 405 473 474 494 ((496)) 500 526 (601) 603 605 608
yir	18 32 53 410 454 460 ((473)) ((474)) ((500)) 526 592
THOSE	
Form	Texts
yo	((27)) 30 ((32)) 115 ((191)) 200 204 ((234)) ((364)) 405 406 ((454)) (473) 474 ((488)) 494 500 589 ((592)) 601 603 605
ya	(4) 32 191 358 364 410 ((460)) ((473)) ((526)) 592 598 603 607 1349
yose	27 175 200 ((204)) ((234)) 405 454 (473) 477 (496) 603
Texts with *yese/yo* as main forms: 200 406 589 601 603	
Texts with *yese/ya* as main forms: 191 364 603	
Texts with *yese/yose* as main forms: 200 603	
Texts with *yise/yo* as main forms: 204 405 474 494 500 603 605	
Texts with *yise/ya* as main forms: 603	
Texts with *yise/yose* as main forms: 405 603	
Texts with *yir/yo* as main forms: none[3]	
Texts with *yir/ya* as main forms: 32 410 592	
Texts with *yir/yose* as main forms: 454	

---

[2] These forms require more attention than they will receive here; I hope to address such problems in the future.
[3] The *yir/yo* combination does appear as a minor system in several texts, viz. Linguistic Profiles 32, 4545, 474, 500 and 502 (of those cited above).

If this material is placed on a schematic map, an interesting distribution results. The map places these texts according to their *LALME* localisations. Bearing in mind that linguistic systems are not necessarily constrained by the county boundaries of government administrators, we can distinguish four major systems in the West Riding. These systems are summarised in Table 6.

Table 6

NW	Central N	NE	Central/Southern
yese/yo	*yese/ya*	*yir/ya*	*yise/yo*

Text 454 (with *yir/yose*) presents a system whose focus is on the Lancashire side of the Yorkshire border, while the mixture of systems in Text 603, no single system is dominant there, represents the kind of confusion which might be expected in intermediate zones.

The *yese/ya* system is a fairly clear compromise between the NW and NE systems.

Rather nicely, these systems map quite neatly onto what we can reconstruct of contemporary settlement patterns. The NW and NE systems are separated by an area of unsettled high ground, and there is a physical connexion – the river-system – between the users (see Darby and Versey 1975: maps 58-61).

The *yir*-type form for THESE is traditionally seen as deriving from Old Norse *þeir*, *þeir(r)a*, – a point made by Trygve Heltviet in the standard study of the form (Heltviet 1953:92-96) – and it is not surprising that it appears in the 'core' area of Norse settlement, the Great Scandinavian Belt. These Norse forms are, of course, generally – if not universally – seen as the ancestors of PDE *they*, *their* as well.

In Old Norse (Gordon 1957:§§109, 111), the paradigms for the third person personal and the demonstrative pronouns were identical in the plural because, as E.V. Gordon says, "the plu[rals of the third person personal pronouns in Old Norse were] originally [and continued in use as] demonstrative pronouns". The Old Norse third person plural forms meaning 'they' and 'their', therefore, functioned also as the plural demonstrative meaning 'those' (King 1997:169).

Intriguingly, of course, *þir* in the West Riding seems to be the proximal, not the distal form, and it is possibly this apparent discrepancy which caused Joseph and Elizabeth Wright to insert a question mark when they cited the origins of the form:

> From the fourteenth century onwards the northern dialects also had *þir* (? from ON. *þeir*) as well as the variants *þire, þeir(e), þair, þier, þer(e), þar(e)*, which has remained in the dialects of Scotland and the northern counties of England down to the present day. (Wright and Wright 1928:171)

It seems likely that the Norse-derived form was perceived as the emphatic form, reinterpreted as a proximal usage. Such differentiations are commonplace, as Leonard Bloomfield pointed out.[4] A comparable distinction may be observed, for example, in Gothic, which distinguishes a 'simple' demonstrative and a 'compound' one – the latter being more emphatic – and "stronger deictic force" (Prokosch 1939:267) seems to have required a kind of compounding using whatever materials lay to hand. Modern German offers the most obvious example of a similar system, where the demonstrative is, as Rudi Keller has said, 'usually' *der/die/das*, with *dieser/jener* retained for more emphatic use (Keller 1974:521).

The semantics of THIS in Middle English would repay closer examination; Chaucer, after all, refers to *this sely carpenter* etc., not *that carpenter*. Something similar seems to be happening in Old English given that *se* etc. is really THE/THAT, as Bruce Mitchell among others has flagged (1985:127), and it is likely that a shift in semantics may be another part of the complex story of the demonstratives, triggering the timing of the change to a clearer proximal/distal distinction.

It may be noted that Mitchell (1985:127) considers this as something to "be left to the lexicographer" (see also Szemerenyi 1996:204-205; on the compounding of the ancient *to-* and *so-*types, and, for the development in Middle English, see importantly Millar 2000). However, there is another, not necessarily mutually exclusive, possibility for the selection of the *thir*-form for proximal use; this possibility will be discussed towards the end of section 1.

---

[4] "Where a speaker knows two rival forms, they differ in connotation, since he has heard them from different persons and under different circumstances" (1935:394).

It is clear that determiners are especially susceptible to processes of analogy and transfer and conflation, e.g. *thon* for *yon* in some varieties of present-day Scots; the extension of an *-e* inflexion to *this* to produce *thise*, *these* in Middle English; the extension of *-r* to produce present-day Yorkshire *thore*; and indeed the origin of the proximal (seen as emphatic) demonstrative in Old English and Gothic. The key thing to note is that all these operations produce variants, which are in turn available for functional selection.

Selection from this variational pool is hardly conscious, but part of the pragmatic negotiation of meaning through monitoring which underpins communication. From these acts of negotiation systems emerge. Some of these systems will survive for a period and thus become available for scholarly observation, being sustained over time and developing in their own way; it is fairly clear that the modern Yorkshire system recorded in *SED* (*thir/thore*) can be seen as deriving rather nicely, by analogy and other phenomena, from one of the systems current in the ME materials of the West Riding. Other systems do not survive.

Why some systems are retained and others have gone away is of course a notorious problem in historical linguistics. Some would argue that functional issues are important here, and I myself would favour a weakish form of functionalism, based on a simple communicative notion: if a speaker uses a form which causes confusion to the hearer then a speaker looks for an alternative mode of expression (cf. Smith 1996:10-11 and references there cited; with reference to demonstratives, see Millar 2000).

In principle, disambiguation between THOSE and THESE could be made by the presence of *-s*, giving *tho - *those; this pattern is, as has already been noted, what might be expected as a straightforward development of OE *þā* - *þās*. Of course the analogous addition of *-s* to *tho*-type forms is a fairly predictable phenomenon for flagging plurality, and can be visualised as a likely variable.

Part of the explanation for the favouring of *-s* types for distal THOSE may have to do with the clash with the word THOUGH as the *gh*-element disappeared in speech, towards the end of the ME period in the South Midlands, flagged by forms such as *þow*, a minor late ME variable; such a suggestion has been made by Robert Millar (2000: 288-289).

Although the two forms belong to different word-classes the opportunities for such a clash exist. Michael Samuels has cited something rather comparable, in the selection of *though* in place of *theigh*-forms for THOUGH, which he linked to propinquity with *they* (for THEY); Samuels cites a good deal of late ME evidence for usages of *they* for both THOUGH and THEY, which – it might be argued – would seem to require therapeutic remedy (Samuels 1972:71). The problem would not arise in those dialects, chiefly northern ones, where an unrounded vowel was retained for THOSE; nor would it arise in those north Midland dialects where another form for THOUGH seems to have arisen early, viz. *þof*.

However, such an explanation would not account for the adoption of *e*-type proximals fairly early on – not as a response to the selection of *-s* type distals – in what looks like a very stable system (i.e. that exemplified in Table 3). Nor would such an explanation account for the adoption of *i*-type forms, e.g. *yir*, in the West Riding.

The key point to make here is that developments are sustained in the history of a language – in general – not for single reasons, but for many reasons: multi-factorial conditioning (see Samuels 1972: chapter 1, *passim*).

It will be argued here that the development of PDE *these/those* or *thir/thore* alternations was favoured, in part at least, by the phonaesthetic associations of front-back vowel-alternation in vowels. Such associations are also found in close-mid alternations, as demonstrated by the present-day Scots alternation *thir-thae*[5] or, for that matter, the Gloucestershire *thick-they* distinction. These phonaesthetic considerations will now be discussed.

2. Sound-symbolism

Linguists have often felt uneasy about sound-symbolism. Not only is the phenomenon hard to classify in terms of 'levels of language' – is it

---

[5] A distinction favoured by the fact that, historically, Scots lacked mid and low long back vowels.

part of morphology or phonology or lexicology? – but also the notion seems, at first sight, to go against a key Saussurean axiom: "The bond between the signifier and the signified is arbitrary [...] The idea of 'sister' is not linked by any inner relationship to the succession of sounds [...] which serves as its signifier" (Saussure 1974:67).

Although Saussure's statement is widely accepted among linguists, there has nevertheless always been an interest in sound-symbolism, generally from those scholars who have worked aslant the fashionable mainstream of linguistic (and literary) enquiry. Perhaps the most important work in this area, from distinct perspectives, was undertaken by Roman Jakobson and J.R. Firth in the middle of the twentieth century. Interestingly, both scholars, somewhat against the grain of their contemporaries, placed issues of meaning at the centre of their interests (see Firth 1964, Jakobson and Waugh 1979). It is only recently that there has been a revival in interest in questions of 'iconicity' in language.

It is generally accepted that there are two kinds of sound-symbolism: onomatopoeia and phonaesthesia. Onomatopoeia is widely understood, and might be exemplified by the birds in the ME alliterative poem *Sir Gawain and the Green Knight* who

> pitosly þer piped for pyne of þe colde (*Sir Gawain* line 747)

Piped, especially in its ME pronunciation, would seem to be quite an accurate representation of the sound the birds are supposed to have made. However, as is very well-known, human languages represent the noises of animals differently. It would seem that onomatopoeic elements are themselves essentially conventional.

Phonaesthesia is a more complex matter, though it has been noticed for a long time.[6] It may be defined as a phenomenon whereby the presence of a particular phonological component seems to correspond regularly – though not consistently – to one particular semantic component. For example, the element (J.R.Firth called it a 'phonaestheme') *gr-*, shared by *grudge, gruff, grumble, gripe, grizzle,*

---

[6] The earliest explicit discussion of the phenomenon is possibly that in John Wallis' *Grammatica Linguae Anglicanae* of 1653.

grim, grunt seems to signal a common semantic component of rudeness, ill-temper and/or taciturnity in the meaning of these words. Now it is easy to find counter-examples – *great* and *grin*, perhaps, although – interestingly – *grin* according to the *Oxford English Dictionary* had an older meaning, "bare one's teeth in rage" (s.v. *grin*). Such counter-examples have caused some linguists to dismiss the phenomenon as linguistically trivial.

Nevertheless, the existence of phonaesthetic patterns would seem to be confirmed from the evidence supplied by large-scale corpora or databases. Thus, for instance, the near-synonyms *begin* and *start* might be examined. Most native speakers of English would hold that *start* is the word used when the act of inception is sudden (cf. *starting pistol* as opposed to **beginning pistol*), and this perception is confirmed through analysis of the form's occurrences in the major PDE corpora, e.g. the *British National Corpus www.natcorp.ox.ac.uk/*. Part of the reason for the choice of *starting* rather than *beginning* in this collocation must have to do with the semantic range covered by the *st-* phonaestheme, and this has been demonstrated by (among others) Liz Reay in her work derived from the *Historical Thesaurus of English* (Reay 1991).[7]

Now that fuzziness and prototypicality rather than clear-cut categorisation are more part of the mainstream of linguistic scholarship, the phenomenon has attracted attention once again. David Crystal, for instance, sees the process as one of extension, whereby "associations [which] may have been accidental at first ... [were] extended to other words of similar meaning" (Crystal 1995:251); thus the basic Saussurean principle of the arbitrary nature of signs is retained. As Firth put it, the notion of phonaesthesia is

> not to be interpreted as a theory of inherent sound symbolism. [...] W]ith the doubtful exception of certain sibilant consonants, there would appear to be no inherent phonaesthetic value in any speech sound. It is all a matter of habit. (Firth 1964:187)

---

[7] See also Käsmann (1992), Reay (1994), Smith (2000) for discussion of other phonaesthetic clusters, e.g. /sl/.

3. Classifying the phonaestheme

The problem of classification remains, of course, and is a complex one: where can phonaesthetics be placed within the levels of language traditionally distinguished? Does a phoneme fulfil (for instance) George Yule's definition of the morpheme, as "... a minimal unit of meaning or grammatical function" (Yule 1996:75)? It is hard to answer this question; but it is not easy to locate phonaesthesia within phonological enquiry either. Like many of the topics which interested Firth, it seems to straddle the traditional 'divisions' adopted by linguists, and resists easy formalisation.

At one time, this inability to locate phonaesthesia in relation to the major levels of language would have been disconcerting. However, the insights of cognitive linguists have demonstrated that an Aristotelian emphasis on discrete categories does not work anyway; as John Taylor has put it,

> Prototype categories have a flexibility, unknown to Aristotelian categories, in being able to accommodate new, hitherto unfamiliar data. With only Aristotelian categories at our disposal, new data would often demand, for their categorization, the creation of new categories, or a redefinition of existing categories. On the other hand, new entities and new experiences can be readily associated, perhaps as peripheral members, to a prototype category, without necessarily causing any fundamental restructuring of the category system ... (Taylor 1995:53)

So the worry about categories, with reference to phonaesthemes, could perhaps be set aside as simply an index of our limited ability to categorise complex phenomena. Just as participles span the verb/adjective divide, or as metaphor sits oddly askew with regard to traditional linguistic enquiry and represents "something of an embarrassment to generative linguists", as Taylor has phrased it (1995:130), so phonaesthesia seems to span the division between phonology and morphology.

It may be argued, though, that this difficulty in classifying the phenomenon does not make it any less useful a notion in accounting for historical developments, and it is to a demonstration of its usefulness for our understanding of the history of THESE/THOSE that this paper will now turn.

4. *Ablaut* and phonaesthesia

A phonaesthetic connexion of front/close vowels with nearness and back/low ones with distance has been made by many scholars, including (interestingly) significant popularisers such as Steven Pinker. Although he did not use the term "phonaesthesia", Pinker has drawn the parallel in *The Language Instinct*:

> ... words that connote me-here-now tend to have higher and fronter vowels than words that connote distance from 'me': *me* versus *you*, *here* versus *there*, *this* versus *that*. (Pinker 1994:167)

At one point, Pinker comes close to linking particular sounds to intrinsic properties:

> When the tongue is high and at the front of the mouth, it makes a small resonant cavity there that amplifies some higher frequencies, and the resulting vowels like *ee* and *i* (as in *bit*) remind people of little things. When the tongue is low and to the back, it makes a large resonant cavity that amplifies some lower frequencies, and the resulting vowels like *a* in *father* and *o* in *core* and in *cot* remind people of large things. Thus mice are *teeny* and *squeak*, but elephants are *humongous* and *roar*. (Pinker 1994:167)

An association rather like this underpins Michael Samuels' discussion of the exceptions to mid-vowel raising in the seventeenth century, whereby most words with medial <ea> underwent a change from /ɛː/ to /eː/, as in PDE *meat, peal, ream, reap* beside *great, steak, break, yea*. Samuels notes (inter alia) the phonaesthetic associations of /iːt/ vs. /-eːt/: /-iːt/ suggests "smallness, daintiness, politeness, dexterity" (*feat, fleet, neat, sweet* etc.), whereas /-eːt/ "suggests the opposite –size, expanse, tangibility, grossness" (*freight, straight, weight* etc.) (Samuels 1972:152).

Given such associations, it would seem clear that frontness and nearness go together. It is, in Firth's words, a matter of habit. It is perhaps not quite so surprising, therefore, that, in standard use, proximal THESE should be *these*, and distal THOSE should be *those*. It would seem at least arguable that the front/back formal distinction which arose as a result of analogy was favoured because of the phonaesthetic associations of the vowels in THESE/THOSE. And indeed something like this explanation – though without theoretical orientation or support from large corpora of data – was argued by Otto Jespersen as long ago as 1922 (1922:402-403; see also Smith 1996:46).

Obviously this argument is hard to prove in the way, but then historical linguistics, like other branches of history, typically begins with hypothetical inference or abduction, followed by testing (see Anttila 1989:196-198). There is indeed some supporting evidence for the semantic role of front/close - back/open vowel-distinctions, to be derived from the history of *Ablaut* variation in the Germanic languages.

One of the most famous discussions of *Ablaut* in the scholarly literature is Prokosch's discussion of its origins, in his *Comparative Germanic Grammar*:

> American nursery talk offers an amusing illustration. A little steam train tries to climb a hill and says cheerfully, 'I think I can, I think I can.' But the hill is too steep, the poor little engine slides back and says sadly, 'I thought I could, I thought I could.' The front vowels [ɪ æ] aptly characterize the active interest in the successful performance, the back vowels [ɔ ʊ] the melancholy retrospect to what might have been. (Prokosch 1939:122)

And Prokosch goes on to cite some contemporary experimental work in "phonetic symbolism" (a phrase, interestingly, which both he and Pinker use) by Sapir and others:

> ... statistics show a definite trend to associate back vowels with concepts of large or dark, front vowels with concepts of small or bright. Obviously, this can be observed only in paired nonsense words, since in actual languages the action of phonetic laws has greatly modified the original conditions. (Prokosch 1939:122)

This account could very easily be recouched in terms of phonaesthetics (cf. Firth's discussion of the 'meaning' of the nonsense forms *oombaloo* and *kikiriki*; see Firth 1957:192-193).

Prokosch's anecdote is a footnote in a much larger discussion, which goes on to note that the distribution of *e*- and *o*-grades in Proto-Indo-European seems to demonstrate an interesting correlation: the *e*-grade, says Prokosch (1939:122), "is characteristic primarily of the present tense of thematic verbs of light bases", while the *o*-grade "belongs chiefly to the singular of the perfect and to various types of verbal nouns and root nouns". This correlation could be seen in grammatical terms, but it is worth recalling that grammar, like the lexicon, is simply a method of expressing meaning, or semantics (see Smith 1996:4). The phonaesthetic connexion is thus implicit, if not explicit, in Prokosch's discussion.

Prokosch's 'explanation' of *Ablaut* has, oddly, never really been superseded. The scholarly literature since has concentrated on discussing how the variant forms might have emerged (e.g. through discussions of pitch/accent relationships), but the process involved in the selection of those forms, and their assignment to distinct semantic categories seems to have been (comparatively) rarely addressed since the nineteenth century, possibly because semantics has been something of a poor relation in historical study. It would seem at least arguable, given the association of particular sounds with particular meanings, that the notion of phonaesthesia offers a useful way of accounting for the pattern. Certainly there seem to be very well-established, long-term correspondences between *Ablaut* and particular semantic categories which are hard to ignore. For instance, we might look at the EModE pattern of strong verbs (see Table 7).

Table 7

write – wrote
creep – crope[8]
bind – bound
bear – bore (beside *bare*)
tread – trod (beside *trad*)
shake – shook

As Michael Samuels has suggested in another context, "Surely we ought at least to consider whether the forms were phonetically and

---

[8] Cf. PDE 'standard' *crept*. *Crope* is recorded as a dialectal form in *SED* (La Do Ha).

phonaesthetically suited to carry their meaning?" (1987:246). The history of THESE and THOSE, with which this paper began, can thus be seen as part of a larger, persisting pattern in the history of not only the English language.

Appendix

Schematic map of forms for THESE/THOSE in the West Riding of Yorkshire (for full details and precise localisations, see *LALME*).

References

Anttila, Raimo. 1989. *Historical and comparative linguistics*. Amsterdam: Benjamins.
Bloomfield, Leonard. 1935. *Language*. London: Allen and Unwin.
Crystal, David. 1995. *The Cambridge encyclopedia of the English language*. Cambridge: CUP.
Darby, Henry C. and George R. Versey. 1975. *Domesday Gazeteer*. Cambridge: CUP.
de Saussure, Ferdinand. [1974]. *Course in general linguistics*. Transl. by Wade Baskin. Glasgow: Fontana.
Firth, John R. 1957. "Modes of meaning". In: *Papers in linguistics 1934-1951*. London: OUP: 190-215.
Firth, John R. 1964. *Speech*. Oxford: OUP.

Gordon, Eric V. 1957. *An introduction to Old Norse*. Oxford: Clarendon.
Heltviet, Trygve. 1953. *Studies in English demonstrative pronouns*. Oslo: Akademisk Forlag.
Jakobson, Roman and Linda Waugh. 1979. *The sound shape of language*. Brighton: Harvester Press.
Jespersen, Otto. 1922. *Language: its nature, development and origin*. London: Allen and Unwin.
Käsmann, Hans. 1992. "Das englische Phonäesthem *sl-*". *Anglia* 110: 307-346.
King, Anne. 1997. "The inflexional morphology of Older Scots". In: Jones, Charles (ed.). *The Edinburgh history of the Scots language*. Edinburgh: Edinburgh University Press: 156-181.
Keller, Rudi. 1974. *The German language*. London: Faber and Faber.
LALME = McIntosh, Angus, Michael L. Samuels and Michael Benskin, with Margaret Laing, Keith Williamson. 1986. *A linguistic atlas of late mediaeval English*. Aberdeen: Aberdeen University Press.
MED = *Middle English Dictionary*. On-line: <http://ets.umdl.umich.edu/m/mec/>
Millar, Robert. 2000. *System collapse, system rebirth: the demonstrative pronouns of English 900-1350 and the birth of the definite article*. Lang: Bern.
Mitchell, Bruce. 1985. *Old English syntax*. Oxford: Clarendon.
OED = *Oxford English Dictionary*. On-line: <http://dictionary.oed.com/>
Pinker, Steven. 1994. *The language instinct*. Harmondsworth: Penguin.
Prokosch, Eduard. 1939. *A comparative Germanic grammar*. Philadelphia: Linguistic Society of America.
Reay, Irene Elizabeth. 1991. *A lexical analysis of metaphor and phonaestheme*. PhD dissertation, University of Glasgow.
Reay, Irene Elizabeth. 1994. "Sound symbolism". In: Asher, Ron and James M. Y. Simpson (eds.). *An encyclopedia of language and linguistics*. Oxford: Pergamon: 4064-4070.
Samuels, Michael L. 1972. *Linguistic evolution*. Cambridge: CUP.
Samuels, Michael L. 1987. "The status of the functional approach". In: Koopman, Willem, Frederike van der Leek, Olga Fischer and Roger Eaton (eds.). *Explanation and language change*. Amsterdam: Benjamins: 239-250.
SED = Clive Upton, David Parry and John D. A. Widdowson. 1994. *Survey of English dialects: the dictionary and grammar*. London: Routledge.
Smith, Jeremy J. 1996. *An historical study of English*. London: Routledge.
Smith, Jeremy J. 2000. "Semantics and metrical form in *Sir Gawain and the Green Knight*". In: Powell, Susan and Jeremy J. Smith (eds.). *New perspectives on Middle English texts*. Cambridge: Brewer: 87-103.
Szemerenyi, Oswald. 1996. *Introduction to Indo-European linguistics*. Oxford: Clarendon.
Taylor, John. 1995. *Linguistic categorization*. Oxford: Clarendon.
Tolkien, John R. R., Eric V. Gordon and Norman Davis (eds.). 1967. *Sir Gawain and the Green Knight*. Oxford: Clarendon.

Wright, Joseph and Elizabeth M. Wright. 1928. *An elementary Middle English grammar*. Oxford: Clarendon.
Yule, George. 1996. *The study of language*. Cambridge: CUP.

Christian Liebl
The A and O of a medieval English sound-change: prolegomena to a study of the origins and early geographical diffusion of /ɑː/ > /ɔː/[1]

1. Introduction

Somewhat surprisingly, no detailed investigation into the origins and early geographical diffusion of the important phonemic shift of OE /ɑː/ > /ɔː/ (as in /stɑːn/ > /stɔːn/ 'stone') has so far been undertaken.[2]

---

[1] The present contribution, which is based on my unpublished M.A. thesis (Liebl 2002) and has profitted greatly from the critical remarks of an anonymous reviewer, represents an abridged version of the paper delivered at ICEHL 13; I hope to be able to publish my comments on the 13th-century situation elsewhere.

[2] '/ɑː/ > /ɔː/' here serves as an umbrella term referring not only to the shift in its effect on isolated /ɑː/, but also all the other relevant contexts, viz. /ɑː/+w and /ɑː/+mb/nd/ng/ld (/ɑ/ > /ɑː/ through Homorganic Lengthening). /ɑ/ > /ɑː/ (through compensatory lengthening) > /ɔː/ seems to be suggested by the place-name form <Hole>, attested in 1293 for Great and Little Hale (< OE halh) in Lincolnshire, alongside <Haal> in 1306 and numerous later o-spellings (Perrott 1979:66f.). This toponomastic evidence, if reliable, would contradict Hogg (1992:§5.124), Dietz (1970:10) and Smith (1956, 2:243f., s.v. walh), but confusion with OE hol(h) cannot be ruled out entirely. Moreover, '/ɑː/' is also meant to subsume ON á (as in vrá, but, *pace* Kristensson 1967:18, not in Ás- = OE Ōs- < Gmc. *ansu-) or L ā (as in OE/L pāpa, which, contrary to Baugh and Cable 2002:86 and n.10, must have been borrowed later than OE nǣp/L nāpus).

Finally, ā in both Old French loans (e.g. *fame*) and words like ME *name* – where /ɑː/ is the result of ME Open Syllable Lengthening (MEOSL) – normally does not become /ɔː/, although there are a few unexplained cases, e.g.:
a) the Old French loan *scorn*, with a confusing distribution of <a> and <o> (*MED*:s.v.; see also Diensberg 1989:53, but cf. *ODEE*:s.v.)
b) several o-spellings for OE *haga* in place-names from the South and East Midlands (see Perrott 1979:376 and Mills 1980:169), possibly as a result of confusion with OE hōh?

Otherwise, though, <a> is preserved, and according to numerous handbooks this fact proves that such loans entered the language after /ɑː/ > /ɔː/, and that the shift also preceded MEOSL (cf. e.g. Strang 1970:§§134f.). Yet an alternative explanation for the failure of operation seems to lie in the different vowel quality: while OE /ɑː/

In this paper, therefore, an attempt will be made to review and supplement the accounts in the standard handbooks, which usually look back to the classic treatments in Luick ([1964]) or Jordan (1974). As we shall see, the occurrence of *o*-spellings in both Anglo-Saxon manuscripts and place-names from Domesday Book now seems to confirm the intuitions of those scholars who advocated an 11th-century date for /ɑː/ > /ɔː/. The traditional views as to the early stages of this innovation in terms of the spread and frequency of *o*-spellings, however, are not entirely borne out by the evidence provided by onomastic material as well as literary texts, glosses and documents.[3]

2. Stress reduction: shortening and phonological changes

For a correct interpretation of our evidence, particularly the onomastic data, it is important to realise, first, that *a*-spellings, notably in compounds, need not necessarily imply the preservation of OE /ɑː/: depending on a variety of complex factors (cf. Campbell 1959:§§87ff.; Hogg 1992:§§2.87ff.; Fulk 1992:§§212f.), they could also be the result of stress reduction and subsequent shortening to /ɑ/ (which would therefore not have qualified as an input for /ɑː/ > /ɔː/). Second, reduced stress may lead to phonological changes which,

---

was a back vowel, OF *a* and ME /aː/ (as the result of MEOSL) were palatal (Pope [1952]:§182; Lass 1976:129f.; *pace* Iglesias-Rábade 2003:§326f.).

[3] The place-name spellings were chiefly culled from the county surveys of the English Place-Name Society (EPNS). Considering the dearth and shortcomings of early ME literary and documentary sources (see Laing 1993, 2000), historical dialectologists have long recognised the potential value of onomastic evidence, which covers the whole of England and, at least theoretically, can be more clearly dated and localised than textual sources. It is not always fully recognised, though, that place-names, apart from possibly preserving more conservative spellings, often occur in later cartulary copies or in sources which are not clearly local but were drawn up by central government scribes, on the spot or in London; they may therefore have been refashioned after their own non-local dialect, especially when the place-name elements were still fully transparent (for a very cautious approach see Clark 1992a). The non-onomastic material consists of spellings from both literary and non-literary manuscripts listed in the catalogues by Ker (1957), Pelteret (1990) and Laing (1993); electronic versions of the *MED* and the *MCOE* have also proved very helpful here.

though yielding *o*-spellings, are not due to /ɑː/ > /ɔː/, but rather examples of the development of Gmc. */ai/ > OE /o(ː)/ (cf. Hogg 1992:§§5.7, 6.4ff., 6.29). This can be observed in a few words such as *nōht* 'nothing' (*pace* Lass 1992:46) and in the second element of original compounds where secondary stress had been lost, as in OE *earfoþ* 'trouble' and, presumably, <ordol> for OE *ordāl* 'ordeal'.[4] Reduced stress may also result in *o*-spellings in the second elements of personal names (like *-bold*, *-wold* or *-ston*); they had thus better be treated with caution, even though Fulk (1992:§213 and pers. comm.), contrary to Hogg (1992:§6.7), considers them to represent /ɔː/.

3. Anglo-Saxon manuscripts and Domesday Book

Klaeber (1902:270f.) seems to have been one of the few scholars to interpret occasional instances of <o> in OE sources as phonetic spellings and evidence for incipient rounding of OE /ɑː/; his findings and the results of my own research are conveniently summarised in Table 1 below.[5]

---

[4] This latter spelling, listed by neither Hogg (1992) nor Brunner (1965:§43, Anm.4), occurs only four times in two 11th-century manuscripts, MS Corpus Christi College, Cambridge 201 (Ker 1957:no.49B; see Liebermann 1903:243, 252, 382; Karaus 1901:§22) and MS Bodleian Library, Junius 121 (Ker 1957:no.338). WGmc. */a/ > /o/ before nasals also belongs here: OE *furlang* ~ *furlong* is thus similarly inconclusive (*pace* Kristensson 1967:16).

[5] For manuscript details see Ker (1957), Pelteret (1990) and Sawyer (1968); CCCC = Corpus Christi College, Cambridge / CUL = Cambridge University Library / BL = British Library / Bodl. Libr. = Bodleian Library. The following erroneous items have been excluded:
1. The *MCOE* entry <on two healfa>, glossing *altrinsecus* in MS BL Cotton Cleopatra A iii (s. x med.; Ker 1957:no.143) and taken from William G. Stryker's 1952 edition, should actually read <on twa healfa> (Philip Rusche, pers. comm.).
2. MS BL Royal 12 D xvii of Bald's *Leechbook* (s. x med.; Ker 1957:no.264) contains various spellings of a plant-name *gotwoþe*; its first element, according to the entry in Hall (1960:s.v. *gōtwoðe*), corresponds to OE *gāt* 'goat', suggesting an early instance of /ɑː/ > /ɔː/. This, however, is quite unlikely, and Bierbaumer (1975:70f.) rightly gives the etymology as "ungeklärt".
3. Moffat (1987:540) interprets <oc> in the English bounds of a badly damaged charter fragment (Sawyer 1968:no.1863) as an instance of *āc* 'oak'; upon closer inspection of the facsimile (Keynes 1991:no.10), though, it turned out that this is not justified.

Table 1. Apparent evidence for /ɑː/ > /ɔː/ in Anglo-Saxon manuscripts

manuscript	text	date	item
CCCC 173	The Parker Chronicle	s.ix/x	on (for OE ān 'one', s.a. 879)
CUL Hh.I.10	Ælfric, Grammar and Glossary	s.xi²	on (2x, for OE ān 'one'; Brüll 1900:§39)
CUL Ii.II.2	translation of the Gospels	s.xi	on (for OE ān 'one'; Trilsbach 1905:n.1/p.53, §21)
CUL Kk.III.18	translation of Bede, Historia ecclesiastica gentis anglorum	s.xi²	on (for OE ān 'one'); adrof (for 1/3 sg.pret.ind. of OE ādrīfan 'drive away')
Exeter Cathedral, Dean & Chapter Library 3501	The Exeter Book: Precepts, Maxims I, Riming Poem	s.x²	mon (3x, for OE mān 'evil deed'; Krapp and Dobbie 1936:143/l.82, 163/l.195, 168/l.62)
	inventory	s.xi²	Stofordtune (for OE stān+ford+tūn in the place-name Staverton)
	manumission and notification	s.xi/xii	mó (for OE mā 'more'; Earle 1888:259); non (for OE nān 'none'; Earle 1888:260)
BL Cotton Augustus ii, no. 25	diploma of William I	1081	orwurþa (for OE ārwurð, -weorð 'pious')
BL Cotton Faustina A x	Ælfric, Grammar and Glossary	s.xi²	goð (for pres.pl. of OE gān 'go'; Brüll 1900:§39)
BL Cotton Julius A ii	Ælfric, Grammar and Glossary	s.xi med.	on (2x, for OE ān 'one'; Brüll 1900:§39)
BL Cotton Otho A vi	translation of Boethius, De consolatione philosophiae	s.x med.	on (2x, for OE ān 'one'; Sedgefield 1899:42/l.9, 78/l.14)
BL Cotton Vitellius A xv	Beowulf	s.x/xi	sole (for OE sāl 'rope', l.302); ón (for OE ān 'one', l.2210; cf. Kiernan 1996:234, Fulk 2005:210)
BL Cotton Vitellius E xviii	interlinear gloss to Vitellius Psalter	s.xi med.	þo (for pl. of OE þā, dem./rel. pron.; Ps. 88.8)
BL Harley 107	Ælfric, Grammar and Glossary	s.xi med.	on (for OE ān 'one'; Brüll 1900:§39)
BL Stowe Ch. 31	charter	s.xi/xii	Northuuold (for OE norð+wald in the place-name Northwold)
Bodl. Libr. Auct.D.2.19	Rushworth[1]	s.x	aswopen (for past part. of OE āswāpan 'sweep away', Matthew 12.44)
Bodl. Libr. Hatton 20	Pastoral Care	890-897	sorig (for OE sārig 'sorry'?)
Bodl. Libr. Junius 11	Genesis A	s.x/xi	wigrode (for OE wīgrād 'war-path'?)

Apart from the predominance of <on> (potentially subject to reduced stress with rounding before nasals, or scribal confusion with the preposition?), also the last two entries need to be commented on. What would be a very early instance of /ɑː/ > /ɔː/ in the *Pastoral Care* is dismissed as "scarcely significant" by Hogg (1992:§5.7, n.2) and has perhaps rightly been called a scribal error by Brunner (1965:§73, Anm.1); the contemporary MS BL Cotton Tiberius B xi (Ker 1957:no.195) has <sarig>. Even so, this *hapax legomenon* was granted a separate entry in Hall (1960:s.v.): "sorig *sorry*". Similarly, while the glossary entry of Doane's edition of *Genesis A* reads "?wíg-ród f. (= wíg-rád? or for wíg-trod n.? [...]) war-road" (Doane 1978:179/l.2084), Hall (1960:s.v.) has an entry "wīgrād (ō) f. *war-path*".

Most of the early onomastic evidence for /ɑː/ > /ɔː/ comes from Domesday Book (see Table 2).[6] Actually consisting of three manuscripts from around 1086, it has been called "the most important source of English place-name forms" (Sawyer 1956:483), but the value of its spellings has often been questioned (cf. e.g. Clark [1995]). Admittedly, the extant manuscripts are only copies of the lost circuit returns, oral statements by local juries of both Normans and Englishmen, taken down by Norman clerks (see Feilitzen 1937:6ff.);

---

[6] A comprehensive investigation of EPNS volumes and some other sources has substantially increased Feilitzen's (1937:45, n.1) list of Domesday Book forms which, "if reliable, seem to point to incipient rounding of $\bar{a}$"; his Snower Hall (Norfolk), however, does not belong here – its etymon being OE *snōr* rather than **snǣr* (cf. Kristensson 1965:154; *pace* Sandred 1996:45) – and Radway (Warwickshire) is equally doubtful (cf. Ekwall 1960:s.v.). Other problematic spellings which have been omitted include: <Longesdune> (Great Longstone in Derbyshire, I/138) and <Elont> (Elland in the West Riding of Yorkshire, III/43), where <o> could also be the reflex of the allophone of OE *a* before nasals; <Sonwic> (Swanage in Dorset, Fägersten 1933:126) and <So(a)neberge> (Swanborough Hundred in Sussex, II/317), the former of uncertain etymology ("*swān* or *swan*", Mills 1993:s.v.), with <o> in both instances possibly a scribal convention for *w*; <Unlouebi> (Anlaby in the East Riding of Yorkshire, 216) and <Hamolde> (Hammill in Kent, Wallenberg 1934:587), where <o> might represent ŏ in unstressed syllables (cf. Feilitzen 1937:335 and §57); and <Humbrestone> (Humberston in Lindsey/Lincolnshire, V/116), which in view of the absence of subsequent *o*-spellings seems unreliable (cf. also Ekwall 1938:160ff.).

still, in the case of our sound-change it is quite likely that the spellings reflect spoken forms largely free of the pressure of Late West Saxon standard orthography, even though Anglo-Saxon charter material might occasionally have been used as well (unlike Bauer 1986:203, Clark 1992b:124f. is however fiercely opposed to the concept of Norman scribes producing "phonetic transcriptions").

Table 2. Apparent evidence for /ɑː/ > /ɔː/ in Domesday Book

county and reference: place-name	element	item
Berkshire II/343: Wifol	fald	Wifol(d)
Buckinghamshire 17: Bradwell	brād	Brodewelle
Cheshire		
IV/58: Tilston	stān	Tilleston
II/223: Cranage	crāwe	Croeneche
Cornwall (Mills 1993:s.v.): Braddock	brād, āč?	Brodehoc
Devon		
II/471: Hennock	āc	Hanoch, Hainoc
I/115: Horwood	hār?	Horew(o)da
II/520: Staverton	stān	Stovretona
Hertfordshire 142: Watton at Stone	wād	Wodtone
Kent (Mills 1993:s.v.): Hadlow	hlāw	Haslow
Leicestershire (Ekwall 1938:165): Prestwold	wald	Prestwolde
Northamptonshire		
56: Radstone	stān	Rodestone
131: Walgrave	wald	Wold(e)grave
Somerset (Sawyer 1956:493, n.1): Stone	stān	Estone
Suffolk (Baron 1952)		
46: Stone Street	stān	Ston
45: Southwold	wald	Sudwolda
West Riding of Yorkshire I/147: South Anston	stān	Litelastone
Wiltshire 109: Sherston	stān	Sorestone

For a proper evaluation of the evidence presented in the two tables above it is important to have a closer look at the phonetic environment of original /ɑː/. Quite obviously, the vicinity of labiovelar /w/ appears to have been highly conducive to the raising and rounding of /ɑː/ (on such influence of /w/ in other contexts see Hogg 1992:§§5.176ff.); moreover, /l/ and /r/, notably when covered, are characterised by backness (cf. Hogg 1992:§§2.73f.; Lass 1994:49f.), and this velar quality might similarly have exerted an influence on the quality of preceding /ɑː/. On the one hand, early *o*-spellings may of course simply be brushed aside as "sporadic, and without significance till after 1100" (Campbell 1959:§132, n.3). On the other hand, it may be suggested, very tentatively, that it was in such highly favourable environments that this sound-change first surfaced, the overall paucity of <o> being at least to some extent also due to the restraining influence of the Late West Saxon *Schriftsprache*. At any rate, while future investigations will no doubt yield additional *o*-spellings, early instances of <o> for OE /ɑː/ already now seem to be attested more frequently than generally assumed, contradicting conventional wisdom, which usually assigns the first written evidence of /ɑː/ > /ɔː/ to the 12th century (e.g. Brunner 1965:§73, Anm.1; Lass 1992:46) – not to speak of the claims in Mossé (1952:§27, Rem.II) and Iglesias-Rábade (2003:§327), who hold that /ɑː/ > /ɔː/ does not appear in spelling until the 13th century.

Luick ([1964], 1:§369) must have been one of the first to remark on the geographical origin of /ɑː/ > /ɔː/, which he located in some part of the West Saxon area and neighbouring Worcestershire as well as Kent, where the rounding is said to have begun in the course of the 11th century, with the /ɔː/-stage reached in the course of the 12th. Yet neither Luick nor later scholars following his dating have ever adduced any evidence for this.[7] Indeed, Luick seems to have based his conclusions chiefly on 12th-century sources, and the reason why he brought in Worcestershire must be connected with the tenacious belief still encountered today (e.g. Lass 1992:46) that the writings by the 'tremulous hand' of Worcester with their abundance of *o*-spellings belong to the (late) 12th rather than the (second quarter of the) 13th century (Franzen 2003). Yet of the manuscripts discussed above only one (CUL Kk.III.18) can definitely be assigned to Worcester, and while Domesday Book has no evidence for early <o> in Worcestershire either, it does have some for Kent. Clearly then, the

---

[7] E.g. Dietz (1989b:135), arguing that /ɑː/ > /ɔː/ "im Süden noch vor 1100 beginnt" – but elsewhere (Dietz 2002:589): "im Süden schon c1150".

material presented in the two tables does not really admit of determining the geographic origin of /ɑː/ > /ɔː/; still, it is interesting to note that *o*-spellings can be found not only in the South (Berkshire, Kent), but also in the Midlands (e.g. Northamptonshire and Cheshire), while being completely absent in some other Southern counties.

4. The 12th century: onomastic and textual evidence

More revealing in terms of the geographical diffusion of the sound-change discussed here is the onomastic data for the 12th century, summed up in Tables 3 and 4.[8]

Table 3. The 12th century: summary of onomastic data (absolute figures)

counties	<a> / <o>		<aw> / <ow>		<amb>/<omb> etc.		<ald> / <old>		total <a>/<o>
	-1150	-1200	-1150	-1200	-1150	-1200	-1150	-1200	
The South									subtotal: 424/49
Berkshire	1/0	19/3	–	3/0	–	12/0	–	3/0	38/3
Devon	0/1	28/4	–	6/0	1/0	20/1	–	2/0	57/6
[Dorset]	12/15	21/0	–	–	4/1	18/0	1/0	–	56/16
[Hampshire]	–	17/0	–	–	1/0	4/1	–	6/0	28/1
[Kent]	10/0	25/5	–	1/1	2/0	15/0	–	10/1	63/7
Surrey	3/0	12/2	–	2/1	1/0	6/0	–	3/0	27/3

---

[8] Despite careful analysis, the figures and percentages will have to be taken with the proverbial grain of salt: for instance, there is no certainty possible as to whether all the *o*-spellings denote local usage, or whether the preservation of <a> before *mb/nd/ng* might not simply be due to failure of Homorganic Lengthening. Incidentally, in those areas where Gmc. *$ă$ before nasals in non-lengthening contexts is known to have been represented by <o> (which was the case not only in the West Midlands; cf. Dietz 1989a:304f.), spellings involving <omb>, <ond> or <ong> have been excluded altogether; this has been denoted by the symbol ~, while – indicates that neither <a> nor <o> is attested. Square brackets enclose counties for which either unpublished EPNS material has been used or only investigations other than EPNS surveys exist (or which have not yet been fully covered by the EPNS). The North Riding of Yorkshire, Cumberland, Westmorland and Lindsey/Lincolnshire have been excluded altogether for lack of native *o*-spellings. In the last columns of Tables 3 and 4, "<a>/<o>" and "<o>" of course subsume all the other contexts, viz. <aw>, <amb, and, ang>, <ald> and <ow>, <omb, ond, ong>, <old>.

Sussex	9/1	21/6	–	2/1	9/0	13/3	3/0	4/0	61/11
Wiltshire	12/0	52/0	1/0	14/0	–	7/0	–	8/2	94/2
The East Midlands and London								subtotal: 477/44
Bedfordshire	–	20/3	–	8/0	–	8/1	–	6/2	42/6
Bucks.	5/0	59/2	–	20/0	2/0	1/0	1/0	10/0	98/2
Cambridgeshire	–	10/0	–	12/1	2/0	1/0	–	4/0	29/1
Essex	5/0	24/0	–	12/0	–	20/1	2/0	4/0	67/1
Hertfordshire	1/0	11/2	–	0/1	–	5/1	–	2/0	19/4
Huntingdonshire	5/0	12/3	–	–	–	–	3/0	8/0	28/3
[London]	3/4	4/1	1/0	–	3/0	5/0	–	–	16/5
Middlesex	2/0	14/0	–	–	–	1/1	–	–	17/1
[Norfolk]	4/0	4/2	–	0/1	–	0/1	–	–	8/4
Northamptontshire	7/0	43/3	–	3/0	–	1/0	2/0	8/2	64/5
Rutland	–	5/0	–	–	1/0	10/4	–	4/0	20/4
[Suffolk]	6/1	33/2	–	4/0	1/0	17/3	2/0	6/2	69/8
The West Midlands								subtotal: 518/63
Cheshire	8/0	34/11	1/0	14/2	~	~	–	13/0	70/13
Derbyshire	10/1?	35/0	3/0	26/2	~	~	3/0	16/0	93/3?
Gloucestershire	13/0	57/10	1/0	3/0	~	~	1/0	9/1	84/11
[Herefordshire]	2/0	1/0	–	–	~	~	–	–	0
Nottinghamshire	4/0	38/4	–	9/0	2/0	11/0	–	3/1	67/5
Oxfordshire	3/0	33/6	1/0	10/4	2/0	24/10	–	11/1	84/21
[Shropshire]	1/0	13/3	1/0	12/1	~	~	–	–	27/4
[Staffordshire]	3/0	13/1	–	–	~	~	–	–	16/1
Warwickshire	2/0	18/3	4/0	19/0	~	~	1/0	3/1	47/4
Worcestershire	2/0	23/1	2/0	–	~	~	–	3/0	30/1
The North and Lincolnshire								subtotal: 682/24
E. R. of Yorks.	12/0	32/0	–	–	5/0	36/4	1/0	19/0	105/4
[Lancashire]	4/0	8/0	–	2/0	~	~	–	2/0	0
[Lincs./Holland]	2/0	13/1	–	–	1/1	20/1	–	4/0	40/3
[Lincs./Kesteven]	6/0	55/4	–	9/0	1/0	31/3	–	2/1	104/8
W. R. of Yorks.	31/0	197/3	2/0	26/1	10/0	128/3?	1/0	38/2	433/9?
								total: 2101/180

Table 4. The 12th century: summary statistics of onomastic data (percentages of <o> spellings, rounded)

counties	<o>		<ow>		<omb, ond, ong>		<old>		total <o>
	-1150	-1200	-1150	-1200	-1150	-1200	-1150	-1200	
The South								subtotal:	10.5
Berkshire	0	14	–	0	–	0	–	0	7
Devon	100	12.5	–	0	0	5	–	0	9.5
[Dorset]	56	0	–	–	20	0	0	–	22
[Hampshire]	–	0	–	–	0	20	–	0	3
[Kent]	0	17	–	50	0	0	–	9	10
Surrey	0	14	–	33	0	0	–	0	10
Sussex	10	22	–	33	0	19	0	0	15
Wiltshire	0	0	0	0	–	0	–	20	2
The East Midlands and London								subtotal:	8
Bedfordshire	–	13	–	0	–	11	–	25	12.5
Buckinghamshire	0	3	–	0	0	0	0	0	2
Cambridgeshire	–	0	–	8	0	0	–	0	3
Essex	0	0	–	0	–	5	0	0	1.5
Hertfordshire	0	15	–	100	–	17	–	0	17
Huntingdonshire	0	20	–	–	–	–	0	0	10
[London]	57	20	0	–	0	0	–	–	24
Middlesex	0	0	–	–	–	50	–	–	5.5
[Norfolk]	0	33	–	100	–	100	–	–	33
Northamptonshire	0	6.5	–	0	–	0	0	20	7
Rutland	–	0	–	–	0	29	–	0	17
[Suffolk]	14	6	–	0	0	15	0	25	10
The West Midlands								subtotal:	11
Cheshire	0	24	0	12.5	~	~	–	0	16
Derbyshire	9?	0	0	7	~	~	0	0	3?
Gloucestershire	0	15	0	0	~	~	0	10	12
[Herefordshire]	0	0	–	–	~	~	–	–	0
Nottinghamshire	0	9.5	–	0	0	0	–	25	7
Oxfordshire	0	15	0	29	0	29	–	8	20
[Shropshire]	0	19	0	8	~	~	–	–	13
[Staffordshire]	0	7	–	–	~	~	–	–	6

Warwickshire	0	14	0	0	~	~	0	25	8
Worcestershire	0	4	0	–	~	~	–	0	3
The North and Lincolnshire								subtotal: 3	
E. R. of Yorks.	0	0	–	–	0	10	0	0	4
[Lancashire]	0	0	–	0	~	~	–	0	0
[Lincs/Holland]	0	7	–	–	50	5	–	0	7
[Lincs/Kesteven]	0	7	–	0	0	9	–	33	7
W. R. of Yorks.	0	1.5	0	4	0	2?	0	5	2?
								total: 8	

Now, while <a> is still clearly predominant in onomastic sources throughout the 12th century, accounting for some 92% of the spellings, it turned out that about a third of the 75 or so manuscripts investigated contain *o*-spellings in varying number. Apart from invoking shortening processes, conservative spelling habits and the *literatim* copying of an OE exemplar to explain the frequency of <a> for OE /ɑː/, we may also point to Clark's (1958:lx) suggestion that, as long as "the *a*-spelling served well enough to distinguish this [ɔː] from [oː] ... there would have been little need to modify the spelling".

Judging by both onomastic and textual evidence, Kent and several other counties of the South(-East) and East Midlands seem to have spearheaded the change. There are a few *o*-spellings in Kentish manuscripts, including the continuous gloss to Eadwine's Psalter (Laing 1993:39; Schlemilch 1914:17), the Vespasian Homilies (Richards 1978; Hall 1920, 2:269ff.), a copy of the West Saxon Gospels (Laing 1993:99; Reimann 1883:§12.3) and the 'Textus Roffensis' (Ker 1957:no. 373; Görnemann 1901:30; Münch 1902:30). <o> (chiefly preceded by *w*) can likewise occasionally be found in some charters from the Winchester Codex Wintoniensis (Laing 1993:61; Sawyer 1968:nos. 242, 359, 938, 1154) as well as in Augustine's *Soliloquies*, possibly also from Hampshire (Laing 1993:84; Carnicelli 1969). In Dorset, the frequency of <o> is conspicuous, but perhaps less significant given that the *o*-spellings all come from a single source, the Sherborne Cartulary. And while <o> is the majority form in the Trinity Homilies and the oldest version of the *Poema Morale* – representing the dialects of Suffolk and Essex (Laing

2000; Hall 1920, 2:317, Strauss 1916) – there are only three instances of /ɑː/ > /ɔː/ in the *Peterborough Chronicle*, all from the Final Continuation of 1155 (Clark 1958:lix, 54ff.); a trilingual glossary, composed perhaps in the same region not much later, has almost always <o> (Laing 1993:107; Hunt 1991:22f.). Yet *o*-spellings in place-names from Cambridgeshire and Essex are curiously underrepresented.

As for the West Midlands, Oxfordshire and the Herefordshire/Shropshire region – the likely home of the Lambeth Homilies, with a fair number of *o*-spellings (Laing 1993:111; Stadlmann 1921) – seem to have been more important than Worcestershire, where <o> is found in merely 3% of the relevant place-names. Similarly, a late-12th-century sermon from Worcester has still predominantly <a> (Stanley 1961), as do the English bounds of some Worcester charters (Kitson 1997:231ff.; Sawyer 1968:nos. 79, 80, 1553). In Cheshire, on the other hand, which already had <o> in Domesday Book, *o*-spellings amount to an unexpected 16%.

Of course, given the uncertainties involving the local nature of numerous *o*-spellings, one must not jump rashly to conclusions; still, the evidence suggests, I believe, that /ɑː/ > /ɔː/, rather than spreading from the South to the North, might have started in Late Old English more or less simultaneously in several counties in the South as well as the East and West Midlands and radiated from there. This view possibly also underlies Ekwall's (1938:165) statement that there is no "reason to place the change very much later in the North Midlands than in the South Midlands or in the South". Similarly, in the context of the Great Vowel Shift it has been shown that ME $\bar{\imath}$ too, was probably affected independently in several areas, with waves spreading from there (see Ogura, Wang and Cavalli-Sforza 1991). And there may be yet another connection, for "it would be tempting to see the two parallel and perhaps roughly contemporaneous sound-changes", viz. /ɑː/ > /ɔː/ and /æː/ > /ɛː/, "as the early indication of an impulse which gained momentum only at the time of the Great Vowel Shift, transforming the system of long vowels by a series of interconnected raisings" (Liebl 2002:48) – "the First Push", as Lutz (2004) recently put it.[9]

References

Baron, Margaret Cynthia. 1952. *A study of the place-names of East Suffolk*. Unpubl. M.A. thesis, University of Sheffield.
Bauer, Gero. 1986. "Medieval English scribal practice: some questions and some assumptions". In: Kastovsky, Dieter and Aleksander Szwedek (eds.). *Linguistics across historical and geographical boundaries: in honour of Jacek Fisiak on the occasion of his fiftieth birthday. Volume I: Linguistic theory and historical linguistics*. Berlin: de Gruyter: 199-210.
Baugh, Albert C. and Thomas Cable. 2002. *A history of the English language*. 5th ed. London: Routledge.
Bierbaumer, Peter. 1975. *Der botanische Wortschatz des Altenglischen. 1. Teil: Das Læcebōc*. Frankfurt/M.: Lang.
Brüll, Hugo. 1900. *Die altenglische Latein Grammatik des Aelfric*. Inaugural-Dissertation, Friedrich-Wilhelms-Universität Berlin. Berlin: Mayer und Müller.
Brunner, Karl. 1965. *Altenglische Grammatik*. 3rd rev.ed. Tübingen: Niemeyer.
Campbell, Alistair. 1959. *Old English grammar*. Oxford: Clarendon.
Carnicelli, Thomas A. (ed.). 1969. *King Alfred's version of St Augustine's Soliloquies*. Cambridge, Mass.: Harvard University Press.
Clark, Cecily (ed.). 1958. *The Peterborough Chronicle 1070-1154*. London: OUP.
-----. 1992a. "Onomastics". In: Hogg, Richard M. (ed.). *The Cambridge history of the English language. Volume I: The beginnings to 1066*. Cambridge: CUP: 452-489.
-----. 1992b. "The myth of 'the Anglo-Norman scribe'". In: Rissanen, Matti et al. (eds.). *History of Englishes: new methods and interpretations in historical linguistics*. Berlin: de Gruyter: 117-129.
-----. 1992 [1995]. "Domesday Book - a great red-herring: thoughts on some late-eleventh-century orthographies". In: Jackson, Peter (ed.). *Words, names and history: selected writings of Cecily Clark*. Cambridge: Brewer: 156-167.
Diensberg, Bernhard. 1989. "On the origin of Late Middle English spellings of the type *chombre, chongi, penonce* for regular *chaumbre, chaungen, penaunce*". *Folia Linguistica Historica* 8: 51-63.
Dietz, Klaus. 1970. "Zur Vokalquantität ae. Wörter des Typus *W(e)alh-W(e)alas*". *Anglia* 88: 1-25.

---

[9] It is gratifying to see that Lutz (2004:219f.) also concurs with me on another issue, viz. the absence of spelling evidence in favour of OE /æː/ > ME /ɛː/ preceding /ɑː/ > /ɔː/, as apparently assumed by Liberman (1966) and Lass (1992:45f.).

-----. 1989a. "Die historische Schichtung phonologischer Isoglossen in den englischen Dialekten: Altenglische Isoglossen". *Anglia* 107: 295-329.

-----. 1989b. "Die historische Schichtung phonologischer Isoglossen in den englischen Dialekten: II. Mittelenglische Isoglossen". In: Fischer, Andreas (ed.). *The history and the dialects of English: Festschrift for Eduard Kolb*. Heidelberg: Winter: 133-175.

-----. 2002. Review of Gillis Kristensson. 2001-2002. *A survey of Middle English dialects 1290-1350: the southern counties*. 2 vols. Lund: UP. *Anglia* 120: 585-589.

Doane, Alger N. (ed.). 1978. *Genesis A: a new edition*. Wisconsin: The University of Wisconsin Press.

Earle, John. 1888. *A hand-book to the land-charters, and other Saxonic documents*. Oxford: Clarendon.

Ekwall, Eilert. 1938. "The Middle English ā/ō-boundary". *English Studies* 20: 147-168.

-----. 1960. *The concise Oxford dictionary of English place-names*. 4th ed. Oxford: Clarendon.

Fägersten, Anton. 1933. *The place-names of Dorset*. Inaugural-Dissertation. Uppsala: Lundequistska Bokhandeln.

Feilitzen, Olof von. 1937. *The pre-Conquest personal names of Domesday Book*. Uppsala: Almqvist and Wiksell.

Franzen, Christine. 2003. "The Tremulous Hand of Worcester and the Nero scribe of the *Ancrene Wisse*". *Medium Ævum* 72: 13-31.

Fulk, Robert D. 1992. *A history of Old English meter*. Philadelphia: University of Pennsylvania Press.

-----. 2005. "Some contested readings in the *Beowulf* manuscript". *The Review of English Studies* 56: 192-223.

Görnemann, Willy. 1901. *Zur Sprache des Textus Roffensis*. Inaugural-Dissertation, Friedrich-Wilhelms-Universität Berlin. Berlin: Mayer and Müller.

Hall, J.R. Clark (with a supplement by Herbert D. Meritt). 1960. *A concise Anglo-Saxon dictionary*. 4th ed. Cambridge: CUP.

Hall, Joseph (ed.). 1920. *Selections from early Middle English: 1130-1250*. 2 vols. Oxford: Clarendon.

Hogg, Richard M. 1992. *A grammar of Old English. Volume 1: Phonology*. Oxford: Blackwell.

Hunt, Tony. 1991. *Teaching and learning Latin in thirteenth-century England. Volume I: texts*. Cambridge: Brewer.

Iglesias-Rábade, Luis. 2003. *Handbook of Middle English: grammar and texts*. München: Lincom Europa.

Jordan, Richard (trans. and rev. by Eugene Joseph Crook). 1974. *Handbook of Middle English grammar: phonology*. The Hague: Mouton.

Karaus, Arthur. 1901. *Die Sprache der Gesetze des Königs Aethelred*. Inaugural-Dissertation, Friedrich-Wilhelms-Universität Berlin. Berlin: Mayer and Müller.

Ker, N.R. 1957. *Catalogue of manuscripts containing Anglo-Saxon*. Oxford: Clarendon.
Keynes, Simon (ed.). 1991. *Facsimiles of Anglo-Saxon charters*. Oxford: OUP.
Kiernan, Kevin S. 1996. *Beowulf and the* Beowulf *manuscript*. Rev. ed. Ann Arbor: University of Michigan Press.
Kitson, Peter R. 1997. "When did Middle English begin? Later than you think!" In: Fisiak, Jacek (ed.). *Studies in Middle English linguistics*. Berlin: de Gruyter: 221-269.
Klaeber, Friedrich. 1902. "Zur altenglischen Bedaübersetzung". *Anglia* 25: 257-315.
Krapp, George Philip and Elliott van Kirk Dobbie (eds.). 1936. *The Exeter Book*. (= The Anglo-Saxon Poetic Records, 3.) New York: Columbia University Press; London: Routledge and Kegan Paul.
Kristensson, Gillis. 1965. "Another approach to Middle English dialectology". *English Studies* 46: 138-156.
-----. 1967. *A survey of Middle English dialects 1290-1350: the six northern counties and Lincolnshire*. Lund: Gleerup.
Laing, Margaret. 1993. *Catalogue of sources for a linguistic atlas of early medieval English*. Cambridge: Brewer.
-----. 2000. "*Never the twain shall meet*: Early Middle English – the East-West divide". In: Taavitsainen, Irma et al. (eds.). *Placing Middle English in context*. Berlin: de Gruyter: 97-124.
Lass, Roger. 1976. *English phonology and phonological theory: synchronic and diachronic studies*. Cambridge: CUP.
-----. 1992. "Phonology and morphology". In: Blake, Norman (ed.). *The Cambridge history of the English language. Volume II: 1066-1476*. Cambridge: CUP: 23-155.
-----. 1994. *Old English: a historical linguistic companion*. Cambridge: CUP.
Liberman, Anatoly S. 1966. "On the history of Middle English $\bar{a}$ and a". *Neuphilologische Mitteilungen* 67: 66-71.
Liebermann, Felix (ed.). 1903. *Die Gesetze der Angelsachsen. Erster Band: Text und Übersetzung*. Halle a.S.: Niemeyer.
Liebl, Christian. 2002. *The origins and geographical diffusion of a medieval English sound-change: a study of $\bar{a} > \bar{o}$, based on onomastic and textual evidence*. Unpubl. M.A. thesis, University of Vienna.
Luick, Karl. 1914-1940 [1964]. *Historische Grammatik der englischen Sprache*. 2 vols. Stuttgart: Tauchnitz; Oxford: Blackwell.
Lutz, Angelika. 2004. "The first push: a prelude to the Great Vowel Shift". *Anglia* 122: 209-224.
MCOE = Healey, Antonette diPaolo and Richard L. Venezky (eds.). 1980. *A microfiche concordance to Old English*. [incl.: *The list of texts and index of editions*]. Toronto: Pontifical Institute of Mediaeval Studies.
MED = Kurath, Hans, Sherman M. Kuhn and Robert E. Lewis (eds.). 1954-2001. *Middle English dictionary*. Ann Arbor: University of Michigan Press.

Mills, Anthony D. 1980. Review of Margaret Gelling. 1978. *Signposts to the past: place-names and the history of England.* London: Dent. *Medium Ævum* 49: 167-170.
-----. 1993. *A dictionary of English place names.* Oxford: OUP.
Moffat, Douglas. 1987. "The occurrences of *āc* 'oak' in Old English: a list". *Mediaeval Studies* 49: 534-540.
Mossé, Fernand (trans. by James A. Walker). 1952. *A handbook of Middle English.* Baltimore: Hopkins.
Münch, Rudolf. 1902. *Die Handschrift H (Textus Roffensis) der Gesetzsammlung König Alfreds des Großen: Eine grammatische Untersuchung.* Inaugural-Dissertation, Vereinigte Friedrichs-Universität Halle-Wittenberg. Halle a.S.: Kaemmerer.
ODEE = Onions, C.T. (ed.). (with the assistance of G.W.S. Friedrichsen and R.W. Burchfield). 1966 [repr. 1969, with corr.]. *The Oxford dictionary of English etymology.* Oxford: Clarendon.
Ogura, Mieko, William S.-Y. Wang and L.L. Cavalli-Sforza. 1991. "The development of Middle English *ī* in England: a study in dynamic dialectology". In: Eckert, Penelope (ed.). *New ways of analyzing sound change.* San Diego: Academic Press: 63-106.
Pelteret, David A.E. 1990. *Catalogue of English post-Conquest vernacular documents.* Woodbridge: Boydell.
Perrott, Michael. 1979. *The place-names of the Kesteven Division of Lincolnshire.* Unpubl. M.A. thesis, University of Nottingham.
Pope, M.K. 1934 [1952]. *From Latin to Modern French with especial consideration of Anglo-Norman: phonology and morphology.* Manchester: Manchester University Press.
Reimann, Max. 1883. *Die Sprache der mittelkentischen Evangelien (Codd. Royal 1 A 14 und Hatton 38.).* Berlin: Weidmann.
Richards, Mary P. 1978. "MS Cotton Vespasian A. XXII: The Vespasian Homilies". *Manuscripta* 22: 97-103.
Sandred, Karl Inge (in collaboration with Barbara Cornford, B. Lindström and P. Rutledge). 1996. *The place-names of Norfolk.* Part II. Nottingham: English Place-Name Society.
Sawyer, Peter H. 1956. "The place-names of the Domesday manuscripts". *Bulletin of the John Rylands Library* 38: 483-506.
-----. 1968. *Anglo-Saxon charters: an annotated list and bibliography.* London: Royal Historical Society.
Schlemilch, Willy. 1914. *Beiträge zur Sprache und Orthographie spätaltengl. Sprachdenkmäler der Übergangszeit (1000-1150).* Halle a.S.: Niemeyer.
Sedgefield, Walter John (ed.). 1899. *King Alfred's Old English version of Boethius De Consolatione Philosophiae.* Oxford: Clarendon.
Smith, Albert H. 1956. *English place-name elements.* 2 vols. Cambridge: CUP.

Stadlmann, Alois. 1921. *Die Sprache der mittelenglischen Predigtsammlung in der Handschrift Lambeth 487*. Wien: Braumüller.
Stanley, Eric G. 1961. "An inedited nativity sermon from Worcester". *English and Germanic Studies* 7: 53-79.
Strang, Barbara M.H. 1970. *A history of English*. London: Methuen.
Strauss, Otto. 1916. *Die Sprache der mittelenglischen Predigtsammlung in der Handschrift B.14.52 des Trinity College, Cambridge*. Wien: Braumüller.
Trilsbach, Gustav. 1905. *Die Lautlehre der spätwestsächsischen Evangelien*. Bonn: Hanstein.
Wallenberg, Johannes K. 1934. *The place-names of Kent*. Uppsala: Appelberg.

Julia Schlüter
A small word of great interest: the allomorphy of the indefinite article as a diagnostic of sound change from the sixteenth to nineteenth centuries*

1. Introduction

It is the aim of this study to shed more light on a set of largely unexplored sound changes that were under way between the sixteenth and nineteenth centuries. For this purpose, the indefinite article with its two allomorphs will be exploited as an indicator of the phonetic quality of the following sound. The analysis rests on the premise that the short form of the article *a* is regularly placed before lexemes that are considered to begin with a consonantal segment, whereas the long form *an* precedes lexemes considered as vowel-initial. Since early Middle English, when the loss of final /n/ before consonants was completed, this distributional rule has remained essentially unchanged, with very little variation as far as Standard English is concerned (cf. Schlüter forthc. a).

The occurrence in English of V-initial content words with first-syllable stress is an innovation of the ME period, which appears to have been fostered (though not initiated) by the influx of French loanwords (cf. Minkova 2000b:506-507; 2003:149-160; and the critical review in Schlüter forthc. a). Even so, the universal preference for syllables to begin with consonantal onsets (cf. Vennemann

---

* I take this opportunity to foreground a person who is very much present in the background of the work that has gone into this paper as well as into all my past (and, for that matter, future) ventures into English linguistics. I dedicate this paper to my supervisor Günter Rohdenburg on the happy occasion of his 65th birthday on 28th July 2005, with congratulations and best wishes. Working under his guidance has always been an immensely inspiring and gratifying experience, for which I owe him my heartfelt thanks. The present research is part of a larger research project under Günter Rohdenburg's direction. I acknowledge the financial support received from the German Research Foundation (DFG; grant number RO 2271/1-3) and the Lise Meitner post-doctoral fellowship awarded by the North-Rhine Westfalian Ministry of Science and Research.

1988:13, 21) has remained in vigour – the allomorphy of the indefinite article being the most visible of its manifestations. It is assumed that the final /n/ of the article transfers (resyllabifies) to the onset of a following V-initial lexeme, thereby optimizing syllable structure (cf. Nespor and Vogel 1986:65; Lutz 1991:61, note 115).

The present contribution contends that a number of sound changes have taken place in the course of the ModEn era that can be subsumed under a tendency to (re-)introduce or strengthen consonantal onsets in formerly V-initial lexemes. Focussing on written Standard English, the analysis will deal with the following phenomena:

(1) Lexemes beginning etymologically with /h/ had apparently lost this initial consonant in the ME era. It has been shown (cf. e.g. Lutz 1991:62, or Schlüter forthc. a) that the loss, frequently attributed to French influence, was more probably a natural continuation of home-grown developments in English and that it was not completed, but left some phonetic traces, which provided the germs of a renewed strengthening in the Modern period (cf. Schlüter forthc. a). It is this restitution of /h/-onsets that will come under closer scrutiny in section 2.1 of this contribution. The influence of French phonology will be discussed as a factor distinguishing the group of Romance loanwords from the native Germanic word stock.

(2) Section 2.2 relativizes the explanatory force of purely etymological arguments in that it points out the sharp contrast between the mainstream development of Romance loanwords and the strikingly exceptional items *hour*, *honour*, *honest* and *heir*, which fail to reintroduce an initial /h/. It also hints at possible explanations for the deviant behaviour of these stems.

(3) Among Germanic as well as Romance <h>-initial words, some evolved an additional glide that came to reinforce the onset, yielding the initial consonant cluster /hj/. Section 2.3 sets out to measure the effect of this privilege with regard to the filling of the onset position.

(4) While (1) to (3) all relate to the prominent class of <h>-initial lexemes, the allomorphy of the indefinite article also tells a story about the evolution of new initial consonants in formerly V-initial lexemes. Due to the methodologically necessary restriction of this study to the written standard language, the cases investigated in

section 2.4 are limited to the development of the /j/-onset in loanwords such as *eunuch, eulogy, Europe* as well as *unit, urine, use*.

Further relevant examples of newly created consonantal onsets known from dialectal usage since the EModE period are the formation of a prothetic /j/ in *yer* for *ere*, *yerst* for *erst*, *yerth* for *earth*, and of a prothetic /w/ in *uonli* for *only*, *wuts* for *oats*.[1] The forms *whole* and *whore*, whose modern spellings may reflect traces of a phonological /w/-glide, also belong here, but are more properly treated together with <h>-words in a study of Standard English (see section 2.1). The only case in point that happens to have been adopted into the standard is the prothetic /w/ in *one* and *once*. However, since *once* is rare after the indefinite article and *one* occurs mostly in fixed collocations like *such a(n) one*, *many a(n) one* and *so* Adj *a(n) one*, where special conditions apply, both have been excluded from this study.

Investigating sound change in written texts is usually a challenging enterprise. In the present case, however, the availability of phonotactically distinct variants of the indefinite article provides a relatively direct clue to the realization of the following sound or sounds. In addition, the extremely high frequency of the article and the availability of electronically readable texts allow us to describe synchronic contrasts and diachronic trends with a precision that surpasses that of earlier approaches, including Dobson's (1968) monumental compilation.

2. Analyses

The data on which the following analyses are based include four collections of dramatic and non-dramatic prose spanning the sixteenth to nineteenth centuries: one drama collection (*English Prose Drama*, *EPD*), and three collections of non-dramatic literature (mostly novels), namely the *Early English Prose Fiction* (*EEPF*), *Eighteenth-Century Fiction* (*ECF*) and *Nineteenth-Century Fiction* (*NCF*) collections. The four centuries under consideration were divided into segments of about 40 years each, with the exception of the longer first subsection,

---

[1] For more comments and further evidence, see Dobson (1968:995-1001), which is the source of the examples given. Cf. furthermore Ihalainen (1994:202, 213).

in which the *EEPF* coverage of the early years is still relatively thin, while the *EPD* collection sets in only in 1540. The years referred to throughout this discussion invariably represent the publication dates of the works or, in the case of plays, the dates of first performances, if they antedate the first printed publications. Table 1 charts the resulting division and the number of texts and word counts for each subsection.

Table 1. Composition of the database

Subperiod	1518-1580	1581-1620	1621-1660	1661-1700	1701-1740	1741-1780	1781-1820	1821-1860	1861-1903
Prose	*EEPF*	*EEPF*	*EEPF*	*EEPF*	*ECF*	*ECF*	*NCF*	*NCF*	*NCF*
No. of works	23	71	52	65	41	52	56	91	103
Million words	1.42	2.67	2.83	3.12	2.30	8.03	7.57	16.38	15.74
Drama	*EPD*	*EPD*	*EPD*	*EPD*	*EPD*	*EPD*	*EPD*	*EPD*	*EPD*
No. of works	6	62	69	172	226	197	388	315	173
Million words	0.19	1.15	1.44	4.38	3.91	2.80	6.28	4.22	2.63
Total									
Million words	1.62	3.82	4.27	7.50	6.21	10.83	13.85	20.60	18.36

These subcorpora were subjected to a set of full-text searches that were directed at both variants of the indefinite article followed by the typical spellings for the onsets under discussion.[2] This procedure excluded all unwanted instances of lexemes with invariant, categorical C- or V-onsets.[3] In a subsequent manual classification of all matches, sporadically occurring words with an unetymological <h>-spelling, e.g. *hidea, horacle, hointment* etc., were discarded. This non-standard phenomenon is beyond the scope of the present study, but receives due attention in Häcker (1998, 2004) and Crisma (forthc.).

---

[2] Besides <h>-initial words, all words beginning with the digraph <wh> (occasionally representing /h/ as in *whole, whore*, etc.) and the graphemes <eu>, <u> and their allographs <ev> and <v> were searched and monitored.
[3] The *EEPF* corpus contains a total of 34 instances of *a* preceding V-initial words, which is a carry-over effect of the evolution of the indefinite article in many non-standard varieties of English. This extremely low number, which compares with over 20,000 occurrences of *an* before V in this corpus, testifies to the close adherence of the corpus texts to the standard norms.

2.1 A salad bowl of etymologies

Descriptions of the status of initial /h/ in Early and Late Modern English typically concentrate on factors such as the presence of stress on the syllable under consideration (cf. Strang 1970:81), the emotional emphasis on a word (cf. Milroy 1992:138-142), dialectal differences (cf. Graband 1965:222; Milroy 1983:39-40; 1992:137; Ihalainen 1994:217) and the increasing social stigma attached to /h/-dropping (cf. Dobson 1968:991; Strang 1970:81; Lutz 1991:59; Milroy 1983:49; 1992:140; Lass 1992:61; Mugglestone 1995:107-150). However, independently of prosodic, stylistic, diatopic and sociolinguistic considerations, the class of English <h>-initial lexemes represents a mixture of items of very diverse origins. Teasing apart the etymological intricacies involved in this heterogeneous class of lexemes is a worthwhile task that has never been addressed in any systematic way.

To start with, a substantial section of the English lexicon goes back to French sources: beginning in the thirteenth, peaking in the fourteenth century and persisting for many centuries, English has been tapping massively into the French vocabulary (cf. Pope 1934:424; Dekeyser 1986:256; Baugh and Cable 1993:164). Native French words are known to have lost the pronunciation of initial <h> since the Late Latin stage; so it follows that they were borrowed into English without a consonantal onset. The question of whether native English lexemes had preserved traces of a consonantal realization in the period of the most substantial borrowing from French is still debated (see in particular Schlüter forthc. a, where an affirmative answer is suggested). For the present study, it will be sufficient to bear in mind that the pronunciation of initial <h> was regaining ground in the course of the EModE and LModE eras.[4]

This suggests the hypothesis that Germanic and Romance <h>-words in the ModE period may have behaved differently in the course of the evolution reinstating their /h/-onsets. For the following

---

[4] In Schlüter (forthc. a), it is argued that this trend cannot be exclusively ascribed to the influence of a normative enforcement of a spelling pronunciation (as is almost unanimously done by linguists at a loss for a better explanation; cf. e.g. Graband 1965:223; Dobson 1968:992; Strang 1970:81; Lutz 1991:60, note 113; Gimson 1994:175).

analyses, it will be proposed that the relative collocation frequencies of these words with *a* and *an* can be taken as a direct clue to the consonantal strength of their onsets: the higher the percentage of *an*, the higher the number of occasions on which an <h>-initial word was judged to be V-initial, and inversely, the lower the percentage of *an*, the higher the number of occasions on which it was judged to be C-initial. For the consistency of this argument, it does not matter whether we assume a homogeneous speech community in which every speaker reacts spontaneously to every instance of an <h>-initial word by variably selecting *a* or *an*, or whether we assume a heterogeneous community in which an individual consistently uses either *a* or *an* in connection with a certain lexical entry. In either case, the statistical picture afforded by a corpus study will be the same. Crucially, however, my argument presupposes a gradient phonetic realization with a categorical phonological interpretation that switches between V and C as a certain threshold of consonantal strength is crossed. Evidence in favour of this claim will accumulate as the discussion proceeds (for further discussion, see Schlüter forthc. a).

Figure 1. The distribution of *a* and *an* before <h>-initial words of Romance (or Greek) and Germanic (or other) origin

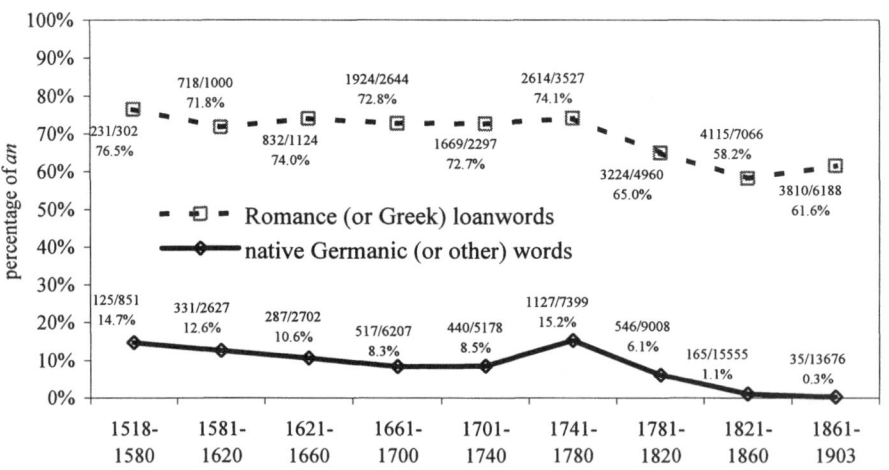

Figure 1 provides a first rough division of all corpus examples of <h>-words preceded by *a/an* according to their etymological sources.

The clear and remarkably constant difference of around 60 percent between the two groups[5] demonstrates that, on the above premise, Romance loanwords typically show a far weaker onset realization than Germanic words. In addition, the figure displays a slight downward trend in the use of *an*, which translates into a reinforcement of initial /h/, both Germanic and Romance. However, this presentation of the data hides some important distinctions, which make the contrast look less categorical and the diachronic trend more pronounced.

For a start, the category of Germanic <h>-words subsumes the stems *whole* and *whore* as well as their derivatives. Their <wh>-spelling, nowadays no more than a variant of <h>, gained currency in the fifteenth and sixteenth centuries and corresponded to a labialized pronunciation that extended also to other <(h)o>-initial words (cf. *OED*: s.v. *wh*; Dobson 1968:997-998). However, the glide-like realization of the onset was only short-lived, while the spelling is perpetuated to the present day. Besides, it should be noted that the category labelled 'native Germanic (or other) words' also comprises all loanwords that are not of Romance or Greek origin. However, members of this subcategory appear only in the eighteenth- and nineteenth-century data and are negligible in number. Persian/Urdu *hindoo* and *hookah*, Romanian *hospodar* and Hungarian *hussar* are cases in point. None of these words however exhibits any quantifiable deviations from the norm of Germanic <h>, so that there is no need for a separate treatment.

In contrast to the Germanic category, which can stand as it is, the only thing that unifies the <h>-words in the Romance (or Greek) category is the fact that they were usually adopted into English (more or

---

[5] The results are highly significant, which is indicated by the fact that the statistical error probability p as calculated by the chi-square test, i.e. the likelihood with which the observed contrast is only a chance distribution, is negligible for each of the chronological corpus sections: 1518-1580: $p = 9.60 \cdot 10^{-89}$ (***); 1581-1620: $p = 1.67 \cdot 10^{-270}$ (***); 1621-1660: $p \approx 0$ (***); 1661-1700: $p \approx 0$ (***); 1701-1740: $p \approx 0$ (***); 1741-1780: $p \approx 0$ (***); 1781-1820: $p \approx 0$ (***); 1821-1860: $p \approx 0$ (***); 1861-1903: $p \approx 0$ (***).

less directly) from French. Yet, this conglomerate is so heterogeneous that the corresponding curve in Figure 1 is no more than an artefact – none of the subgroups actually behaves in the way suggested by the curve. For one thing, the data subsume words of different Romance provenances, including above all Old French, but also Classical, Late and Mediaeval Latin, as well as many learned words of Greek origin, which typically arrived in English by the mediation of French.

More importantly, there is another subgroup that contrasts sharply with all others, namely those words that French had previously adopted from the Germanic languages spoken on the continent. Not surprisingly, the number of these lexemes is far from negligible, considering that Norman French in particular had undergone a strong influence from Frankish plus a slight one from Old Norse (cf. Pope 1934:13-14). Following the etymologies given in the *OED*, examples include *habergeon, halberd, halt, hamlet, harbinger, hardy, harlequin, harquebus, haste, hasty, hatchet, haunch, heinous, helmet, herald, heron* and *hobby*. Pope (1934:15, 41, 56, 94) claims that even in French, these lexemes preserved a pronounced initial /h/ as late as the sixteenth or seventeenth century. This fact can be expected to be mirrored in a deviant behaviour after their adoption into English.

Figure 2 below extracts the Romance loanwords of Germanic origin and juxtaposes them with the category of straightforward Germanic words, which is reproduced from Figure 1 as a standard of comparison.

The data indicate that the detour taken by the doubly borrowed words remains without a noticeable effect on the realization of their onsets: the initial /h/ turns out to be practically identical in strength with that of their less travelled congeners.[6] This seems to corroborate Pope's view that the words concerned preserved the consonantal onset inherited from Germanic during their stopover in the French system.

---

[6] The results of the chi-square test show no noteworthy differences between the two groups, with the exception of the subperiod 1781-1820, in which straightforward Germanic words are slightly ahead in the strengthening of /h/: 1518-1580: $p = 0.51$; 1581-1620: $p = 0.71$; 1621-1660: $p = 0.96$; 1661-1700: $p = 0.63$; 1701-1740: $p = 0.74$; 1741-1780: $p = 0.12$; 1781-1820: $p = 0.04$ (*); 1821-1860: $p = 0.52$; 1861-1903: $p = 0.47$.

Incidentally, the etymological complication has left intact not only the peculiar onset but also the substance of the lexemes: thus, native *helm* and re-borrowed *helmet*, native *halter* and re-borrowed *halt*, native *hard* and re-borrowed *hardy* share so many phonological, morphological and semantic features that a limited period of spatial separation is unlikely to have obliterated the connection holding between them. On the diachronic dimension, Figure 2 furthermore shows that throughout the three centuries from 1518 to 1820, there is very little change in the pronunciation of initial <h> in Germanic words: there continues to be a residue of cases with a subliminal realization that only disappears in the course of the nineteenth century.

Figure 2. The distribution of *a* and *an* before originally Germanic <h>-initial words re-borrowed from French compared to straightforward native Germanic <h>-words

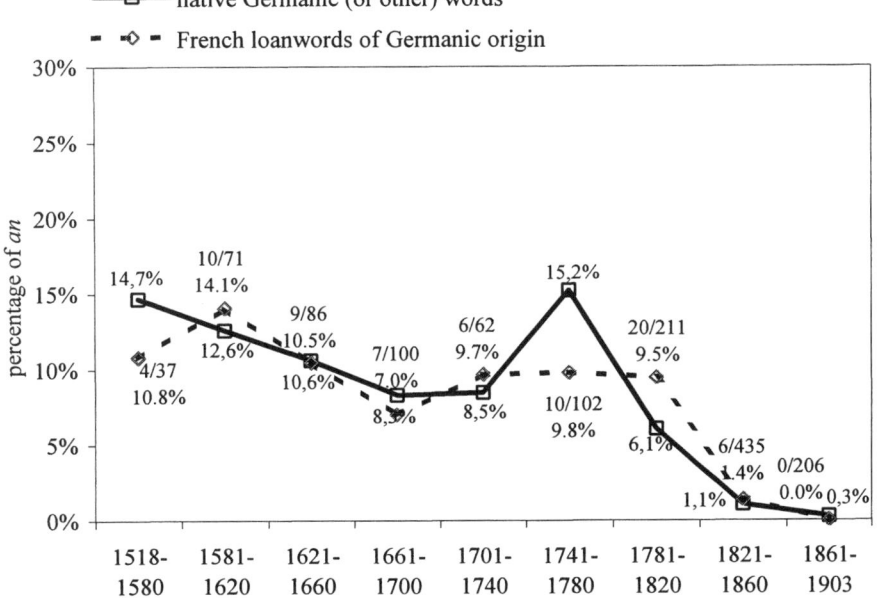

This concludes the analysis of the historical origins of English <h>, albeit in a preliminary way. As we have seen, the English lexicon

might be more adequately compared to a salad bowl of etymologies rather than a melting pot: the ingredients do not assimilate to an undifferentiated norm, but preserve the marks of their provenance. Thus, a major contrast between Germanic and Romance etymologies has been observed that cuts across the group of loanwords adopted from French.

2.2 They never come back: mute initial <h>

Even after the exclusion of words of Germanic origin from the group of Romance (plus Greek) loanwords in Figure 1, we are left with a varied set.

Figure 3. The distribution of *a* and *an* before Romance (or Greek) loanwords with a 'pronounced' or 'mute' initial <h>

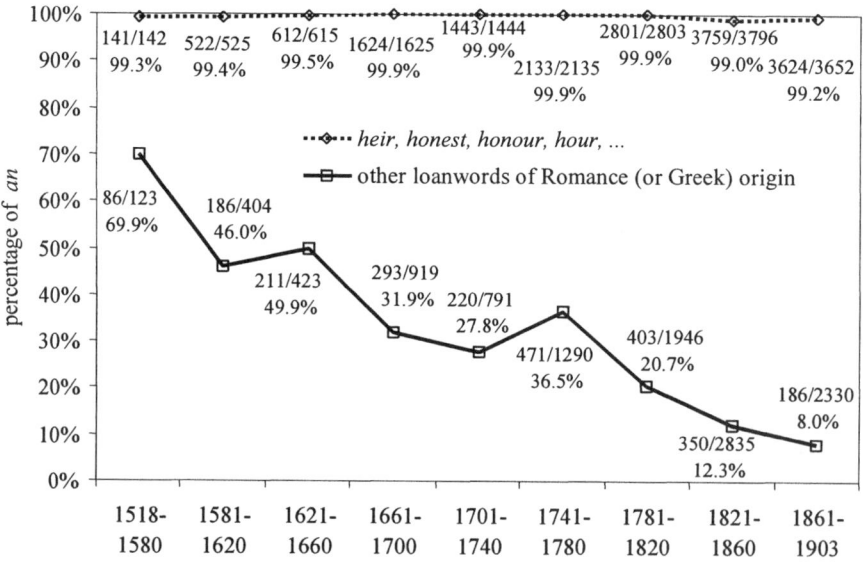

Down to the present day, there is a split between Romance and Greek loanwords that have re-adopted a pronounced <h> and such that have been remarkably resistant to it, including first and foremost the group *heir*, *honest*, *honour*, *hour* and their derivatives. Figure 3 differentiates between the two groups on the basis of the present-day situation in Standard British English (in American English, *herb* and possibly *hom(m)age* would be further candidates for the second category).

The results show a stagnant situation among the four stems that separates them from the remaining lexemes of Romance or Greek origin. While in the former group, there are never any signs of even an incipient comeback of pronounced initial /h/, in the latter, this change already has a firm foothold in the earlier part of the sixteenth century and catches on slowly but continuously.[7] As a result, in the late nineteenth century, an almost categorical distinction can be observed between two classes of Romance loanwords, which cannot be explained as an effect of etymological differences.

A closer look at the data for individual lexemes shows that the reintroduction of initial /h/ spreads by lexical diffusion: not all lexemes are affected at the same time and at an equal rate. Thus, *hospital*, *host(ess)*, *hotel* and *humble* as well as some non-initially stressed adjectives (*habitual*, *hereditary*, *heroic*, *historic(al)*, *hysteric(al)*) are among the last to consistently introduce a pronounced consonantal onset. This effect may in large part be due to the increasing influence of prescriptive norms in the eighteenth and nineteenth centuries.[8] However, what is still at stake is an account of the striking divergence between the groups depicted in Figure 3.

---

[7] The statistical difference between the two groups is very highly significant throughout: 1518-1580: $p = 1.01 \cdot 10^{-11}$ (***); 1581-1620: $p = 4.77 \cdot 10^{-80}$ (***); 1621-1660: $p = 9.73 \cdot 10^{-84}$ (***); 1661-1700: $p \approx 0$ (***); 1701-1740: $p = 1.73 \cdot 10^{-305}$ (***); 1741-1780: $p \approx 0$ (***); 1781-1820: $p \approx 0$ (***); 1821-1860: $p \approx 0$ (***); 1861-1903: $p \approx 0$ (***).

[8] In their detailed survey of eighteenth-century English grammars, Sundby, Bjørge and Haughland (1991:177-178) find partly conflicting orthoepic pronouncements on whether to use *a* or *an* before different Romance and Greek <h>-words: before *habitual*, *Herculean*, *honest*, *humble* and *humoursome* some recommend the use of *an*; before *heroic*, *hideous* and *horrid*, but again also *humble*, *humorous* and *humoursome* others recommend the use of *a*, which illustrates the somewhat arbitrary nature of normative precepts.

A suggestive remark comes from Graband (1965:224), who relates the exceptionality of the stems *heir, honest, honour* and *hour* to their extreme frequency of occurrence. A glimpse at the absolute numbers included in Figure 3 gives an impression of this striking imbalance between the two groups: tokens representing only these four stems are on average 1.5 times as frequent in the collocation with the article as all other tokens taken together, even though the latter category contains an incommensurately larger number of stems and derivatives (e.g. *haberdasher, habit, hackney, halo, harass, harlot, harmony, harpoon, haughty, haunt, hazard*, to give just a few examples from the beginning of the list). The effect of frequency is investigated in more detail in Schlüter (forthc. a). Suffice it to say at this point that a moderate correlation can be detected between a high frequency of the string *a/an* + <h>-lexeme and an /h/-less pronunciation. This effect can be explained by the high degree of contextual predictability of the items and the economy of articulatory effort in frequent collocations. In addition, items that are current in ordinary spoken discourse can be expected to be particularly immune to the influence of spelling on their pronunciation. Thus, *honest* and *honour* and the extraordinarily frequent *hour* have a particular predisposition to remain /h/-less (the same is less true of *heir*). The explanatory potential of frequency becomes manifest also among other loanwords of Romance or Greek origin: the more frequent they are, the slower they are to reintroduce a pronounced initial /h/ (cf. Schlüter forthc. a).

2.3 More equal than others: /hj/-clusters

In early Middle English, the three /h/-containing stem-initial consonant clusters /hn/, /hl/ and /hr/ inherited from Old English (e.g. *hnutu* 'nut', *hlud* 'loud', *hræfn* 'raven') had been reduced to /n/, /l/ and /r/ as a first step in the weakening process of initial /h/ (cf. Lutz 1991:29-37; Lass 1992:62). Since /h/ had from then on no longer clustered with any other consonants, assessing the consonantal force of lexeme onsets has so far only taken into account /h/ alone. However, in the course of the EModE period, the new cluster /hj/ evolved as a consequence of a phonetic change in a ME vowel: by the end of the fifteenth century, the native diphthongs /iu/ and /eu/ and the loan phoneme /y:/ (from Old French /y/), which had in all but the most cultivated registers merged with the former, had only one common realization /iu/. Due to a lengthening of the second element, the phoneme developed into the glide plus vowel combination /ju:/ (cf. Dobson 1968:700-713; Lass 1992:50-55; 1999:99). According to Lass (1999:100), this shift took place between 1650 and 1700; in contrast, Dobson's (1968:709) evidence indicates that it began "at least as early as the last decade of the sixteenth century (and probably as early as the 1560's)" and first affected vowels in initial position. The increased rate of change at the beginnings of words can be explained with reference to the preference for filled onsets: English words typically carry stress on the first (stem-initial) syllable, which is therefore particularly prominent, and loanwords tended to assimilate to this pattern relatively fast (cf. Minkova 2000a:440, 451). Thus, an empty onset under the primary stress can be expected to constitute a particularly serious infraction of the preference for filled onsets, and the development of a glide came in handy to amend this. Dobson (1968:705) furthermore informs us that the /ju:/ pronunciation was considered "barbarous" by orthoepists of the EModE period, so that we have to reckon with a delayed penetration of the change into the standard language that was at the basis of written texts. As to the date of the completion of the change, Dobson remains silent, but towards the end of the seventeenth century, he considers /ju:/ more likely than /iu/ (1968:712).

The concordances of <h>-words studied in the previous sections contain a considerable number of lexemes, of both native and foreign origin, whose first vowel underwent the evolution just described, so that they standardly begin in /hju:/ in the present day.[9] Examples of Germanic origin include mainly *hewer* and *hue*, and the most frequent Romance loanwords concerned are *huge*, *human/-e/-ity*, *humility/ -iation/-iating* and *humour/-ist/-ous*. Compared to other <h>-initial lexemes with a pure /h/-onset followed by a vowel (/hV/), these items

---

[9] On the variant realization of the cluster /hj/ as [ç], see Gimson (1994:192) and Lutz (1991:57, notes 103 and 104).

by hypothesis boast a stronger onset, combining the consonantal force of an increasingly articulated /h/ and the newly forming glide /j/.

Focusing on Romance (or Greek) words,[10] the dataset represented by the black curve in Figure 3 (already excluding the group *heir, honest, honour, hour*) can be split up further into two subcategories: the /hj/-items can be predicted to be ahead of /hV/-items of the same etymological provenance in the abandonment of the long variant of the indefinite article. Figure 4 illustrates the results of this subdivision.

Figure 4. The distribution of *a* and *an* before Romance (or Greek) loanwords with /hV/- and /hj/-onsets

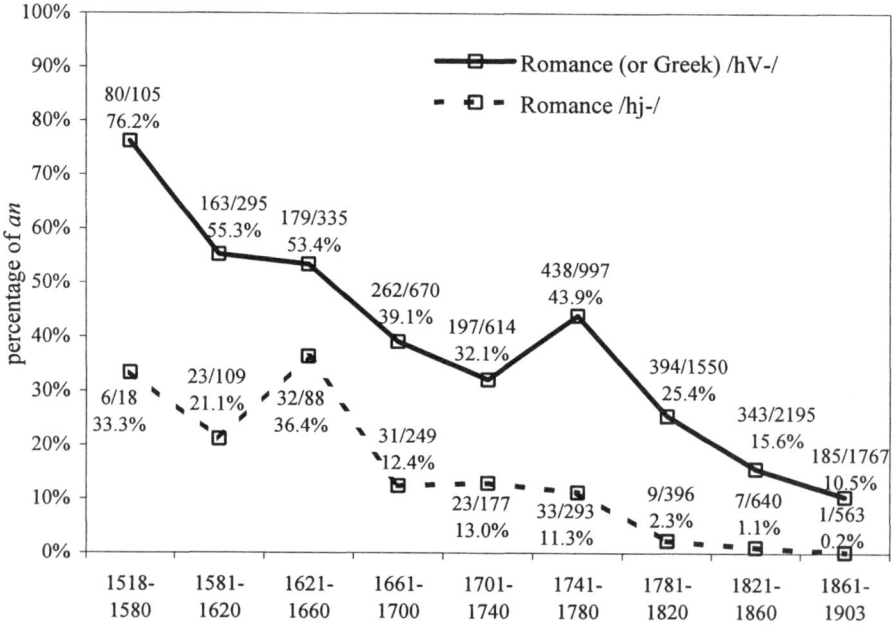

The figure shows a clear internal differentiation within the class of loanwords in the expected direction: in every diachronic subsection of the corpus, we find a statistically highly significant contrast between

---

[10] Parallel findings have emerged from a study of native lexemes, which is not described here since the amount of data for Germanic /hj/-onsets is less satisfactory.

the respective proportions of *an*-selection.[11] This indicates that the development of the /j/-glide out of the diphthongal nucleus in the first syllable increases the adequacy of the onset to function as fully consonantal. After the exclusion of the /hj/-items, the remaining Romance or Greek <h>-words appear even more conservative as far as the reinforcement of initial /h/ and the concomitant abandonment of *an* in favour of *a* is concerned.

Diachronically, Figure 4 suggests that the impact of the glide formation was clearly noticeable even in the earliest subcorpus, which confirms Dobson's early dating of the change. The implementation of the change, however, just like the resurrection of initial /h/, seems to have spanned an extended period of far more than three centuries. Astonishingly, while /hj/-items virtually behave like full consonant-initial words by the turn of the nineteenth century, items with a pure /h/-onset still preserve a considerable margin of variability, indicating that the reintroduction of initial /h/ across the board is still incomplete at the end of the century.[12]

In sum, closer analysis of Romance <h>-initial lexemes shows that the formation of a glide on the basis of the LME diphthong /iu/ – which proceeds simultaneously with but independently of the re-emergence of pronounced /h/ – gives rise to an inequality among members of these two etymological categories: the combination of two consonantally weak, but stabilizing sounds significantly boosts the consonantal strength of the onset cluster /hj/, leaving single /h/ far behind. This concludes the discussion of the richly varied category of <h>-initial words and leads over to a study of two related sets of vowel-initial lexemes.

---

[11] The chi-square test yields the following error probabilities: 1518-1580: $p = 0.00022$ (***); 1581-1620: $p = 9.77 \cdot 10^{-10}$ (***); 1621-1660: $p = 0.0044$ (***); 1661-1700: $p = 1.29 \cdot 10^{-14}$ (***); 1701-1740: $p = 5.92 \cdot 10^{-07}$ (***); 1741-1780: $p = 1.77 \cdot 10^{-24}$ (***); 1781-1820: $p = 3.50 \cdot 10^{-24}$ (***); 1821-1860: $p = 8.03 \cdot 10^{-23}$ (***); 1861-1903: $p = 4.27 \cdot 10^{-15}$ (***).

[12] The non-negligible remains of weak initial <h> in Present-Day English are analyzed in detail in Schlüter (2003:83-88; forthc. b). Suffice it to say that the absence of stress on the initial syllable is the main factor raising the percentage of *an*-selections, in particular in British English.

2.4 Upstart onsets: the development of /juː/

The emergence of the glide plus vowel combination /juː/ can also be traced in the evolution of lexemes without an initial <h>. There are two classes of lexemes that are at issue here. One class goes back to French loanwords etymologically beginning in /y/, which had commonly been replaced by ME /iu/, as has already been pointed out. To this class belong the lexemes *union/-que/-form*, *unit/-y/-ed*, *universe/-ity/-al/-ality*, *use/-ful/-less*, *usual/-rer*, *usurper/-ation* and *unanimous/-ity*. The second, smaller, class goes back to Greek roots, which also arrived in English via Latin and French and had an initial diphthong /ɛu/ in Middle English (cf. Dobson 1968:799; Lass 1992:50). The principal representatives of this class that can be found following the indefinite article are *eulogy/-ium*, *eunuch* and *European*. According to Dobson (1968:798-799), the first component of the ME diphthong /ɛu/ was raised, passing through /eu/ and eventually merging with the reflex of /iu/. As shown above, this latter sound must at that time have been developing the initial glide /j/, and former /ɛu/ followed suit. Dobson suggests that the loss of the distinction between the two phonemes began possibly as early as the end of the fourteenth century in Northern and Eastern dialects, spread to the South in the sixteenth century, and affected the more conservative careful standard pronunciation around the mid-seventeenth century. According to this chronology, the realization /juː/ must have appeared earlier for the <u>-words than for the <eu>-words, but the difference should have been neutralized by the late seventeenth century. In Lass' (1999:100) account of the chronology, the merger and the development of /juː/ coincided in the second half of the seventeenth century. The <u>-initial words would correspondingly be expected to develop the initial glide no earlier than the <eu>-words.

The corpus study outlined in Figure 5 measures the choice of the allomorphs of the indefinite article as a diagnostic of the transition of the two word classes from V-initial to C-initial realizations.

Figure 5. The distribution of *a* and *an* before two categories of originally V-initial lexemes forming new /j/-onsets

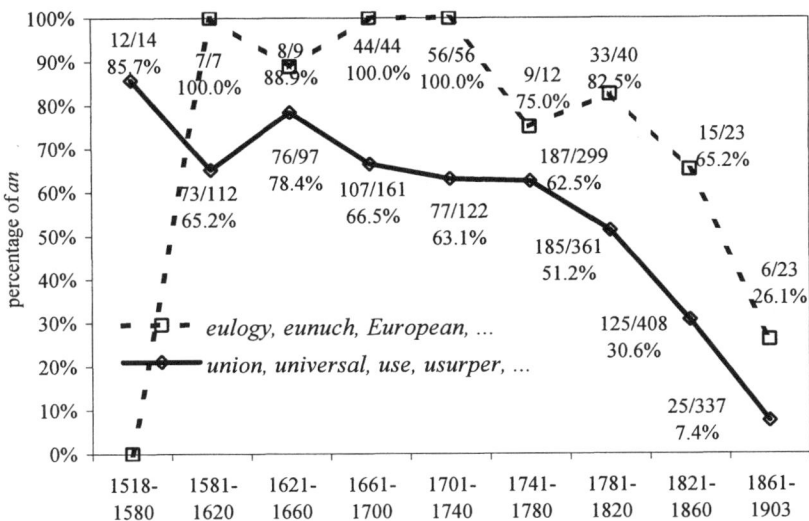

The graph reveals the expected continuous establishment of a consonantal onset, making the full form of the article increasingly superfluous. As already stated in section 2.3, the effects of the change are visible long before Lass' (1999:99) dating. It is also obvious that the <u>-words were more advanced than the <eu>-words, as a consequence of the fact that former /ɛu/ joined into the evolution of /ju:/ only in the mid-seventeenth century.[13] A comparison of the <u>-initial words to the <hu>-initial words in Figure 4 (the grey curve) moreover exhibits an obvious difference between these categories, which follows from the summation of the consonantal properties

---

[13] The results of the chi-square test are statistically highly significant in all subcorpora in which the dataset is sufficiently large. In some subsections, the rarity of <eu>-words makes the test not applicable (n.a.). 1518-1580: –; 1581-1620: n.a.; 1621-1660: n.a.; 1661-1700: p = $7.60 \cdot 10^{-06}$ (***); 1701-1740: p = $1.46 \cdot 10^{-07}$ (***); 1741-1780: n.a.; 1781-1820: p = 0.00017 (***); 1821-1860: p = 0.00057 (***); 1861-1903: p = 0.0020 (**).

contributed by both the /h/- and /j/-sounds: the developing glide on its own takes considerably longer to acquire a full consonantal status than in combination with the glottal fricative.[14]

While Dobson's dating of the incipient change is largely confirmed by the corpus data portrayed in Figure 5, the further time course disagrees with his findings in two respects. For one thing, the establishment of /ju:/ in <u>- as well as <eu>-words gains momentum mainly as late as the nineteenth century, and its endpoint is still pending at the turn of the twentieth century. For another, even in the last subperiod investigated, we witness a robust and statistically reliable difference between the reflexes of former /iu/ and /ɛu/. This necessitates a substantial revision of the chronology proposed by Dobson (1968:798), who dates the last convincing piece of evidence of a distinction very precisely to a description by the orthoepist Owen Price in the year 1668.

While this is not the place to discuss the problem of phonemic mergers in any detail, suffice it to point to a way in which the discrepancy between empirical measures and the judgement of members of a speech community can be reconciled. Labov (1994:349-418) adduces six examples of 'near mergers', i.e. cases in which speakers of various contemporary dialects consistently produce a difference between two sounds that they are at the same time unable to distinguish perceptually. If Dobson's information drawn from orthoepists' observations holds true, and if the indefinite article is a valid measure of the realization of onsets as well, this suggests the conclusion that we are dealing with a production-perception asymmetry of the kind described as a 'near merger', which may have been carried to completion only in the twentieth century.[15]

---

[14] The difference between <u>- and <hu>-words is statistically highly significant throughout: 1518-1580: $p = 0.0030$ (**); 1581-1620: $p = 3.87 \cdot 10^{-11}$ (***); 1621-1660: $p = 7.21 \cdot 10^{-09}$ (***); 1661-1700: $p = 1.28 \cdot 10^{-29}$ (***); 1701-1740: $p = 1.75 \cdot 10^{-19}$ (***); 1741-1780: $p = 4.01 \cdot 10^{-38}$ (***); 1781-1820: $p = 1.29 \cdot 10^{-53}$ (***); 1821-1860: $p = 7.19 \cdot 10^{-45}$ (***); 1861-1903: $p = 3.46 \cdot 10^{-10}$ (***).

[15] The status of /h/ in Middle English is argued to be another instance of a near merger in Schlüter (forthc. a).

3. Conclusion

The discussion in this contribution has focussed on a set of sound changes stretching all across the EModE and LModE eras and sharing the characteristic of adding a consonantal onset to formerly V-initial lexemes. This leads to a gradual reduction of the range of application of the long form of the indefinite article. The functional motivations promoting these changes can be assumed to include a tendency to optimize the syllable structure of the lexemes concerned as well as a minimization of the necessity to resyllabify the final /n/ of the article (which negatively affects the phonological integrity of both the article and the following word).

The two principal changes considered here are the reintroduction or reinforcement of initial /h/ in lexemes containing this sound in their etymologies (sections 2.1–2.3) and the new formation of the glide /j/ in reflexes of the ME vowels /iu/, /eu/, /y/ and /ɛu/ (sections 2.3–2.4). The analysis in section 2.3 has shown that the effects of the two changes add up in environments where both overlap. As additional factors, the etymological origin and the frequency of <h>-initial words have been brought into play. Section 2.1 has provided evidence in favour of a strong effect of the phonology of the language of origin, which remains noticeable in loanwords for a long time after their adoption. Thus, Romance loanwords preserve a particularly weak /h/ for several centuries in English, and Germanic loanwords re-adopted from French also preserve the marks of their provenance in the form of an undiminished consonantal value of their onset, which is indicative of a continued realization of /h/ in French. Section 2.2 has demonstrated the conservative effect of high frequency, which opens up an avenue to explaining the continued /h/-lessness of the stems *hour, honour, honest* and *heir*.

The interpretation of the statistical data presented in this contribution is open as to the source of the variation observed: it can be put down to variation in the individual language user, who responds spontaneously to the conditions obtaining in a particular instance of the lexical items discussed, or it can be ascribed to interindividual variation with every speaker (or writer) adhering to an invariable lexical representation of each item that includes or excludes an onset consonant. The former view suggests a homogeneous speech community, the latter implies a heterogeneous one, but the most likely hypothesis is that both types of variability combine to produce the highly complex picture painted by the above analyses. Though there is no direct evidence, we have reason to assume that the actual phonetic strength of a consonantal onset plays a major role in judging a lexeme to be either C- or V-initial. This binary distinction (which is mirrored in the selection of *a* or *an*) depends on whether a certain threshold of consonantal strength is crossed.[16] Consonantal strength, however, is a gradual phenomenon dependent on systematic parameters that are beyond the conscious control of language users. Thus, even educated speakers of Early Modern English and Late Modern English can hardly be expected to be aware of the etymological distinction between native, borrowed and re-borrowed lexemes. In addition, lexeme frequency is a gradual phenomenon that translates into stochastic probabilities rather than into unique lexical representations. Finally, the additive treatment of developing /h/- and /j/-onsets speaks clearly in favour of an account in terms of phonetic strength that comes to bear in the assignment of *a* or *an* to the lexeme in question.

To summarize the combined effects of this set of factors, a relative chronology of the changes studied can be established: when the relevant curves from Figures 2 to 5 are superimposed on each other, there is practically no crossover between two lines (with the exception of straightforward and re-borrowed Germanic <h>-words, which are virtually indistinct). On the basis of these data, a hierarchy of consonanthood can be established, which is visualized in Table 2. This hierarchy is consistent on the synchronic as well as diachronic dimensions, i.e. a higher hierarchical position translates into both a

---

[16] The competing interpretation according to which the variability is an artefact of a categorical change in lexical representations distributing along a social and historical dimension cannot be completely excluded. However, the phonetic parameters underlying the change and the systematic character of the variation pattern are accommodated more easily in a model in which the interplay of several functional factors enables language users to come to phonetically grounded decisions in every single instance of the lexemes considered.

relatively higher level of consonanthood at a given point in time and a chronologically earlier transition to a C-initial status.

Table 2: Hierarchy of consonantal force for the onsets studied

least consonantal					most consonantal
Romance loanwords with 'mute' <h>	Romance or Greek loanwords with /ɛu/ > /ju:/	Romance loanwords with /iu/ > /ju:/	Romance loanwords with /hV/	Romance loanwords with /hiu/ > /hju:/	Native Germanic or other words with /h/
hour, honour, honest, heir, ...	*Eulogy, eunuch, European,* ...	*union, universal, use, usurper,* ...	*habit, hackney, heroic, historical, hospital,* ...	*huge, human, humility, humour,* ...	*hair, hand, house, husband, whole, whore,* ... *hindoo, hookah,* ... *halberd, halt, hardy, haste, heinous,* ...

What remains to be said in conclusion is that the allomorphy of the indefinite article has proved to be a particularly instructive diagnostic of sound changes in progress. Its frequency and accessibility to electronic full-text searches have allowed us to refine the categorization of the lexemes at the centre of the analysis step by step and to establish and quantify a phonetically plausible synchronic and diachronic gradation of their onsets. The suitability of the indefinite article as a tool for measuring historical sound change is what makes this small word so deserving of linguistic interest.

References

Electronic text databases

Early English Prose Fiction (*EEPF*). 1997. Electronic Book Technologies Inc. and Chadwyck-Healey. Cambridge. In association with the Salzburg Centre for Research on the English Novel SCREEN.
Eighteenth-Century Fiction (*ECF*). 1996. Electronic Book Technologies Inc. and Chadwyck-Healey. Cambridge.

English Prose Drama (EPD). 1996/1997. Electronic Book Technologies Inc. and Chadwyck-Healey. Cambridge.
Nineteenth-Century Fiction (NCF). 1999/2000. Electronic Book Technologies Inc. and Chadwyck-Healey. Cambridge.

Secondary sources

Baugh, Albert C. and Thomas Cable. 1993. *A history of the English language.* 4th ed. London: Routledge.
Crisma, Paola. (forthc.). "Were they 'dropping their aitches'? A quantitative study of *h*-loss in Middle English". *English Language and Linguistics.*
Dekeyser, Xavier. 1986. "Romance loans in Middle English: a re-assessment". In: Kastovsky, Dieter and Aleksander Szwedek (eds.). *Linguistics across historical and geographical boundaries: in honour of Jacek Fisiak on the occasion of his fiftieth birthday. Volume I: Linguistic theory and historical linguistics.* Berlin: de Gruyter: 253-265.
Dobson, Eric J. 1968. *English pronunciation 1500-1700. Volume II: Phonology.* 2nd ed. Oxford: Clarendon.
Gimson, Alfred Charles. 1994. *Gimson's pronunciation of English.* 5th ed., revised by Alan Cruttenden. London: Arnold.
Graband, Gerhard. 1965. *Die Entwicklung der frühneuenglischen Nominalflexion: Dargestellt vornehmlich auf Grund von Grammatikerzeugnissen des 17. Jahrhunderts.* Tübingen: Narr.
Häcker, Martina. 1998. "Why is there no /h/-dropping in Scots? Loss and insertion of /h/ as a contact phenomenon in British English dialects". In: Strässler, Jürg (ed.). *Tendenzen europäischer Linguistik: Akten des 31. Linguistischen Kolloquiums, Bern 1996.* Tübingen: Niemeyer: 71-76.
Häcker, Martina. 2004. "Intrusive [h] in Present-Day English accents and ⟨h⟩-insertion in medieval manuscripts: hypercorrection or functionally-motivated language use?" In: Kay, Christian (ed.). *New perspectives on English historical linguistics,* vol. II. Amsterdam: Benjamins: 109-123.
Ihalainen, Ossi. 1994. "The dialects of England since 1776". In: Burchfield, Robert (ed.). *The Cambridge history of the English language. Volume V: English in Britain and overseas: origins and development.* Cambridge: CUP: 197-274.
Labov, William. 1994. *Principles of linguistic change. Volume I: Internal factors.* Oxford: Blackwell.
Lass, Roger. 1992. "Phonology and morphology". In: Blake, Norman (ed.). *The Cambridge history of the English language. Volume II: 1066-1476.* Cambridge: CUP: 23-155.
Lass, Roger. 1999. "Phonology and morphology". In: Hogg, Richard (ed.). *The Cambridge history of the English language. Volume III: 1476-1776.* Cambridge: CUP: 56-186.

Lutz, Angelika. 1991. *Phonotaktisch gesteuerte Konsonantenveränderungen in der Geschichte des Englischen.* Tübingen: Niemeyer.
Milroy, James. 1983. "On the sociolinguistic history of /h/-dropping in English". In: Davenport, Michael, Erik Hansen and Hans Frede Nielsen (eds.). *Current topics in English historical linguistics.* Odense: Odense University Press: 37-53.
Milroy, James. 1992. *Linguistic variation and change: on the historical sociolinguistics of English.* Oxford: Blackwell.
Minkova, Donka. 2000a. "Middle English prosodic innovations and their testability in verse". In: Taavitsainen, Irma, Terttu Nevalainen, Päivi Pahta and Matti Rissanen (eds.). *Placing Middle English in context.* Berlin: de Gruyter: 431-459.
-----. 2000b. "Syllable ONSET in the history of English". In: Bermúdez-Otero, Ricardo, David Denison, Richard M. Hogg and Chris B. McCully (eds.). *Generative theory and corpus studies: a dialogue from 10 ICEHL.* Berlin: de Gruyter: 499-540.
-----. 2003. *Alliteration and sound change in Early English.* Cambridge: CUP.
Mugglestone, Lynda. 1995. *'Talking proper': the rise of accent as social symbol.* Oxford: Clarendon.
Nespor, Marina and Irene Vogel. 1986. *Prosodic phonology.* Dordrecht: Foris.
OED 2 on CD-ROM. 1995. Version 1.13. Oxford: OUP and Rotterdam: AND Software B.V.
Pope, Mildred K. 1934. *From Latin to Modern French with especial consideration of Anglo-Norman: phonology and morphology.* Manchester: Manchester University Press.
Schlüter, Julia. 2003. "Phonological determinants of grammatical variation in English: Chomsky's worst possible case". In: Rohdenburg, Günther and Britta Mondorf (eds.). *Determinants of grammatical variation in English.* Berlin: de Gruyter: 69-118.
-----. (forthc. a). "Consonant or 'vowel'? A diachronic study of initial ⟨h⟩ from Early Middle English to nineteenth-century English". In: Minkova, Donka (ed.). *Phonetic and phonological weakness in the history of English* (working title).
-----. (forthc. b). "Rhythm and grammar". In: Rohdenburg, Günter and Julia Schlüter (eds.). *One language, two grammars? Differences between British and American English.* (SEL.) Cambridge: CUP.
Strang, Barbara M.H. 1970. *A history of English.* London: Methuen.
Sundby, Bertil, Anne Kari Bjørge and Kari E. Haughland. 1991. *A dictionary of English normative grammar 1700-1800.* Amsterdam: Benjamins.
Vennemann, Theo. 1988. *Preference laws for syllable structure and the explanation of sound change: with special reference to German, Germanic, Italian, and Latin.* Berlin: de Gruyter.

Philip Durkin
Loanword etymologies in the third edition of the *OED*: the benefits of the application of a consistent methodology for the scholarly user

The etymologies given for loanwords in *The Oxford English Dictionary* (*OED*) provide the basis, directly or indirectly, for a great deal of further work in historical linguistics. It is therefore valuable for the dictionary's policies to be identified as clearly as possible, so that members of the scholarly community are aware of the conventions and the methodology employed, and can have the opportunity to make suggestions for changes or improvements to the dictionary's approach in certain cases. The *OED* is currently in the process of a complete revision. The text of 1989, which brought together the first edition of 1933 and its four-volume *Supplement* of 1972-1986, is now being reviewed from top to bottom, with quotations and definitions supplemented and reassessed, and all etymologies reconsidered and essentially rewritten. The results of this revision are being published online in quarterly instalments, currently covering the alphabetical range from the beginning of the letter M to ORATURE in the middle of the letter O, which is roughly one tenth of the full text of the dictionary.[1]

The present paper deals in some detail with questions of lexicography, but is intended primarily to provide information which will be of use to the *OED*'s readership in interpreting its data, and if possible to provoke debate on how this data should best be compiled and interpreted in order to serve the needs and interests of that readership. (On the complementary issue of the presentation of this data in *OED* etymologies, i.e. the stylistic conventions which are employed, see Durkin (2004).) This paper proceeds from the premise that it is of great importance to know not only what the evidence is

---

[1] Publication details given for *OED* reflect the date of this conference paper, August 2004. For further information on the *OED* project see www.oed.com, and also two recent accounts in Simpson et al. (2004) and in Simpson (2004); the latter also includes a select bibliography of publications relating to the *OED* revision process.

that supports an etymology, but also which sources of information will have been consulted, and how their relative merits will have been assessed.

When one is preparing etymologies within a dictionary format there is an inevitable tension between researching each word as far as is humanly possible, and trying to ensure that there is some parity in how words are treated: firstly so that the best use is made of inevitably limited editorial time, but secondly and just as importantly, so that readers can be confident that they are comparing like with like when using our etymologies. The *OED* team is large, and our revision work will take a good few years yet, but this still only yields a finite amount of time that can be spent on any given word, especially as the second edition has a total wordlist of 291,500 headwords, which is being added to all the time. Obviously, it would be absurd to allot a fixed quota of research time to each word, but we still need to work within guidelines to ensure both that the available time is well invested and that the results are as even as possible, and do not show the caprices of a particular researcher on a particular day.

Before moving on to some concrete examples, I should also take a moment to discuss how I will be using the term "etymology", and how it is understood within the working methodology of the *OED*. The *OED* presents a history of the lexis of English on a lexeme by lexeme basis, giving an overview of the meanings and spellings of any word at any point in its history, and of its distribution in different varieties of English. At the earliest possible stage, it is useful to know how far this internal history has been shaped or otherwise affected by influences both from other English words and from other languages, and I will use the word "etymology" in its broadest sense to refer to all of the area of lexicographical work which examines these influences, as well as the more traditional focus on both the immediate and the ulterior origin of any English word. So far as the *OED*'s etymology work is concerned, it is the immediate origin of a word and any continuing external influences during the course of its history which are the factors of vital importance. Ulterior etymologies are certainly not ignored, but here our work will tend much more to be a digest of existing scholarship, summarizing for the student of English what is known of the further etymology of a donor word. Our own original research efforts will be concentrated much more on examining direct foreign-language influence on English, whether on a word's form or its meaning. In the course of doing this, new etymologies in the narrower sense do certainly come to light. Very frequently we will discover that what appeared to be a derivative formation within English is in fact a borrowing from an existing word in the donor language (or alternatively, is formed within English on the model of the foreign-language word), rather than being formed in isolation within English. Sometimes we will also make radical reassessments of the etymologies of base words.[2] But this is not the 'be all and end all' of our etymology work.

For internal formations (such as an English compound formed from word A plus word B, for instance NARROW GAUGE *n.*, or a derivative such as OBTRUSIVENESS *n.*) the documentation tends to be fairly straightforward and is presented up-front in one or more *OED* entries; i.e., one can look at each of the parent entries to ensure that the currency of each supposed parent fits with the assumed derivation.

For inherited words (that is to say, for words which are present from the OE period and are not identified as loans within Old English) the available dictionaries and other resources will be squeezed for all that they can give, and the usual hypothesis or hypotheses will be reassessed on this basis. A useful illustration may be given by two relatively difficult OE etymologies, OOZE *n.*[1] 'wet mud or slime' and OOZE *n.*[2] 'juice from a plant' (all material quoted from *OED Online* www.oed.com; the etymology of OOZE *n.*[1] given here has been abbreviated; in earlier editions of the dictionary the order of the two headwords is the reverse):

OOZE *n.*[1] (Old English *wāse*):

> [Cognate with Old Frisian *wāse* mud (prob. reflected by West Frisian *weaze*), Old Icelandic *veisa* wetness, mud, marshy ground, Norwegian (Nynorsk) *veis* strip of moist (marshy) soil, *veise* moist

---

[2] For a selection of examples of both types see Durkin (1999).

(marshy) soil, Danish regional *vejs* oozy bottom, Swedish regional *vesa*, *ves*, *veis* (viscous and sticky) mud or sludge; further etymology uncertain and disputed.

... Rhymes in the ME period and the 16th cent. show open $\bar{o}$ as the regular (southern) development of OE $\bar{a}$. The modern pronunciation shows raising to the reflex of ME close $\bar{o}$, prob. as a result of the influence of preceding *w* (which was subsequently assimilated), although association with the semantically close OOZE *n.*² is also likely to have played a part. For evidence from the early modern period for pronunciations with the reflexes of both open $\bar{o}$ and close $\bar{o}$ see E. J. Dobson *Eng. Pronunc. 1500-1700* (ed. 2, 1968) II. §153, although the possibility of inexact rhymes cannot be ruled out.]

OOZE *n.*² (Old English *wōs*):

[Cognate with Middle Low German *wōs*, *wōse* foam, scum, Old Swedish *ōs*, Danish *ōs* (Danish regional *os*) juice from a plant; further etymology uncertain and disputed. (Prob. not related to Old Icelandic *vás* wetness, toil, fatigue from storm, etc.) β forms show assimilation of *w* to the following vowel. The 17th-cent. forms *oaze*, *oze* may result from association with OOZE *n.*¹ (see discussion s.v.).]

Neither of these words has a huge number of cognates in other Germanic languages, and in the case of OOZE *n.*¹ in particular I am very grateful to the staff of the *Svenska Akademiens ordbok* for having provided a lot of very useful information on North Germanic dialectal material for a word which they have yet to publish in their own dictionary. Nevertheless, the basic principle is simple: we will work through available sources of data for the Germanic languages in order to provide a satisfactory set of cognates. Wherever possible, forms will be checked in primary dictionaries for each language, rather than being taken on trust from other etymological dictionaries. Normally, a restricted set of languages will be taken as sufficient for illustrative purposes; hence, for the North Germanic languages, normally just Old Icelandic, Danish, and Swedish. However, where cognates are rather thin on the ground, as is the case with these two words, we will cast our net much more widely, and will include any information which helps to fill out the picture. These two words also illustrate how internal semantic and formal influence of one word upon another can be documented within the dictionary format, with notes on possible formal influence occurring in the etymology section of each word (and notes on semantic overlap also occurring in the definitions of the first sense of each, not quoted here).

With loanwords the methodology is perhaps less transparent. To put the methodology at its simplest, we will work through all relevant resources for each language for each English word where that language is relevant. But the word "relevant" occurs twice in this formulation, and in both cases its meaning is, to say the least, open to interpretation. To begin with, what counts as a "relevant" resource for the *OED*'s research? For many languages the answer to this question is simple: there are few resources available to us, and we will use all of them gratefully each and every time, often calling upon the help of a specialist consultant as well to see whether any extra information can be extracted from any other source. For some of the most important donor languages, however, the situation is very different, and there is almost an *embarras de richesses* – or at least, there are so many different potential sources of information that to check each and every one for every word would be prohibitively time-consuming, and arguably of little real benefit.

To take the biggest single donor language, and also the best documented, this paper simply would not allow the space to give a comprehensive list of all the available resources for French. There are numerous dictionaries and related resources, such as the *Trésor de la langue française* (*TLF*; giving comprehensive modern coverage and selective historical coverage (which is soon to be revised) for those words which survive into modern French), the *Französisches etymologisches Wörterbuch* (*FEW*; giving detailed etymological treatment and fairly comprehensive historical treatment for most words), the 48 volumes of *Datations et documents lexicographiques* (*DDL*) supplementary to *TLF* (now mercifully searchable online as well), Tobler-Lommatzsch *Altfranzösisches Wörterbuch* for Old French, a series of new online subject-specific dictionaries for Middle French (for which see www.atilf.fr/blmf), the *Anglo-Norman*

Dictionary for insular developments (sadly, not conceived as an historical dictionary, and so not giving earliest examples of words or senses), Huguet *Dictionnaire de la langue française du XVIe siècle* for the sixteenth century; in addition, numerous gleanings can be found for modern words in dictionaries such as the Robert *Dictionnaire alphabétique et analogique de la langue française* for items excluded from the *TLF*, and likewise for older (especially nineteenth-century) vocabulary in Littré *Dictionnaire de la langue française*. This list of dictionary resources is still at this length selective and representative only. Furthermore, there are now corpora such as *Frantext* available (http://atilf.atilf.fr/frantext.htm), and other electronic databases such as *Gallica* (searching the Bibliothèque Nationale's collections; http://gallica.bnf.fr/), searchable texts of individual authors (such as the electronic Rabelais, http://134.59.31.3/rabelais.html), assorted encyclopedias (most notably the *Encylopédie* of Diderot at http://portail.atilf.fr/encyclopedie/), or searchable dictionaries from the early modern and modern periods (as for instance those made available through the *Dictionnaires d'autrefois* project at http://dictionnaires.atilf.fr/dictionnaires/). In addition, there are hints and clues to be pursued from our own English data (for example, a quotation from a work which is translated from a French original, a reference to a use by a French scholar or scientist, etc.).

All of these resources, and more, are used in the course of the compilation of our etymologies. However, as I hope will by now be obvious, it is simply impossible for every one of these resources to be checked for every item in our wordlist of approximately 300,000 words (and rising) for which a French etymology or other French influence is likely.[3] The *OED*'s response to this problem is to work through a small core of key resources in a preferred order, and then

---

[3] Rothwell (2001) suggests that the *OED* should also "do its own research in the Anglo-French field, using primary rather than secondary material" (Rothwell 2001:540). Such a task would be well beyond the resources of an English dictionary, much as it doubtless would further enrich our coverage. However, as more such material becomes searchable online in a corpus (www.anglo-norman.net), then there will be much more realistic possibilities for targeted searches for further data.

select which subsidiary sources to look at according to date, milieu, etc., but also crucially on the basis of what we have found out so far.

Initially there is a raft of pre-editorial checking, to ascertain whether the information from the *TLF* is supplemented by other modern dictionaries or Littré, and also whether there is anything in any of the *DDL* volumes. At the editing stage *TLF* will always be consulted, and for words of any complexity also *FEW*, and then other period-specific resources when (a) the English word is first attested in the corresponding period or slightly earlier, and (b) there are gaps in the picture given by *TLF* and *FEW*; in other words, if what we know about the English word raises questions not adequately answered already by the basic documentation in *TLF* and *FEW*. The *Anglo-Norman Dictionary* will of course also always be consulted to check for insular evidence for any word that it is medieval.

As an illustration, in the entry OPPOSE *v.* the etymology is determined on morphological grounds, the English word showing a reflex of French *opposer*, which in turn shows a formation from classical Latin *ob-* plus French *poser* on the model of classical Latin *oppōnere* (the cross-reference to POSE *v.* will in turn explain that the French simplex *poser* is in fact the formal descendant of Latin *pausare*, but shows the effects of that verb having become confused semantically with *pōnere* in Vulgar Latin):

> [< Anglo-Norman *opposer*, *oposer* to question, to oppose, object, and Middle French, French *opposer* to object (12th cent. in Old French as *oposer*), to set oneself in opposition, resist (*c*1224), to set something against or opposite (1321), to place as an obstacle (1580) < classical Latin *ob-* OB- + Old French, Middle French, French *poser* POSE *v.*, after classical Latin *oppōnere* to set against (see OPPONE *v.*; cf. COMPOSE *v.*, DEPOSE *v.*, etc.). With branch I., cf. post-classical Latin *opponere* to dispute (freq. *c*1282-*c*1592 in British sources), to appose, examine (*a*1410 in a British source). These were the chief senses of *oppose* in Middle English, varying with APPOSE *v.*^{1}, which later became the established form in these senses. Branch II, which is rare in English before the late 16th cent., ult. represents senses of classical Latin *oppōnere*: see OPPONE *v.* Before 1600 OPPONE *v.* was chiefly used in these senses, but subsequently *oppose* became commoner, as also with

compose, depose, dispose, expose, and other words taken to be representatives of classical Latin *pōnere.* Cf. Catalan *oposar* (14th cent.), Old Occitan *opausar*.]

As regards its semantics, the English verb shows influences from both French *opposer* and Latin *opponere*; in this particular instance, all of the relevant information on French is readily available in the first port of call, the *TLF*. For such a major word the other key sources have of course been checked, but here they do not yield anything else of great importance for the English word history.

For the related word OPPOSITION *n.*, either French or Latin are plausible as etymons on formal grounds, and the etymological formula that we present is the result of careful comparison of dates of senses in each language:

[< Middle French, French *opposition* contrary argument, objection (*c*1165 in Old French as *oposicion*; cf. Anglo-Norman *opposicioun* irrelevant question), position opposite something (late 12th cent.), opposition of two celestial objects (1269-78), (in rhetoric) antithesis (1567), logical opposition of propositions (1721), movement of the hand by which one wards off a fatal blow (1765), antonymy (1921 in the passage translated in quot. 1925, sense 9a), functional contrast between phonological elements (1931 in *Travaux du Cercle Linguistique de Prague* 4 311) and its etymon post-classical Latin *opposition-, oppositio* contradiction (Vetus Latina, Vulgate, translating Greek αντίθεσις ANTITHESIS *n.*), (in rhetoric) antithesis (6th cent., translating Greek αντίθεσις), opposition of two celestial objects (1120, 1686 in British sources), disputation, examination (*a*1215 in a continental source, from 1357 in British sources) < classical Latin *opposit-*, past participial stem of *oppōnere* to set against (see OPPONE *v.*, OPPOSE *v.*) + *-iō* - ION¹. Cf. Italian *opposizione* (1282), Spanish *oposición* (1288), both in sense 1.

The specific senses relating to astronomy (1) and rhetoric (6a) are recorded earlier than the more general senses in English.]

For this word, the information on senses in French results from a careful collation of what the French dictionaries have, giving a composite picture which could not be duplicated from any single source. The criterion for mentioning a sense is that it should seem plausible that it has had an effect on the development of the word within English, or (more rarely) that it provides an indispensable link in explaining the development within French of other senses which have had an influence on the English word. The result is thus very far from a repetition of what will be found in the French dictionaries, even if all of their evidence is brought together; for instance, in modern French an important strand of meaning relates to the political opposition in a deliberative assembly, but since this meaning is developed in French on the model of earlier use in English in the early eighteenth century, and cannot be shown to have exercised any significant subsequent influence on the English word in this sense, it is not mentioned in the *OED* etymology.

In addition, some of the information is not found in French dictionaries, but has been added from other sources. For the sense "A functional, or potentially functional, contrast between linguistic (esp. phonological) elements", research for *OED Supplement* in the 1970s unearthed evidence of use in French in 1931 in the *Travaux du Cercle Linguistique de Prague*, while for the slightly earlier sense "antonymy" careful inspection of our quotations shows that the earliest example is in fact in an English translation of Vendryès, and pursuing this in libraries gives us the date 1921. (*TLF* does in fact record the former sense, "functional contrast", but only from 1951 onwards.) Thus we have gained an impression of the extent of continuing French influence on the English word through (a) selective extraction of material from the French dictionaries, focusing on those senses which are most closely related to the English sense development, and (b) further gleaning of information from our own research in the specialist literature, and through hints and clues in our own English documentation.

Further examples could show every possible gradation in the available evidence, but the opposite end of the 'French' spectrum in *OED*'s research work is perhaps best illustrated by a word such as OPPOSAL *n.*, which has in *OED3* the etymology "[< OPPOSE *v.* + -AL¹.]" with, obviously, no French component whatever. However, since the base word is borrowed partly from French, the suffix is not alien to French, and the formation seems at least conceivable for French, we have carefully checked all of our available resources for the relevant period just to make sure that there is no potential etymon in French. We have even examined the original sources translated in two quotations for this word from Lydgate's *Fall of Princes* to check that his *opposaile* does not reflect a parallel in the French sources which he is translating (which it does not).

This example also illustrates the answer to the second rather vague use of the word "relevant" in my earlier formulation: what determines for *OED3* that it is "relevant" to check the resources for a particular language when researching a particular English word? In a case such as this, we will always search for possible parallels in French, and likewise in Latin, for any word which could conceivably be French or Latin. Doubtless human error will sometimes occur, but the resulting picture should give as full an impression of the extent of French and Latin influence as the resources available today allow one to give. However, we will not carry out the same 'blanket coverage' checking for other Romance languages or for Germanic languages, still less for languages geographically and culturally more remote from the traditional centres of English use. What we do here instead is to check for possible pointers in the entry; firstly, by looking at the cultural context of the word's meaning (although with a language as well investigated as English, this will normally fall into the category of rechecking in cases where previous investigators have been unable to find anything, unless one is working on a very recently introduced word), but also more subtly, by looking at our quotation evidence, to see whether we have early examples in translated sources, or whether a particular cultural context is suggested by one or other of our early examples. These triggers will lead to checking in dictionaries and in some cases corpora as well, and also very often to the pursuit of primary leads: for instance, checking the original of a translated text, or the documentary records or official history of a foreign place or institution with which the word appears to be associated, or the biography of a named individual.

As an illustration of what we can do when the resources are very limited indeed, German will serve as a surprisingly good example.

The native, Germanic component of the vocabulary of German is obviously very well covered by dictionaries. However, because of the biases and rather narrow focus which have historically been found in the lexicography of German, it is more difficult to document the German contribution to the language of science in the course of the past two centuries. I give below as a sample very brief summaries of the etymologies given for the first 15 of the 25 words in the June 2004 quarterly release of *OED3* material which are given as loans directly from German, as well as two representative examples from the slightly larger group of words which are given as being formed within English on German models. For each word a short 'thumbnail sketch' of the meaning is given here (not the full *OED* definition), followed by the relevant part of the etymology. The formulae which follow the German etymons tell their own story: those which have a date followed by "or earlier" show the results of searching on electronic corpora, library catalogues, etc.; those which refer to a particular bibliographical location show the results of pursuing the etymology back through clues in the primary literature of the discipline in question; those with "[date] in the passage translated in quot. [date]" show this methodology in its plainest form.

OLM *n.* large, blind, aquatic salamander [< German *Olm* (first used in this sense by L. Oken *Lehrb. der Naturgeschichte* (1816) III. 189; 11th cent. in Old High German as *olm*...]

OMA *n.* grandmother [Prob. partly < German *Oma* (1870 or earlier).., and partly < Dutch *oma* (1900 or earlier)...]

OMI *n.*/2 grandmother [< German *Omi* < *Om-* (in *Oma* OMA *n.*) + *-i*, hypocoristic suffix (cf.-Y/6)...]

OMMATIN *n.* (Biochemistry) type of ommachrome [< German *Ommatin* (E. Becker 1939, in *Biol. Zentralbl.* **59** 622...]

OMMATOPHORE *n.* (Zoology) part of an invertebrate animal [< German *Ommatophor* (1878 in the source translated in quot. 1878)...]

OMMIN *n.* (Biochemistry) type of ommachrome [< German *Ommin* (E. Becker 1939, in *Biol. Zentralbl.* **59** 611...]

OMMOCHROME *n.* (Biochemistry) type of invertebrate pigment [< German *Ommochrom* (E. Becker 1942, in *Zeitschr. f. Indukt. Abstammungs- u. Vererbungslehre* **80** 179...]

OMPHACITE *n.* (Mineralogy) a green foliated pyroxene [< German *Omphazit* (A. G. Werner in C. A. S. Hoffman *Handb. der Mineral.* (1815) II. 302)...]

ONCOSINE *n.* (Mineralogy) aluminosilicate of potassium, other alkali metals, and magnesium [< German *Onkosin* (F. von Kobell 1834, in *Jrnl. f. Prakt. Chem.* **2** 296)...]

ONOFRITE *n.* (Mineralogy) sulphide and selenide of mercury [< German *Onofrit* (W. Haidinger *Handb. der Bestimmenden Mineral.* (1845) 565)...]

ONOMASIOLOGY *n.* [< German *Onomasiologie* (A. Zauner *Die Romanischen Namen der Körperteile* (1902) 4)...]

ONOMATOPOESIS *n.* onomatopoeia [< German *Onomatopoesis* (1880 in the passage translated in quot. 1885)...]

ONTOGENESIS *n.* development of the individual organism [< German *Ontogenesis* (E. Haeckel *Gen. Morphol. der Organismen* (1866) I. 55)...]

OOBLAST *n.* (Biology) oocyte [< German *Ooblast* (L. Will 1885, in *Zeitschr. f. Wissenschaftliche Zoologie* **41** 316)...]

OOID *n.* (Geology) oolith [< German *Ooid* (E. Kalkowsky 1908, in *Zeitschr. f. Deutsch. Geol. Ges.* **60** 72)...]

OMBROPHILOUS *a.*[1] (Botany) able to withstand prolonged rainfall [< OMBRO- + -PHILOUS, in sense 1 after German *ombrophil* (J. Wiesner 1893, in *Sitzungsber. der Kaiserlichen Akad. der Wissensch. Wien: Math.-Nat. Klasse* Abth. I. **102** 509);...]

OMBROPHILY *n.* (Botany) property of being ombrophilous [< OMBRO- + -PHILY, after German *Ombrophilie* (1898 in the passage translated in quot. 1903)...]

Ultimately, this is a pragmatic approach, which looks to eliminate scope for caprice in pursuing one word to the neglect of another, but which does allow flexibility in the use of available resources. The resources will differ greatly from word to word: a few will have received individual consideration in the article literature; some will be well served by foreign-language dictionaries, and others less so. Other words again will have a secondary literature of their own, and this will not be neglected,[4] even if it means that this lexical item therefore receives 'special treatment' in comparison with others. During the course of the *OED* project, new resources will become available, and we will certainly not neglect to use these when revising S simply because they were not available when we revised P; similarly, a good many of our resources at present only cover part of the alphabet – for instance, the *Dictionnaire étymologique de l'ancien français* covers only G, H, and I. We therefore cannot achieve a total evenness of treatment, but what we can and do strive to do is to approach each word with the same aims and with a well-thought-through methodology. Imbalances in the available documentation are inevitable in a project which dares to try to compare the lexis of one language with the lexis of a large number of other languages. What the *OED* etymologists must do in the face of this is ensure that our methodology is as regular as possible, so that our readership continues to have confidence in the results offered.

References

Altfranzösisches Wörterbuch. 1925-2002. Eds. Adolf Tobler, Erhard Lommatzsch and Hans H. Christmann. Wiesbaden: Franz Steiner.
Anglo-Norman Dictionary. 1977-1992. Eds. Louise W. Stone, T. B. W. Reid and William Rothwell. London: The Modern Humanities Research Association.
Datations et documents lexicographiques: Matériaux pour l'histoire du vocabulaire français. 1959-1965, 2nd series 1970-. Eds. Bernard Quemada and P. Rézeau. Paris: Klincksieck. Searchable online at: http://atilf.atilf.fr/jykervei/ddl.htm
Dictionnaire alphabétique et analogique de la langue française: Les mots et les associations d'idées. 2nd ed., 1985. Ed. Alain Rey. Paris: Robert.
Dictionnaire de la langue française. 1863-1872. Ed. Émile Littré. Paris: Hachette.

---

[4] At least, it will not be neglected if the relevant discussion is known to the *OED* editors. See Simpson (2004) for a recent plea for notification of any lexically related studies so that we can ensure that the *OED* files are as comprehensive as possible and provide the soundest possible basis for our editorial work.

Dictionnaire de la langue française du XVIe siècle. 1925-1973. Ed. Edmond Huguet. Paris: Didier.

Dictionnaire étymologique de l'ancien français. 1971- (beginning at G, published to end of I). Eds. Kurt Baldinger and Frankwalt Möhren. Tübingen: Niemeyer.

Durkin, Philip. 1999. "Root and branch: revising the etymological component of the *OED*". *Transactions of the Philological Society* 97: 1-50.

-----. 2002a. "Changing documentation in the third edition of the *Oxford English Dictionary*: sixteenth-century vocabulary as a test case". In: Fanego, Teresa, B. Méndez-Naya and E. Seoane (eds.). *Sounds, words, texts and change. Selected papers from 11 ICEHL, Santiago de Compostela, 7-11 September 2000*. Amsterdam: Benjamins: 65-81.

-----. 2002b. "'Mixed' etymologies of Middle English items in OED3: some questions of methodology and policy". *Dictionaries: the Journal of the Dictionary Society of North America* 23: 142-155.

-----. 2004. "Loanword etymologies in the third edition of the *OED*: towards a classification". In: Kay, Christian, Carole Hough and Irene Wotherspoon (eds.). *New perspectives on English historical linguistics. Selected papers from 12 ICEHL, Glasgow, 21-26 August 2002, Volume II: Lexis and transmission*. Amsterdam: Benjamins: 79-90.

Französisches etymologisches Wörterbuch: Eine Darstellung des galloromanischen Sprachschatzes. 1922-1978; 2nd. ed. in course of publication. Founding editor Walther von Wartburg. Basel: Zbinden.

OED = Murray, Sir James A. H., Henry Bradley, Sir William A. Craigie and Charles T. Onions. 1884-1933. *The Oxford English Dictionary*. Supplement, 1972-1986, ed. by Robert W. Burchfield; 2nd. ed., 1989, ed. by John A. Simpson and Edmund S. C. Weiner. Additions Series, 1993-1997, ed. by John A. Simpson, Edmund S. C. Weiner and Michael Proffitt; 3rd ed. (in progress) *OED Online*, March 2000-, ed. by John A. Simpson. Oxford: OUP.

Rothwell, William. 2001. "*OED*, *MED*, *AND*: the making of a new dictionary of English". *Anglia* 119: 527-553.

Simpson, John. 2004. "The *OED* and collaborative research into the history of English". *Anglia* 122: 185-208.

Simpson, John, Edmund Weiner and Philip Durkin. 2004. "The *Oxford English Dictionary* today". *Transactions of the Philological Society* 102: 335-374.

Trésor de la langue française: Dictionnaire de la langue du XIXe et XXe siècle (1789-1960). 1971-1994, 16 vols. Ed. Paul Imbs and Bernard Quemada. Paris: Gallimard. Searchable online at: http://atilf.atilf.fr/tlf.htm

Online resources:

ATILF/Équipe "Moyen français et français préclassique", 2003-2005, *Dictionnaire du Moyen Français (DMF)*. Base de Lexiques de Moyen Français (DMF1). Site internet http://www.atilf.fr/blmf.

Dictionnaires d'autrefois http://dictionnaires.atilf.fr/dictionnaires/
Encyclopédie http://portail.atilf.fr/encyclopedie/
Frantext http://atilf.atilf.fr/frantext.htm
Gallica: la bibliothèque numérique. Bibliothèque nationale de France
    http://gallica.bnf.fr/
Rabelais et son temps http://134.59.31.3/rabelais.html
The Anglo-Norman On-Line Hub www.anglo-norman.net

Michael Bilynsky
Getting a diachronic view on synonymy: verbs and deverbatives

1. Introduction

Relations of synonymy – which are established through sense proximity between different lexical items – are rooted in the very nature of language signs, which exhibit what is known as asymmetric dualism. At the same time, changes in these relations, such as the rise of parallel formal signifiers for a single signified, represent intrinsically diachronic phenomena. The discipline which studies the lexical resources available for expressing specific concepts at different historical stages is known as diachronic onomasiology. It is also concerned with the expansion and/or reduction of these resources over time, and – by recovering lists of synonymous words available to the previous generations of speakers – provides insights into the minds of those who spoke the language in earlier stages of its evolution.

One method for reconstructing the historical development of relations of lexical synonymy is taking the words in a specific semantic field (Kay and Samuels 1975) and charting the earliest uses of these words, at least to the extent to which they are recoverable from first quotations in the *Oxford English Dictionary* or similar sources (e.g. the *Middle English Dictionary*). That method opens a diachronic perspective for onomasiology (Hüllen 1996), and has resulted in the compilation of a *Historical Thesaurus of English*, which is still in progress. The semantic fields from *Roget's Thesaurus* are given a diachronic dimension, reflecting the different means for expressing them that were available at different stages of lexical history. This mammoth task has necessitated the development of specific software (Wotherspoon 1992) and frameworks of data presentation (Kay and Wotherspoon 2002). It has also made it possible to better address such issues in historical onomasiology as the question how changing world views are reflected in changing lexical inventories (Kay 1994), to describe the moving thesaurus format of specific semantic fields throughout history (Fischer 1992; Sylvester

1994; Coleman 1999) or specific periods (Sylvester 1998; Tissari 1998), as well as to tackle the problem how cultural components of meaning (Kay 1997) and semantic prototyping (Kay 1998) are reflected in the changing lexicon.

In this paper I argue that the semantic relations established by strings of synonymous words deserve to be studied in historical lexicology as well. I describe the diachronic sequence in which verbs that form strings of synonyms emerged and compare it to the sequence in which words derived from such synonymous verbs emerged. In particular, I attempt to develop a framework for presenting and assessing similarities and differences between the historical order in which synonymous verbs emerged and the order in which synonymous words derived from them made their historical appearances.

2. Sources of evidence

My starting point is the entire list of 6,329 strings of synonymous verbs from *Webster's New World Thesaurus* (Laird 1985). In this way the semantic field limitations common in historical lexicology are avoided and the issue of macro-semantic diachronic expansion can be addressed. This study is based on the earliest occurrences of verbs and deverbatives attested in the *Oxford English Dictionary*.[1] Of derivatives, only those that are clearly related to the common-root verb are taken into account. For the sake of clarity, I disregard spelling variation and adopt the spelling of the *OED* lemmas in presenting the historical material. The spelling of verbal strings is preserved as in Laird (1985).

In most cases the *OED* gives exact dates for the earliest attestations of lexemes. When it gives only approximate dates (indicated by *a* (*ante*) and *c* (*circa*), as in *lisp a* 1100 and *weeder c* 1440), such dates are treated as precise for the purposes of this study. Century dating (e.g. 13.. as in *display 13..*) is replaced by the next *OED* attestation of the word in question (e.g. *display* 1320), if it falls within the same

---

[1] The second electronic CD-ROM edition, version 3.

century, or otherwise taken to indicate the very end of the century (e.g. *staking 13..*, 1399). In the rare cases of period dating (e.g. *procession* 1103-23), the earlier date is accepted.

3. Constructing an historical thesaurus of verbal strings

A synchronic string of synonyms is an ordered list of lexemes which starts with a head-word (string dominant), and in which each subsequent constituent is semantically farther from the dominant than the previous one. By contrast, the order of items on a diachronic string of synonyms reflects the age of its constituents rather than their semantic proximity to the headword. Thus, a dictionary of diachronic strings of synonymous verbs amounts to an historical thesaurus.

In presenting strings I use two symbols: '⊂' follows the string dominant and separates it from the other string constituents; → stands between different types of strings (between a synchronic string of synonyms and its diachronic counterpart, or between a string of verbal synonyms and a related string of synonymous deverbal derivatives). Wherever the string dominant is polysemous the relevant meaning is indicated in square brackets.

Unsurprisingly, the succession of constituents in a synchronic present-day string is seldom the same as the one in the corresponding diachronic string (as, for example, in **gape** ⊂ *goggle, gaze, peer* → **gape 1220** ⊂ *goggle* 1380, *gaze* 1386, *peer* 1591). More typically, the transformation of a synchronic string into a diachronic one changes the order of constituents. When synchronic strings are restructured on diachronic criteria, two things may happen. First, the synchronic dominant may also be the historically oldest constituent: e.g. **abate** ['to grow less'] ⊂ *lessen, decline, diminish* → **abate** 1270 ⊂ *decline* 1325, *lessen* 1399, *diminish* 1417. On the other hand, it may not. Then, another word becomes the headword in the diachronically restructured string, and the dominant of the synchronic string may occur on any position of the string, including the last one of course, which would indicate that the present-day dominant is in fact the youngest member of the string. When the contemporary dominant is not the oldest constituent of the diachronic string, it is marked by subscript (cd) in the diachronic string, while the diachronic headword gets the present-day dominant as a subscript index: e.g. ***commend*** ⊂ *laud, support, acclaim* → ***acclaim*** 1320 (commend) ⊂ *commend* 1325 (cd), *laud* 1377, *support* 1382; ***exterminate*** ⊂ *eradicate, annihilate, abolish* → **abolish** 1490 (exterminate) ⊂ *annihilate* 1525, *exterminate* 1541 (cd), *eradicate* 1564; ***coincide*** ['to correspond'] ⊂ *accord, harmonize, match* → ***accord*** 1123 (coincide) ⊂ *match* 1362, *harmonize* 1483, *coincide* 1673 (cd).

When several verbs are attested in the same year they are listed alphabetically in the historical string: ***jump*** ['to pass over'] ⊂ *cover, take, skip, traverse, remove, nullify* → ***take*** 1100 (jump) ⊂ *cover* 1275, remove 1300, skip 1300, *traverse* 1325, *jump* 1511 (cd), *nullify* 1595; ***digest*** ['to summarize'] ⊂ *survey, abstract, abbreviate* → **abbreviate** 1450 (digest) ⊂ *digest* 1450 (cd), *survey* 1467, *abstract* 1542.

Diachronic strings that share constituents (either as dominants or not) due to polysemy make up clusters of strings in the historical thesaurus: e.g. ***acclaim*** 1320 ⊂ *commend* 1325, *laud* 1377, *celebrate* 1534; ***acclaim*** 1320 (applaud) ⊂ *commend* 1325, *applaud* 1536 (cd), *aggrandize* 1634; ***acclaim*** 1320 (approve) ⊂ *approve* 1340 (cd), *recommend* 1377; ***wink*** ['to twinkle'] 897 ⊂ *sparkle* 1200, *gleam* 1225, *blink* 1300; ***wink*** ['to close one's eye'] 897 ⊂ *blink* 1300, *flirt* 1553, *squint* 1599, *nictate* 1691, *nictitate* 1822; ***wink*** 897 (hint) ⊂ *whisper* 950, *signify* 1250, *acquaint* 1297, *advise* 1297, *inform* 1320, *broach* 1330, *prompt* 1340, *imply* 1374, *impart* 1471, *infer* 1526, *suggest* 1526, *insinuate* 1529, *intimate* 1538, *recall* 1575, *foreshadow* 1577, *adumbrate* 1581, *remind* 1645, *hint* 1648 (cd), *indicate* 1651, *cue* 1928.

Sometimes a polysemous dominant of a set of contemporary strings will turn out to be the oldest constituent in some but not all historical strings, e.g. ***abet*** ['to help'] ⊂ *assist, befriend, encourage* → **abet** 1380, *encourage* 1483, *assist* 1514, *befriend* 1559; ***abet*** ['to excite'] ⊂ *inspire, encourage, entreat* → ***entreat*** 1340 (abet) ⊂ *inspire* 1340, *abet* 1380 (cd), *encourage* 1483.

Most strings are etymologically heterogeneous. Although the dominant of a historical string tends to be a native lexeme (e.g. ***abdicate*** ⊂ *relinquish, withdraw* → ***withdraw*** 1225 (abdicate) ⊂

relinquish 1472, *abdicate* (cd) 1541), there are etymologically mixed strings where this is not the case. Again, the dominant of a contemporary string can either retain its position in the diachronic counterpart (e.g. ***abate*** ['to grow less'] ⊂ *lessen, decline, diminish*→ ***abate*** 1270 ⊂ *decline* 1325, *lessen* 1399, *diminish* 1417) or be substituted by another lexeme (e.g. ***secure*** ⊂ *achieve, acquire, grasp* → ***achieve*** 1325 (secure), *grasp* 1382, *acquire* 1435, *secure* 1593 (cd)).

In 1,568 strings of synonymous verbs the present-day dominant is also the oldest string constituent. In the remaining 4,751 strings the oldest constituent and the present-day dominant do not coincide. This is actually to be expected, since no verb has been there forever but must have emerged at some point, so that as one goes back in time, one will necessarily find successively fewer of the verbs that are present-day dominants.

4. Construing an historical thesaurus of deverbatives

Existing dictionaries of synonyms fail to reflect that derivatives of synonyms may also be synonyms. Like items from which they are derived, synonymous derivatives can be listed on synonym strings.[2] One way of constructing such strings of deverbatives is to take a historical string of verbal synonyms, to identify categorical positions in the word-forming family of each of its constituents, and to identify the lexemes that occupy those positions.

A deverbal word-formation family is the set of all lexemes sharing a single verbal root, i.e. it comprises both the verb (D_0) itself, and all coinages (D_n) derived from it. For the purposes of this study, I have entered verbs and their derivatives into a kind of lattice. In that lattice separate positions represent different categories of deverbatives. Categories of deverbatives have been established on the basis of their paraphrases.

---

[2] Possible semantic divergences occurring between the derivatives of synonymous verbs are interesting but will be disregarded for the purposes of this study. Thus, strings of synonymous verbs may yield strings of parallel coinages that are sometimes not synonymous in the same way as the verbs. Such cases may even indicate the need for re-conceptualising the notion of structural-semantic solidarity.

In strings of deverbatives no difference is made between English coinages and deverbatives that entered English as complete chunks. For the purposes of diachronic onomasiology their role in a string of deverbatives from synonymous verbs is identical.

Deverbal classes are identified by numbers, which is necessary for the electronic processing of strings. It is also practical because it helps to keep homonymous nominal and participial coinages in *-ing* apart, and does the same for sporadic cases of suffix substitution. The latter occur primarily between agent and patient coinages as well as between agent nouns and deverbal adjectives.

In the domain of deverbal nouns I attribute separate slots to action nouns (D_1), and action nouns that admit of being lexicalised into factitive nouns (D_2). Both types of derivatives are typically based on the same suffixes: (1) D_1 *-ing* (e.g. *moaning* 1586), *-ion* (e.g. *abdication* 1552), *-ment* (*e.g, exposement* 1632), *-ance* (e.g. *usherance* 1711), *-age* (e.g. *ownage* 1576); D_2 *-ing* (e.g. *beholding* 1225), *-ion* (e.g. *injection* 1541), *-ment* (e.g. *obtainment* 1571), *-ance* (e.g. *acceptance* 1574), *-age* (e.g. *stowage* 1390).

Action nouns that are subject to lexicalisation (D_2) sometimes end in *-ture* (e.g. *coverture* 1393) or *-al* (e.g. *refusal* 1474). Action nouns free of factitive lexicalisation occasionally take on the suffix *-ery* (e.g. *gaugery*$^{*(now\ arch)}$ 1608).

Agent nouns (D_3) end in *-er* (e.g. *blower 897*), less often in *-or* (e.g. *admiror* 1603), sporadically in *-ant* (e.g. *assistant* 1483) and *-ive* (e.g. *digestive* 1386).

Patient nouns (D_4) end in *-ee* (e.g. *leasee* 1481), sometimes in *-er* (e.g. *locker* 1417), and very rarely in *-ant/-ent/-and* (e.g. *analysant* 1933, *confident* 1619, *degradand* 1891) or *-ed* (e.g. *beloved* 1526).

In the adjectival domain, deverbal adjectives (D_5) are derived by means of the suffixes *-ive* (e.g. *abusive* 1583), *-ory* (e.g. *revisory* 1846), *-ous* (e.g. *founderous* 1767), *-ant/-ent* (e.g. *accordant* 1315, *coalescent* 1655), *-ful* (*fretful* 1593), *-y* (e.g. *twisty* 1857).

The lexicalised (adjectivised) present participle (D_6) has the suffix *-ing* (*blowing* 1175).

Passive modal adjectives (D_7) end in the allomorphic variants *-able* (e.g. *addable* 1678) or *-ible* (e.g. *coercible* 1656).

Lexicalised (adjectivised) past participles (D_8) end in -ed (e.g. *abused* 1473).

From each of the four adjectival classes adverbs may be derived, respectively D_9, D_{11}, D_{13}, D_{15} (e.g. *attractively* 1604, *pushingly* 1847, *ascertainably* 1863, *worriedly* 1924). The adverbs are derived by the suffix -*ly* attached to the adjectival or participial suffixes.

Also nouns can be derived from deverbal adjectives. Like adverbs, such nouns are secondary derivatives. Nouns derived from adjectives (D_{10}) and passive modal adjectives (D_{14}) are formed with the help of the alternative suffixes -*ness* and -*ity* attached to the adjectival suffixes (e.g. (D_{10}) *forgetfulness* 1398, *repugnantness* 1727, *discontinuousness* 1865, *accumulativeness* 1862, *dissipativity* 1879, (D_{14}) *allowableness* 1692, *coercibleness* 1864, *combinability* 1900, *addibility* 1690). Nouns derived from participles (D_{12}, D_{16}) are formed with the help of the suffix -*ness* (e.g. *probingness* 1800, *uprootedness* 1927).

Factitive nouns (D_{17}) conclude the list. They are often homonymous with action nouns and have chronologically coincident or divergent first attestation (cf. the examples given here and those under D_2): e.g. *beholding* 1440, *injection* 1607, *obtainment* 1829, *acceptance* 1574, *stowage* 1547. There are also factitive nouns for which action noun readings are not attested, e.g. *arrearage* 1315, *obtainal* 1803.

Usually suffixes are simply attached to verbs. Sometimes, however, deverbalisation is coupled with some morphemic restructuring of the verbal root: cf. (D_0) *imagine* 1340 and (D_5) *imaginative* 1374; (D_0) *abjoint* 1887 and (D_1) *abjunction* 1887; (D_0) *renunciate* 1656 and (D_2) *renunciance* 1837.

When a slot representing an onomasiological category is filled by a single deverbal derivative it is selected for being entered into a respective string of coinages derived from synonymous verbs. Cases of suffix rivalry within an onomasiological category are resolved by selecting the oldest coinage for entering it into the categorial string: e.g. (D_3) _represser_ 1449, *repressor* 1611; _abettor_ 1514, *abetter* 1611; _disputant_ 1393, *disputer* 1434, *disputor* 1637; (D_5) _operatory_ 1556, *operative* 1598; _tormentous_ 1583, *tormentive* 1653; _repentant_ 1290, *repentive* 1620, *repentful* 1631; (D_7) _vendible_ 1382, *vendable* 1400;

(D_{14}) <u>coerciveness</u> 1727, coercivity 1898. Among present participles (D_6), however, some coinages (e.g. *following* 1300) are first attested with the formative -*nd*: *a*1300 *Cursor M.* 11378 (Cott.) *Þe nest yeire foluand*. They are nevertheless taken as coinages in -*ing*.

Among action nouns, coinages with rival suffixes may find themselves in different slots if one of them admits of factitive interpretation. If there is additional suffix rivalry within the slots, the older coinage is once again given preference, e.g. (D_1) <u>regaining</u> <u>1548</u>, regainment 1642; (D_2) <u>reinforcement</u> <u>1607</u>, reinforcing 1611. The same principle holds for factitive nouns: (D_{17}) <u>coverture</u> <u>1225</u>, covering 1375, coverage 1912; <u>reinforcement</u> <u>1646</u>, reinforcing 1966.

In cases when two derivatives are attested in the same year I have selected the one with the more highly productive suffix: e.g. (D_3) <u>accuser</u> <u>1340</u>, accusor 1340, accusant 1611; (D_7) <u>detectable</u> <u>1655</u>, detectible 1655.

Generally, it seems to me that selecting the older derivative in a given deverbal category for entering into a string of deverbal synonyms is more in line with diachronic onomasiology than a strictly formal strategy based on suffix identity. The latter strategy would have two disadvantages. Synonym strings construed in this way would not only be missing older derivative(s) from (a) verb(s) which employed more than one suffix, but also many synonymous derivatives with suffixes that happen not to have been selected for forming the string. For instance, the string of the verbs (D_0) **interrupt** ['to break in on'] 1412 $\subset$ interfere 1530, infringe1533, intrude 1534, obtrude 1555, intervene 1588 would yield the following string of synonymous adjectives with the suffix -*ive*: (D_5) **interruptive** 1651$\subset$ intrusive 1647, obtrusive 1667, interventive 1890. However, if synonymous suffixes are admitted into the string, it would contain two more coinages in -*ent*, and the last constituent in -*ive* would have a much earlier counterpart in -*ent*: **interruptive** 1651 $\subset$ interferent 1876, infringent 1886, intrusive 1647, obtrusive 1667, intervenient 1605.

The sufficient and necessary condition for listing a chronological sequence of deverbatives is that there must exist at least two coinages from verbs in the parent string. To make derivational gaps in the strings of deverbatives explicit, I repeat the base verbs in angled brackets where no derivative has been attested: e.g.(D_0) ***appear*** 1250 (ensue) ⊂ *ensue* 1398 (cd), *result* 1432, *occur* 1527 → (D_3) ***appearer*** 1608 ⊂ *ensuer* 1550, <*result* 1432>, <*occur* 1527>. This also holds for cases where the historical dominant itself does not produce a coinage: e.g. ***overcome*** 725 (reduce) ⊂ *conquer* 1230, *reduce* 1374 (cd), *subdue* 1387 → (D_5) <*overcome* 725> ⊂ *conquerous**$^{(now\ arch)}$ 1571, *reducent* 1805, <*subdue* 1387>. Where there are no derivational gaps, the constituent sequences of the verbal synonym string and the deverbal one may be parallel: e.g. (D_0) ***blast*** 1300 ⊂ *shatter* 1330, *wreck* ['cast on shore'] 1420, *annihilate* 1525, *blight* 1695 → (D_8) ***blasted*** 1552⊂ *shattered* 1666, *wrecked* 1729, *annihilated* 1769, *blighted* 1664.

Such parallelism – which reinforces the impression of the synonymy obtaining among lexemes – may also be observed between strings of primary and secondary deverbatives (e.g. (D_8) ***debased*** 1594 ⊂ *depraved* 1594, *abased* 1611, *perverted* 1667 → (D_{16}) ***debasedness*** 1720 ⊂ *depravedness* 1612, *abasedness* 1900, *pervertedness* 1828) and, in a more distant manner, between strings of verbs and their secondary (deadjectival or departicipial) coinages (e.g. (D_0) ***allow*** ['to grant a request or assertion'] 1300 ⊂ *approve* 1340, *support* 1382, *recognize* 1456 → (D_{14}) ***allowableness*** 1692 ⊂ *approvableness* 1812, *supportableness* 1660, *recognizability* 1873; (D_0) ***daze*** 1325 (bemuse) ⊂ *muddle* 1550, *bewilder* 1684, *bemuse* 1735 (cd) → (D_{15}) ***dazedly*** 1300 ⊂ *muddledly* 1918, *bewilderedly* 1846, *bemusedly* 1896).

5. Sketching a formalised framework

In order to estimate the similarity or dissimilarity between two derivationally related strings of lexemes I compare the relative chronological location of the corresponding constituents on those strings. The results of such a comparison are presented in a matrix.

In order to construct the similarity matrix, the constituents of one string are ordered horizontally, and the constituents of the other vertically (in corresponding order), so that they define the rows and columns of a table. The cells are created at the intersections of the rows and columns of the matrix. A cell gets marked with a plus if the relative chronological positions of the constituents that label its row and column are similar. This is the case if the ordinal numbers (indicating the year of its first attestation) of the constituents in the column and the row coincide, or when the ordinal number of the *i*th constituent from the column is larger than the ordinal numbers of the row constituents located leftwards of its common-root counterpart and, conversely, when it is smaller than the ordinal numbers of the constituents located to the right of its common-root counterpart in the row string. Otherwise, the relative chronological positions of the constituents are regarded as different, and the respective cell in the matrix is marked with a minus.

This procedure amounts to checking for each derived item if its chronological position relative to a specific synonym is similar to the chronological position of its root on the corresponding synonym string of base verbs.

To exemplify this, let us assess the similarity between the verbal string ***acclaim*** 1320 $_{(extol)}$ $\subset$ *laud* 1377, *exalt* 1400, *extol* 1494 $_{(cd)}$, *eulogize* 1810, and a string of the agent nouns derived from it. The chronological string of verbs and the compared string of agent nouns are put down as the row and column in the matrix (Figure 1). The constituents in the column are written in the succession of the corresponding constituents in the row, i.e. non-chronologically: *acclaimer* 1869, *lauder* 1611, *exalter* 1471, *extoller* 1626, *eulogizer* 1837.

The convention of ordering derived string constituents to reflect the order of constituents in the base string seems like a technical detail. However, it helps to reveal that in the common semantic space of word-forming families the historical dominant in derivational classes may often fall on different constituents. In our example, the string of agent nouns has a succession which is different from that in the string of verbs.

Though the verb *acclaim* 1320 is the oldest among its synonyms the derived noun *acclaimer* 1869 is the youngest in its own string. This means that the age of the noun *acclaimer* 1869 relative to any of its synonyms is different from the age of *acclaim* relative to any of its synonyms. Thus, all relevant cells in the matrix are marked negative. Likewise, from the viewpoint of the order of nouns, the verb *acclaim* 1320 is in the wrong place, and its relatedness to all relevant positions in the string of nouns (first column of cells in the matrix) is negative.[3]

If it were to reflect the order of the verbal string, the noun *lauder* 1611 should be younger than the noun *acclaimer* 1869 and older than the remaining three nouns. However, it is older than the noun *acclaimer* 1869 (the sign minus with respect to the verb *acclaim* 1320) and younger than the noun *exalter* 1471 (the sign minus with reference to the verb *exalt* 1400). The noun *lauder* 1611 is younger than the other remaining two nouns *extoller* 1626 and *eulogizer* 1837 just as the verb *exalt* 1400 is younger than the verbs *extol* 1494 and *eulogize* 1810 (plusses in the relevant cells). The noun *exalter* 1471 is the oldest in the string of nouns. However, the verb *exalt* is younger than the verbs *acclaim* 1320 and *laud* 1377 (minuses in the relevant cells). There are plusses that show that the verbs *extol* 1494 and *eulogize* 1810 are younger than the verb *exalt* 1400 in the same way as the nouns *extoller* 1626 and *eulogizer* 1837 are younger than the noun *exalter* 1471. If it were to reflect the order on the verbal base string, the noun *extoller* 1626 should be younger than the previous three nouns and older than the fifth noun. All this is true with the exception of its relatedness to the noun *acclaimer* 1869. Hence it gets three plusses and one minus. Finally, the noun *eulogizer* 1837 also gets one minus, as it is older than the noun *acclaimer* 1869 contrary to the correlation between the respective verbs where *acclaim* 1320 is older than *eulogize* 1810. The remaining correlations of the noun *eulogizer* 1837 with agent nouns in terms of the relative chronology of their appearance in the string are the same as those of the verb *eulogize* 1810 and its respective synonyms (plusses in the relevant cells).

---

[3] These observations show that the matrix is symmetric. Its upper right and lower left triangles map onto each other when folded across the diagonal.

Figure 1. Temporal similarity of the expansion of two strings in diachrony: matrix row – verbs (D_0); matrix column – agent nouns (D_3)[4]

EXTOL		1. acclaim 1320	2. laud 1377	3. exalt 1400	4. extol 1494	5. eulogize 1810
5. acclaimer	1869	▓▓▓	–	–	–	–
1. lauder	1611	–	▓▓▓	–	+	+
2. exalter	1471	–	–	▓▓▓	+	+
3. extoller	1626	–	+	+	▓▓▓	+
4. eulogizer	1837	–	+	+	+	▓▓▓

So much about the way in which similarity matrices are constructed. Of course, the procedure can be modified in various ways. In our case, for example, we might have placed the nouns in the row, left their order intact and rearranged the order of verbs in the columns. Thereby we would have used the deverbal nouns, rather than the verbs, as the basis of our comparison. Also, there are of course cases in which not every constituent has a counterpart in the string that is chosen for comparison. This happens when there are gaps in derivational paradigms. If in such cases the verbal string is selected as the basis of comparison (i.e. the row in the matrix), then the base-string constituents from which no derivative has been formed will result in empty cells. If, on the other hand, a string of deverbatives is placed in the row of the matrix, only those verbs that gave rise to the respective derivatives will enter the matrix column, and all cells will be filled.

How are the results of string comparisons as we have just outlined them to be assessed? Generally, it should be expected that derived strings reflect the chronological order of appearance characterising

---

[4] The layout of the matrix has been modified for better interpretability. The format put out by the specifically designed software is somewhat less user-friendly. As the reproduction below shows, 'rows' appear as left columns, and the actual matrices are small and unlabelled:

```
Example   EXTOL

ACCLAIM              1320   ACCLAIMER    X----      1869
LAUD                 1377   LAUDER       -X-++      1611
EXALT                1400   EXALTER      --X++      1471
EXTOL                1494   EXTOLLER     -++X+      1626
EULOGIZE             1810   EULOGIZER    -+++X      1837
```

base-strings. A divergence from the base sequence strikes one as somewhat unnatural, but may be pragmatically motivated. Of course, there are special cases of divergence, such as instances of reverse word-forming directionality when a deverbative is attested before the motivating verb: e.g. (D_0) ***advance*** 1230 (assert ['to maintain']) $\subset$ *allege* 1300, *cite* 1483, <u>*assert*</u> <u>1604</u> (cd) → (D_3) ***advancer*** 1496 $\subset$ *alleger* 1579, *citer* 1591, <u>*asserter*</u> <u>1449;</u> (D_0) ***show*** 1000 $\subset$ *confirm* 1290, <u>*demonstrate*</u> <u>1552</u>→ (D_8) ***showable*** 1400 $\subset$ *confirmable* 1525, <u>*demonstrable*</u> <u>1400</u>. The assessment of all such cases in the expansion of strings of synonymous verbs and their derivatives can be put on a quantitatively more secure basis with the help of similarity matrices like the ones introduced here.

6. Software

Work on the electronic implementation of the analytic approach presented here was begun in 1995. First, all verbs and deverbatives as well as strings of synonymous verbs were manually entered into a database, which contained no scanned material nor any fragments of downloaded material from electronic lexicographical resources. Then a programme package was designed within FoxPro RDBMS. It consists of three components. The first component construes strings of coinages from synonymous verbs in each class of deverbatives and puts them together in the alphabetic historical thesaurus format. The resulting *Historical Thesaurus of Verbs and Deverbatives* contains entries with the typical structure of one parent and seventeen derived strings. In some cases, there can be a single derivative instead of a string in an onomasiological category. Derivational gaps within the strings and strings that are missing altogether owing to derivational constraints on all verbal constituents are marked as empty positions. This allows one to visualise the unrealised proportion of the onomasiological potential in different word-formation families. The *Historical Thesaurus of Verbs and Deverbatives* exists in a book format and also as a database. It is possible to partition the latter according to the age of the strings' constituents to obtain period thesauri, or by the thematic and/or etymological features of base verbs.

The second component of the programme package juxtaposes the historical sequences of verbs and deverbatives and compares the ordinal positions of their constituents. Historical strings are construed from present-day strings. They can be recovered from the database by their contemporary dominants. Each string of verbs is put into a matrix with a string of deverbatives of a chosen categorical affiliation. The compared strings as well as their similarity matrices are all downloadable.

The third component is aimed at constructing, storing and analysing matrices for categorical pairs of strings. Length limitations on either string or both of them can be imposed. The location of the strings in the matrix is reversible, and each of the strings to be compared can be put either into the matrix row or its column. A corpus of matrices for a specific categorical comparison is subject to a ten-partite division reflecting the similarity of the column-string sequence to that of the row string. The numeric power for each section of this division is established with the possibility of downloading individual strings, complete sets of examples as well as their similarity matrices. The matrix can be juxtaposed with the compared historical strings as in Footnote 4. Within this piece of software it is possible to make queries about precedent, exhaustive or void verification of a calculus of routes of successive vocabulary expansion accompanied by derivational re-categorisation. The queries are also aimed at finding out to what extent classes of deverbalisation expanded differently from the expansion of parent strings under conditions of identical string length and whether strings of the same deverbal class revealed expansion distinctions depending upon the number of their constituents.

7. Discussion

The comparison of all verbal and deverbal strings yields a vast number of matrices and creates the risk of getting lost in plain descriptivism. On the other hand, the factual evidence obtained by the methods described in his paper may make it possible to discern distributional patterns and to try and find explanations for them.

There are almost four hundred verbs that have only one synonymous lexeme in the studied thesaurus. In some cases each of these verbs produces exactly one coinage in a specific category. In such cases the compared strings can be either similar or different. No finer distinctions are possible. In the adduced illustrations, two examples display a parallelism between the emergence of coinages and the emergence of their bases and and two do not: e.g. (D_0) ***search*** 1330 (rummage) $\subset$ *rummage* 1544 (cd) → (D_3) ***searcher*** 1382 $\subset$ *rummager* 1544; (D_0) ***wade*** 993 $\subset$ *paddle* 1530 → (D_3) ***wader*** 1673 $\subset$ *paddler* 1611; (D_0) ***behove*** 890 $\subset$ *suit* 1450 → (D_7) ***behovable*** *(now arch)* 1460 $\subset$ *suitable* 1555; (D_0) ***claim*** 1300 $\subset$ *demand* 1382 → (D_7) ***claimable*** 1611 $\subset$ *demandable* 1576.

Pairs of secondary deverbatives typically correlate with their immediate adjectival/participial bases: e.g. (D_7) ***observable*** 1608 $\subset$ *compliable* 1635 → (D_{13}) ***observably*** 1646 $\subset$ *compliably* 1684; (D_7) ***supposable*** 1643 $\subset$ *presumable* 1692 → (D_{13}) ***supposably*** 1866 $\subset$ *presumably* 1646; (D_8) ***weaned*** 1440 $\subset$ *detached* 1706 → (D_{16}) ***weanedness*** 1617 $\subset$ *detachedness* 1768; (D_8) ***presented*** 1592 $\subset$ *produced* 1644 → (D_{16}) ***presentedness*** 1925 $\subset$ *producedness* 1862. The succession of secondary deverbatives correlates with that of their ultimate verbal bases as well: e.g. (D_0) ***keep*** 1000 $\subset$ *sustain* 1290 → (D_{14}) ***keepability*** 1898 $\subset$ *sustainability* 1972; (D_0) ***dissolve*** 1374 $\subset$ *separate* 1432 → (D_{14}) ***dissolvability*** 1836 $\subset$ *separability* 1640; (D_0) ***lavish*** 1542 $\subset$ *squander* 1593→ (D_{11}) ***lavishingly*** 1585 $\subset$ *squanderingly* 1847; (D_0) ***vanish*** 1303 $\subset$ *dissolve* 1374 → (D_{11}) ***vanishingly*** 1870 $\subset$ *dissolvingly* 1822.

Both primary and secondary deverbatives may also correspond to motivating strings of arbitrary length with derivational gaps in all but two slots: e.g. (D_0) ***abound*** 1374 (bristle) $\subset$ *swarm* 1386, *exuberate* 1471, *bristle* 1480 (cd) → (D_3) ***abounder*** 1755 $\subset$ *swarmer* 1844, <*exuberate* 1471>, <*bristle* 1480>. (D_0) ***dismember*** 1297 $\subset$ *disjoint* 1420, *dissect* 1607, *amputate* 1638 → (D_6) ***dismembering*** 1861 $\subset$ <*disjoint* 1420>, *dissecting* 1854, <*amputate* 1638>; (D_0) ***transcend*** 1340 $\subset$ *excel* 1430, *surpass* 1555 → (D_9) ***transcendently*** 1623 $\subset$ *excellently* 1340, <*surpass* 1555>; (D_0) ***coerce*** (blackmail) 1475 $\subset$ *exact* 1529, *extort* 1529, *blackmail* (cd) 1880 → (D_{10}) ***coerciveness*** 1727 $\subset$

exactiveness 1628, *<extort* 1529>, *<blackmail* 1880>; (D_6) **wasting** 1230 ⊂ *losing* 1519, *consuming* 1535, *spending* 1589, *dissipating* 1818 → (D_{12}) **wastingness** 1900 ⊂ *<losing* 1519>, *consumingness* 1662, *<spending* 1589>, *<dissipating* 1818>; (D_8) **approved** 1380 (recognized) ⊂ *sanctioned* 1799, *recognized* 1826 (cd) → (D_{15}) **approvedly** 1611 ⊂ *<sanctioned* 1799>, *recognizedly* 1861.

In the case of two derivatives the formed matrix has just two squares. Among the synonymous pairs, 41 percent of all adjectives deviate – with respect to the relative chronology of their emergence – from the temporal sequence followed by their base verbs, while only 37 percent of participles and 28 percent of nouns do so. The mean percentage of primary derivatives deviating in this manner is 32 percent. Among pairs of secondary derivatives (both adverbs and nouns) almost 35 percent of the sequences of emergence deviate from that of their motivating adjectives or participles and about 42 percent do so with regard to their base verbs.

The temporal similarity of semantic field expansion between verbal and deverbal strings becomes more finely gradable when there are at least three constituents in the compared strings.

In assessing the similarity between three-member strings of derivatives four degrees of similarity can be distinguished. There can be zero (e.g. (D_0) **shun** 950 (eschew) ⊂ *eschew* 1340 (cd), *abstain* 1380 → (D_3) **shunner** 1806 ⊂ *eschewer* 1578, *abstainer* 1535), two (e.g. (D_0) **conclude** 1300 ⊂ *complete* 1530, *terminate* 1589 → (D_3) **concluder** 1601 ⊂ *completer* 1701, *terminant* 1589), four ((D_3) **abide** 1000 ⊂ *anticipate* 1532, *expect* 1560 → (D_0) **abider** 1543 ⊂ *anticipator* 1598, *expecter* 1584), or only plusses ((D_0) **chide** 1000 ⊂ *rebuke* 1325, *reprimand* 1681 → (D_3) **chider** 1377 ⊂ *rebuker* 1420, *reprimander* 1867) in the matrix cells.

The frequency with which the four possibilities are realised suggests that a lack of similarity between verbal and corresponding deverbal synonym strings is the marked case: it occurs less frequently than cases of synonym strings that exhibit similarity in the temporal order of expansion.

Four-member strings provide us with the possibility of complete similarity (e.g. (D_0) **misconstrue** 1374 ⊂ *pervert* 1374, *exaggerate*

1533, *distort* 1586 → (D$_5$) **misconstruous** 1632 ⊂ *perversive* 1693, *exaggeratory* 1759, *distortive* 1823) and dissimilarity (e.g. (D$_0$) **worry** 725 (perturb) ⊂ *perturb* 1374$_{(cd)}$, *irritate* 1531, *pester* 1536 → (D$_7$) **worriable** 1882 ⊂ *perturbable* 1800, *irritable* 1662, *pesterable**$^{(now}$ $^{arch)}$ 1540), as well as with five degrees of weaker similarity (see examples in Figure 2 below for the D$_0$ → D$_6$ strings).

Figure 2. Exemplification of the degrees of temporal expansion similarity with verbs in four-member strings of present participles

BEWITCH		1. *bewitch* 1205	2. *beguile* 1225	3. *enthrall* 1576	4. *capture* 1795
2. *bewitching*	1561		+	+	+
3. *beguiling*	1593	+		+	+
4. *enthralling*	1871	+	+		−
1. *capturing*	1800	+	+	−	
CLAP		1. *clap* 1300	2. *bang* 1550	3. *slap* ('smack; hit') 1632	4. *slam* 1691
2. *clapping*	1583		−	+	+
1. *banging*	1560	−		+	+
4. *slapping* ('smack; hit')	1812	+	+		−
3. *slamming*	1796	+	+	−	
RULE		1. *rule* 1225	2. *conduct* 1400	3. *control* 1475	4. *dictate* 1592
3. *ruling*	1648		−	−	+
2. *conducting*	1632	−		−	+
1. *controlling*	1576	−	−		+
4. *dictating*	1709	+	+	+	
SUNDER		1. *sunder* 950	2. *part* 1225	3. *separate* 1432	4. *split* 1576
4. *sundering*	1870		−	−	−
1. *parting*	1377	−		+	+
3. *separating*	1694	−	+		−
2. *splitting*	1593	−	+	−	

REVERSE	1. reverse 1315	2. repeal 1325	3. nullify 1595	4. invalidate 1649
4. *reversing* 1804	▓▓▓▓	–	–	–
3. *repealing* 1735	–	▓▓▓▓		
1. *nullifying* 1681	–	–	▓▓▓▓	+
2. *invalidating* 1716	–	–	+	▓▓▓▓

In five-member strings it becomes already possible to measure degrees of string similarity in terms of 10-percent steps: e.g. the similarity between the verbs in (D_0) ***shun*** 950 $\subset$ *evade* 1513, *neglect* 1529, *dodge* 1568, *ignore* 1611 and the deverbal nouns (D_1) ***shunning*** 1546 $\subset$ *evading* 1669, *neglecting* 1552, *dodging* 1593, *ignoring* 1615 is between 70 and 80 percent, while the similarity between the verbal string (D_0) ***weigh*** 897 $_{(gauge)}$ $\subset$ *gauge* 1420 $_{(cd)}$, *check* 1393, *calculate* 1570, *calibrate* 1864 and the nominal string (D_1) ***weighment*** 1878 $\subset$ *checking* 1535, *gaugery*$*^{(now\ arch)}$ 1608, *calculating* 1710, *calibrating* 1870 is between 60 and 70 percent.

The longer the strings, the more finely can differences between base string and derived string be measured. For example, a 100-cell matrix with a similarity between 70 and 80 percent contains twenty-four instances of negative temporal similarity (Figure 3).

Specific categories of deverbatives fail to provide examples of some degrees of similarity. For instance, patient nouns in the four-member strings exhibit only four degrees of weakened similarity when compared to the respective strings of base verbs.

Getting a diachronic view on synonymy 95

Figure 3. Exemplification of the similarity scores in the compared strings of verbs and factitive nouns

INJECT		1. *add* 1374	2. *infuse* 1420	3. *introduce* 1475	4. *insert* 1529	5. *instill* 1533	6. *implant* 1541	7. *imbue* 1555	8. *interject* 1578	9. *inject* 1599	10. *impregnate* 1605	11. *interpolate* 1612
1. *addition*	1366	▨	+	+	+	+	+	+	+	+	+	+
3. *infusion*	1532	+	▨	+	+	+	+	+	−	+	+	+
4. *introducement*	1536	+	+	▨	+	+	+	+	−	+	+	+
8. *insertion*	1624	+	+	+	▨	−	−	+	−	−	+	+
5. *instillation*	1540	+	+	+	−	▨	+	+	−	+	+	+
6. *implantation*	1578	+	+	+	−	+	▨	+	−	+	+	+
10. *imbuement*	1693	+	+	+	+	+	+	▨	−	−	−	−
2. *interjection*	1430	+	−	−	−	−	−	−	▨	+	+	+
7. *injection*	1607	+	+	+	−	+	+	−	+	▨	+	+
9. *impregnation*	1641	+	+	+	+	+	+	−	+	+	▨	+
11. *interpolation*	1675	+	+	+	+	+	+	−	+	+	+	▨

In a next analytical step, all matrices measuring the temporal similarity between the formation of nominal, adjectival and participial strings on the one hand, and the rise of the respective strings of verbs on the other, were divided into two sets. The set of matrices containing from three to nine constituents (Figure 4) and the set of matrices with over nine constituents (Figure 5). To an extent, this division is arbitrary. In fact, the corpus format allows to select any length in either of the compared strings. At the same time, however, the division is well-grounded intuitively. It unites strings of deverbatives that stay within the operational limit of memory amounting to seven ± two lexemes in compliance with the so-called Ingve depth hypothesis.

The horizontal axis on the charts in Figures 4 to 5, and 7 to 8 represents the actual number of matrices for the strings in each deverbal category and the motivating strings; the vertical axis shows the degrees of similarity in 10 percent ranges. The table on the right-hand side of the charts provides the list of deverbal categories (for convenience numeric indices were replaced by verbal definitions) and length specifications for the similarity between strings of primary deverbatives placed in the matrix row, and their verbal base strings.

Similarity scores in the upper half of the vertical axis in shorter strings (Figure 4) are more densely filled with matrices than in the longer strings (Figure 5). The quota of matrices with lower similarity scores in shorter strings (Figure 4) is also considerably bigger than in longer ones (Figure 5). This leads to a seemingly paradoxical conclusion. Clearly, longer strings of derivatives stand a greater chance of deviating (with respect to the temporal order of expansion) from the verbal base string than shorter ones. At the same time they typically preserve up to fifty percent of sequence correspondences.

The maximum string length for examples of the lowest range of similarity stands at five derivatives. That happens to be the lower value of the limit of operational memory. The latter query is heuristic as the established value is not visible on the chart of Figure 4.

Some generalisations concerning differences between deverbal classes in the degrees to which deverbal synonym strings preserve the order of base strings are borne out by our empirical evidence as well. Thus, strings of action nouns which admit of factitive lexicalisation are more likely to diverge than those failing to do so. Agent noun strings are more likely to display a divergent order of expansion than both classes of action nouns. Factitive nouns are more likely to diverge than action nouns. Deverbal adjectives are more likely to diverge than participles. There are minimal differences between present and past participles and larger difference between deverbal adjectives and passive modal adjectives. By and large adjectives and participles are less chronotropic than nouns. Although such discrepancies seem to be rooted in the conceptual distances between deverbal classes, so far it is hard to suggest a consistent explanation for them.

Figure 4. Distribution of the degrees of temporal expansion similarity with verbs in strings of deverbatives containing up to nine constituents

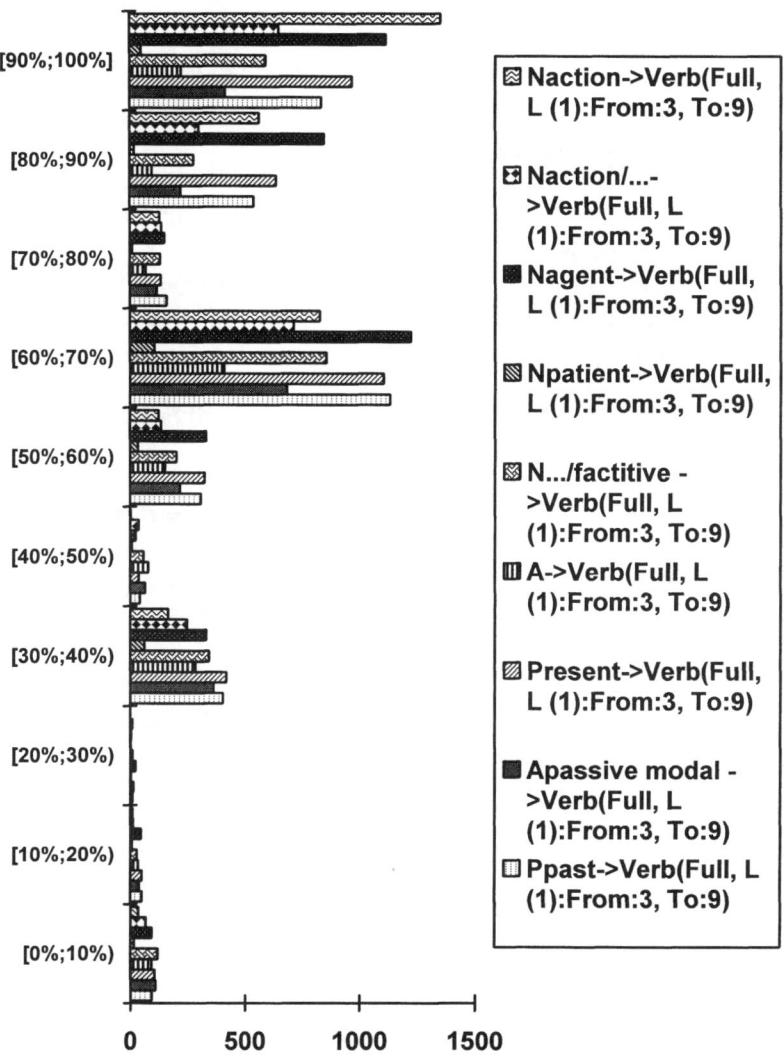

Figure 5. Distribution of the degrees of temporal expansion similarity with verbs in strings of deverbatives containing more than nine constituents

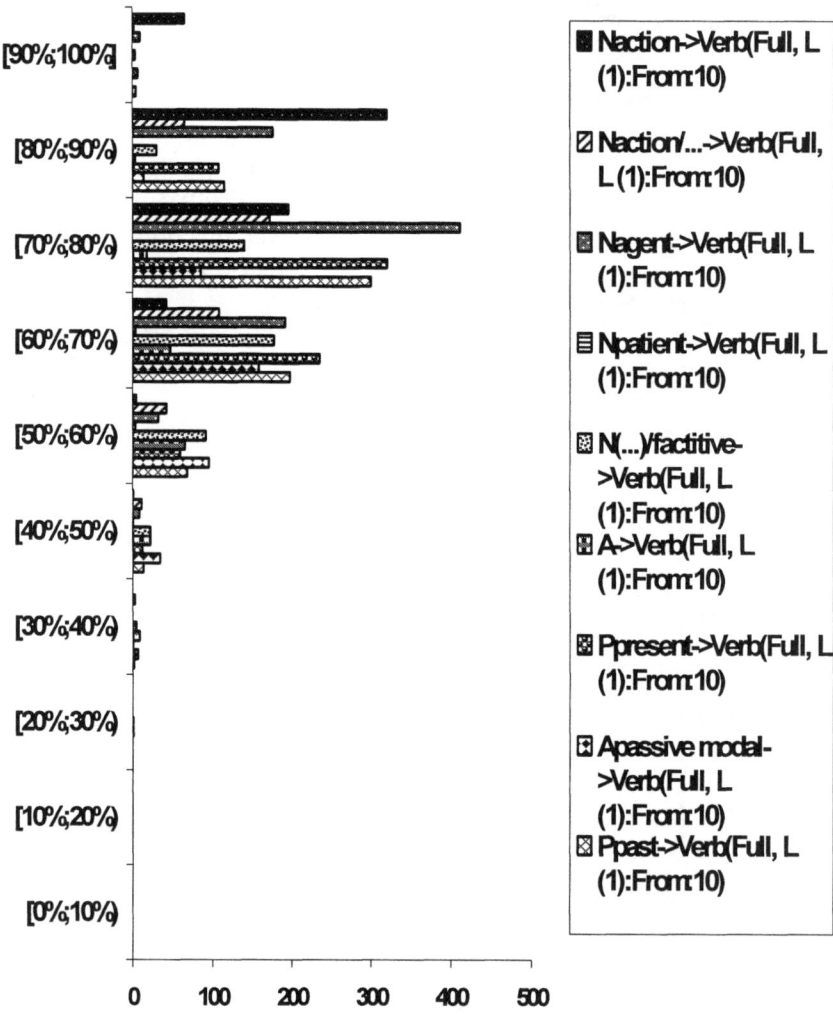

Getting a diachronic view on synonymy 99

The applied procedure yielded over 30,000 matrices. In shorter strings, complete similarity or similarity exceeding 90 percent of matrix cells is quite common. Nevertheless, in all deverbal classes but action nouns the biggest proportion of matrices falls on the similarity range between 60 and 70 percent. In longer strings, this rise is visible in the range of 60 to 70 percent.

Strings of secondary deverbatives reveal discrepancies both between themselves and strings of their immediate adjectival or participial bases, and between themselves and their verbal base strings (cf. the pairs of matrices in Figure 6).

Figure 6. Exemplification of temporal expansion similarity of secondary deverbatives to the immediately and ultimately motivating strings

COERCE	1. restrictive 1400	2. repressive 1597	3. coercive 1600	4. suppressive 1778
1. restrictively 1610	▓	+	+	+
3. repressively 1846	+	▓	−	−
2. coercively 1661	+	−	▓	+
4. suppressively 1837	+	−	+	▓

COERCE	1. repress 1374	2. suppress 1380	3. coerce 1475	4. restrict 1535
3. repressively 1846	▓	−	−	−
4. suppressively 1837	−	▓	−	−
2. coercively 1661	−	−	▓	−
1. restrictively 1610	−	−	−	▓

CAJOLE	1. flattering 1386	2. wheedling 1668	3. coaxing 1704	4. cajoling 1715
1. flatteringly 1387	▓▓▓	+	+	+
4. wheedlingly 1856	+	▓▓▓	−	−
2. coaxingly 1713	+	−	▓▓▓	+
3. cajolingly 1853	+	−	+	▓▓▓

CAJOLE	1. flatter 1225	2. coax 1586	3. cajole 1645	4. wheedle 1661
1. flatteringly 1387	▓▓▓	+	+	+
2. coaxingly 1713	+	▓▓▓	+	+
3. cajolingly 1853	+	+	▓▓▓	+
4. wheedlingly 1856	+	+	+	▓▓▓

Mostly, the sequence in which new items are added to strings of secondary deverbatives is more similar to the expansion of strings of their immediate adjectival or participial bases than to that of verbal base strings. Thus, the lower part of the vertical axis is better represented in Figure 8 than in Figure 7.

The information about the expansion of strings of synonyms lays the foundation for quantitative diachronic onomasiology. Although this branch of historical lexicology is still at its early stages, the question mark which Hüllen put at the end of the title of his 1996 article can now be replaced by three dots. Vast empirical evidence is obtainable at the cross-roads of historical and onomasiological lexicography, and it can be both insightful and misleading. It provides us with new heuristic challenges that would have been impossible to address without sufficiently powerful, and at the same time simple, corpus research tools.

Figure 7. Distribution of the degrees of temporal expansion similarity with motivating adjectives/participles in strings of secondary deverbatives

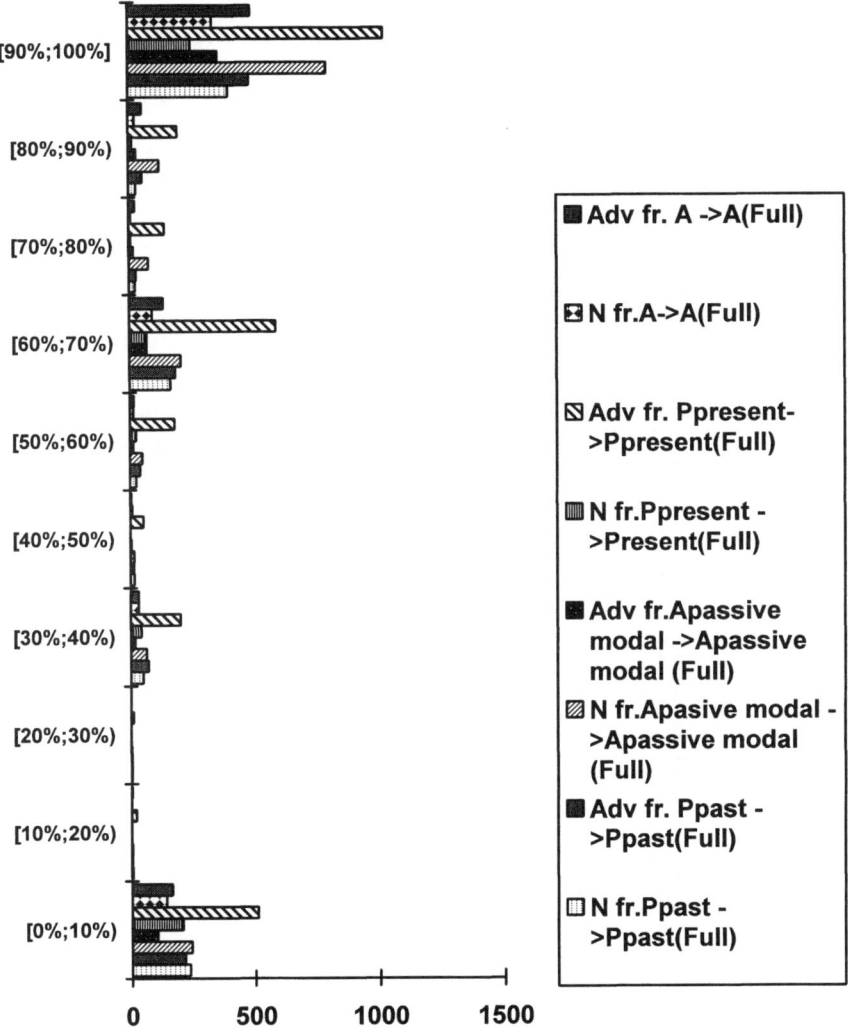

Figure 8. Distribution of the degrees of temporal expansion similarity with verbs in strings of secondary deverbatives

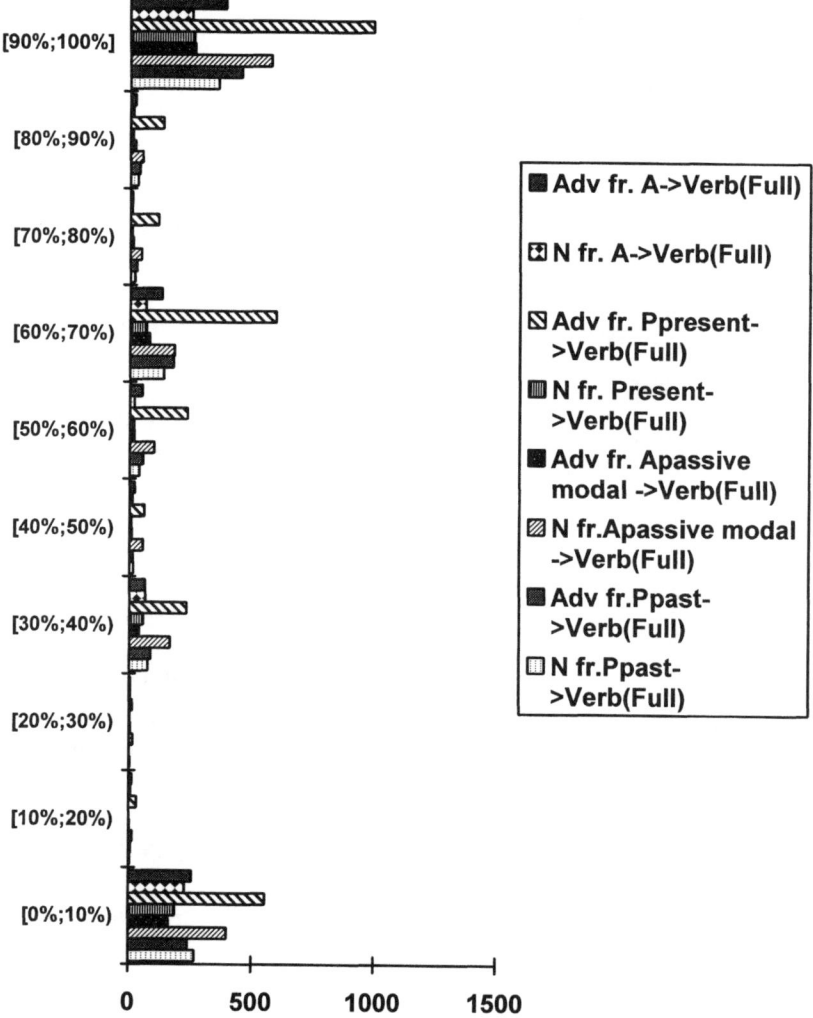

8. Concluding remarks

The discrepancies between diachronic strings of verbal synonyms and strings of deverbal synonyms derived from them give evidence of changes in the inventory of signifiers created by the lexical system and available to speakers over time. The approach outlined in this paper illustrates some of the epistemological possibilities presently available in the sphere of diachronic corpus lexicology. It addresses the problem that "within a word-family, we must examine the relationship of different parts of speech, especially where their dates of currency differ widely" (Kay and Wotherspoon 2002:113).

I have considered the case of verbs and deverbatives. Extending the investigation to pairs of deverbal strings will increase the number of construable similarity matrices considerably. These will provide a testing-ground for revealing similarity in routes of successive expansion between types of deverbal derivations. It is possible to repeat the experiment with other dictionaries of synonyms containing strings of verbs. Sequential deficiency can also be assessed in terms of the mean rates of divergence between strings and/or the age differential between constituents in pairs of strings of specific categorical affiliation and length. Finally, the investigation once again confirms how inexhaustible the number of uses is to which the diachronic textual prototypes from the *OED* can be put.

References

Coleman, Julie and Christian J. Kay (eds.). 1998. *Lexicology, semantics and lexicography. Selected papers from the fourth L.G. Brook Symposium.* Amsterdam: Benjamins.

Coleman, Julie. 1999. *Love, sex and marriage. A historical thesaurus.* Amsterdam: Rodopi.

Fischer, Andreas. 1992. "Laughing and smiling in the history of English". In: Busse, Wilhelm G. (ed.). *Anglistentag 1991 Düsseldorf Proceedings.* Tübingen: Niemeyer: 51-62.

Hüllen, Werner. 1996. "An onomasiological version of the OED?". *Henry Sweet Society Newsletter* 27: 15-16.

Kay, Christian J. and M.L. Samuels. 1975. "Componential analysis in semantics: its validity and application". *Transactions of the Philological Society* 74: 49-81.

Kay, Christian J. 1994. "Word lists for a changing world". In: Hüllen, Werner (ed.). *The world in a list of words.* Tübingen: Niemeyer: 67-75.

Kay, Christian J. 1997. "Historical semantics and material culture". In: Pearce, Susan M. (ed.). *Experiencing material culture in the western world.* London: Leicester University Press: 49-64.

Kay, Christian J. 1998. "Historical semantics and historical lexicography: will the twain ever meet?". In: Coleman, Julie and Christian J. Kay (eds.): 52-68.

Kay, Christian J. and Irené A. W. Wotherspoon. 2002. "Turning the dictionary inside out: some issues in the compilation of a historical Thesaurus". In: Díaz Vera, Javier E. (ed.). *A changing world of words. Studies in English historical lexicography, lexicology and semantics.* Amsterdam: Rodopi: 109-135.

Laird, Charlton. 1985. *Webster's new world thesaurus.* Prepared by Ch. Laird, updated by W.D. Lutz. New York: Prentice Hall Press.

OED = *Oxford English Dictionary* (Second Edition) on CD-ROM Version 3,0. 2002. Oxford: OUP.

Roget's Thesaurus = *Roget's Thesaurus of English words and phrases.* New edition prepared by Susan M. Lloyd. 1982. Harlow: Longman.

Sylvester, Louise. 1994. *Studies in the lexical field of expectation.* Amsterdam: Rodopi.

-----. 1998. "The vocabulary of consent in Middle English". In: Coleman, Julie and Christian J. Kay (eds.): 157-178.

Tissari, Heli. 1998. "Five hundred years of love: a prototype semantic analysis. In: Coleman, Julie and Christian J. Kay (eds.): 127-156.

Wotherspoon, Irené. 1992. "Historical Thesaurus database using Ingres". *Literary and Linguistic Computing* 7(4): 218-225.

Ewa Ciszek
-dōm in medieval English

1. Introduction

The area of OE and ME word-formation is still almost as neglected as it was fifty years ago, and no detailed synthetic treatment of either OE or ME derivation has so far appeared in print. Thus, even when one looks at allegedly simple problems in the field, it often turns out that relatively little is known about them, and that there is no agreement about either facts or interpretations. I would like to illustrate this in the present paper on the basis of the development of *-dōm* from Late Old English (950-1150) to the end of the ME period (1150-1500). Specifically, this paper focuses on three issues. First, it discusses whether *-dōm* had the status of a suffix already in Old English. Secondly, it sketches the semantic evolution of the suffix. And, finally, it attempts to establish if the suffix was still productive in Early Middle English.

The data used for analysis come from various corpora. In order to obtain a broader context for our investigation, the occurrence and behaviour of *-dōm* is examined on the basis of the *Toronto Corpus of Old English Texts*, the *Dictionary of Old English* (letters A-F)[1], and Bosworth and Toller (1898-1921) for the late OE period, and on the basis of the *Middle English Dictionary online* (*MED*) for Middle English.

Unlike Ciszek (2004), this paper will discuss productivity in terms of the number of types rather than tokens (cf. Dalton-Puffer and Cowie 2002). This reflects the assumption that the productivity of native suffixes in a given period is most directly reflected in the number of new transparent types in that period. It also means that we shall define productivity in rather straightforward terms, and consider a suffix as productive as long as new derivatives involving it appear. Our approach seems to be supported by Bauer (2001:41), who claims that

---

[1] I.e. Cameron et al (eds.) 1986. Itself based on the *Toronto Corpus of Old English Texts*.

> [p]roductivity is all about potential. A process is productive if it has the potential to lead to new coinages, or to the extent to which it does lead to new coinages. We are aware of productivity only through the new coinages and the patterns of familiar and unfamiliar words coined by the relevant process.

While Bauer correctly points out that type frequency is a very ambiguous productivity measure in synchronic studies (because a high number of types at any specific point in time may reflect both past and present productivity), such ambiguity does not arise in diachronic studies. Thus, in our investigation we use the *Toronto Corpus of Old English Texts*, which comprises all preserved OE texts, as a starting point and lexical background, against which the developments taking place in Middle English will be held. If a lexeme occurs in the *MED* but not in the *Toronto Corpus*, we shall conclude that it represents a new ME coinage.

Although this paper will focus primarily on type frequency, token frequency will not be completely neglected either. Instead, just as in Ciszek (2004), the number of tokens will be of interest in the case of hybrids, which are also vital indicators of the suffix's productivity.

2. Old English -*dōm*

2.1 Previous studies

2.1.1 The word *dōm*

In Old English *dōm* existed as an independent word, and can be found in historical as well as etymological English dictionaries, such as Bosworth and Toller (1898-1921), Holthausen (1934), Borden (1982), the *Oxford English Dictionary online* (*OED* 1989), Roberts and Kay (1995), Hall (1894 [2000]), and the *Dictionary of Old English* (1986). They list the following meanings:

> Bosworth and Toller (1898-1921:207):
> doom, judgement, judicial sentence, decree, ordinance, law; ... a ruling, governing, command; ... might, power, dominion, majesty, glory, magnificence, honour, praise, dignity; ... will, free will, choice, option; ... sense, meaning, interpretation.

Holthausen (1934:74):
"Urteil, Beschluß, Erklärung; Gesetz, Sitte; Gerechtigkeit; Meinung, Rat; Wahl, Bedingung; Macht, Gewalt; Ruf, Würde, Ruhm, Glanz; Hof, Versammlung"

Borden (1982:299):
doom, judgement, decree, decision, commandment, choice, order, sentence, law, ordinance; custom, equity, opinion, advice; choice, option, free-will; condition; justice, propriety; majesty, might, reputation, dignity, honour, splendour; meaning, significance; court, tribunal, assembly; interpretation; authority, power.

OED (1989)[2]:
a statute, law, enactment; a judgement or decision, esp. one formally pronounced; the action or process of judging (as in a court of law); justice, equity, righteousness; power or authority to judge.

Roberts and Kay (1995:882):
the course of human affairs; judgement, forming of opinion; appraisal, appraising; choice, election; reputation, frame; exposition, making clear by explanation; authority; a rule, order, precept, tenet, principle; judicial body, authority; law, action of the courts; a sentence, judgement, ruling; unfavourable judgement, condemnation.

Hall (1894 [2000]:86):
doom, judgement, ordeal, sentence; ... decree, law, ordinance, custom; ... justice, equity; ... option, advice: choice, option, free-will: condition: authority, supremacy, majesty, power, might...: reputation, dignity, glory, honour, splendour...: court, tribunal, assembly: meaning, interpretation.

Dictionary of Old English ("D", pp. 464-466):
judgement, the exercise of judicature, binding decision, sentence, decree; systematic justice, promulgated law, the laws; jurisdiction, the right to administer justice; God's judgement, especially the Last Judgement; manifestation on earth of divine judgement; dues, levy; testimony, witness; self-doom, choice unlimited by jurisdiction or arbitrament; loosely 'very much'; good sense, right

---

[2] OE section of the *OED* entry.

judgement (other than in matters of law), discernment, discretion; in poetry: favourable judgement, i.e. fame for good; interpretation of dreams; authority, sway, majesty, power (merging with senses glory, fame); often used of divine justice; favourable judgement (esp. after death), glory, fame, victory (in poetry more commonly than in prose).

The word has survived as *doom* until today. Naturally, OE *dōm* could also occur in compounds. In a number of instances, where it occurred as the second element, it seems to have lost its original meaning in the course of Old English, and eventually changed into a suffix with the sense 'dominion, power, authority, property, right, office, quality, state, condition' (Bosworth and Toller 1898-1921:207). Although Marchand (1969:205) maintains that *-dōm* should be regarded as a fully nominal second element of compounds until Middle English, most scholars are of a different opinion and consider it as a genuine suffix already in Old English.

2.1.2 *-dōm*

The OE suffix *-dōm* has never been discussed at any length. Of the authors who have discussed it at all, some limit themselves to defining it as a denominal, or denominal and deadjectival abstract suffix, and give some examples (Wright 1914:304, Mossé 1945:125, Koziol 1937:161), while others emphasize its high frequency (Quirk and Wrenn, 1955:113), or add information on etymology (Kluge 1926:85-86, and Carr 1939:358). As far as its syntactic classification is concerned, some authors view *-dōm* as a 'semi-suffix' that developed into a suffix in Middle English (Faiss 1978:187-190), or "as a suffixoid, if not a suffix" (Kastovsky 1992:384) which became a true suffix by the time of Middle English (Sauer 1992:15, 144, 221-222, 229-231). Marchand (1969:262-264) is the only one who considers *-dōm* as a truly nominal element forming compounds rather than as a suffix.

Among the senses assigned to *-dōm* by scholars there are: 'state (condition), authority' (Kluge 1926:85-86 and, similarly, Marckwardt and Rosier 1972:145), 'state, condition, fact of being, action of' (Kastovsky 1992:184) and 'state, dignity, sphere' or a 'collective body' (Jespersen 1942:461). Koziol (1937:158) is the only one to indicate that the suffix could have a concrete sense as in *lǣcedōm* 'medicine, medicament'.

Dorskiy (1960) offers the most comprehensive treatment of OE *-dōm* (1960:119-128). He argues that there were three types of *-dōm* and that the suffix was in transition. Originally, it formed a group of unrelated compounds whose meanings combined one of the senses of the independent word *dōm*, namely 'decree, judgement, sentence, judging', and the sense of whatever was the first element of the compound. Apart from *cynedōm, dryhtdōm, bisceopdōm, worulddōm, seonoðdōm,* and *wohdōm*, also *wiccedōm, witedōm, witegdōm, wiccungdōm, lǣcedōm* and *wīsdōm* belong to this group. The meanings of such X-*dōm* compounds can be paraphrased as 'a judgement, sentence, etc. by X'. Next, the 9th century, and initially such texts as King Ælfred's *Pastoral Care* and the older part of the *Anglo-Saxon Chronicle*, gave rise to productive formations in which the first part was a personal noun and *dōm* assumed a function similar to that of a suffix with the meaning 'state, condition'. Here Dorskiy (1960:123) lists 19 nouns, e.g., *abbuddōm, cāserdōm, cyfesdōm, dryhtendōm, ealdordōm, hlāforddōm* and *pāpdōm*. The 'state, condition'-meaning, which the instances of *-dōm* in this group carry, became a base for the development of further senses. At that stage *-dōm* formations underwent a reanalysis: *-dōm* began to be regarded a proper suffix in the majority of constructions, and also started to be used to form abstract nouns from adjectives. Dorskiy (1960:126) lists 10 deadjectival coinages, e.g., *cristendōm, dysigdōm, frēodōm* and *hāligdōm*. The final group has concrete nouns as derivational bases, and includes *campdōm, frēolsdōm, friðdōm, rīcedōm, þēowutdōm, þrymdōm* and *swicdōm*.

As demonstrated above, the existence of the independent OE word *dōm* motivated some scholars to consider *-dōm* as a second element of nominal compounds in Old English and quite often also in Early Middle English (e.g., Sauer 1992:229-231). However, as far as we can judge, *-dōm* already had the status of a genuine suffix in Late Old

English.[3] This seems to follow from the fact that some of its senses differed from those of the independent noun *dōm*. The *Dictionary of Old English* clearly shows that the meaning 'state, condition', which was attributed by various authors to the independent word *dōm* did not exist except in derivatives.[4] At the same time, the meaning 'state, condition' is the most frequently attested sense of the LOE suffix *-dōm* (see also the section below).[5]

2.2 Semantics of *-dōm* in Old English

Since the outlook of this paper is primarily descriptive, we shall refrain from committing ourselves to a specific theory of meaning or semantic representation. Instead, we shall steer a pragmatic course and describe the range of textual (and contextually co-determined) meanings which *-dōm* was apparently able to express in attested instances of use from both the OE and the ME periods. At the same time, this will allow us to draw on descriptions produced in historical lexicography, since makers of historical dictionaries typically follow a similar strategy.

In the *Toronto Corpus of Old English Texts*, there are 46 types of *-dōm* formations. 36 of them are derived from nouns, 8 from adjectives, one from a verb and one from a pronoun. Not very surprisingly, one finds these results confirmed if one looks at the material from the *Dictionary of Old English* (letters A-F), which is after all based on the *Toronto Corpus*.[6] Some of the OE words in *-dōm*

---

[3] There also existed compounds with *dōm* such as, e.g., *sinoþdōm* 'decree of a synod' (see also note 6). These, however, are excluded from our analysis.

[4] Bosworth and Toller's (1898-1921) definition (see also above), which is considered as the most traditional one, is misleading in this respect and may have caused misunderstandings.

[5] The view that OE *-dōm* could function as a suffix is supported in a recent study of the development of *-dōm* as a result of grammaticalization by Bongetta (2003). However, since Bongetta used neither the *Toronto Corpus* nor the *Helsinki Corpus* her study lists only 19 OE *-dōm* coinages.

[6] The entry for *-dōm* in the *Dictionary of Old English* starts like this:
Masculine suffix forming abstract nouns
See also: abbod- arcebisceop-, bisceop-, camp-, canon-, cāser-, cifes-, cristen-, cyne-, cyning-, dryhten-, dysig-, eald-, ealdor-, eorl-, flēam-, frēo-, frēols-, gāste-,

could have more than one sense, and the following meanings seem to have been associated with the suffix (*Dictionary of Old English*:s.v. *-dōm*):

1. in denominal derivatives:

a. 'status, a rank, an office': *abbotdōm* 'abbacy, the rule or authority of an abbot', *arcebisceopdōm* 'archiepiscopal dignity, archbishopric', *bisceopdōm* 'bishopric, the rank of bishop, episcopal see', *canondōm* 'a canonship, office of a canon', *caserdōm* 'rule of the emperor, imperial reign', *cynedōm* 'royal authority, sovereignty, kingship; figurative: supreme authority of God, Christ', *cyningdōm* 'royal authority, sovereignty', *dryhtendōm* 'majesty, princely or divine glory', *ealdordōm* 'authority, power; primacy, pre-eminence; rule, sovereignty, lordship, office', *eorldōm* 'the dignity or office of an *eorl*', *hlāforddōm* 'dominion, lordship, jurisdiction', *lāreowdōm* 'the authority or office of a teacher', *lādteowdōm* 'leadership, guidance, conduct', *mægsterdōm* 'office of a master or teacher', *pāpdōm* 'the papacy', *reccenddōm* 'ruling, directing, governance', *ricedōm* 'power, rule, dominion' (17 derivatives);

b. 'state, condition': *campdōm* 'warfare, military service, also figurative: warfare, struggle (ref. to spiritual battle)', *cifesdōm* 'concubinage', *cristendōm* 'Christianity, the Christian faith'; 'membership in a Christian congregation', *flēamdōm* 'the condition of a fugitive', *frēolsdōm* 'freedom (from taxation)', *geongordōm*

---

geongor-, hālig-, hæfte-, hæþen-, hlāford-, hōr-, lār-, lāreow-, lātteow-, læce-, magister-, martyr-, mīn-, pāp-, reccend-, rīce-, sceac-, self-, sinoþ-, sundorfrēo-, swic-, þēow-, þēowot-, þrym-, unriht-, unwīs-, wicce-, wiccung-, wīs-, wīteg-, woruldþēow-, woruldwīs-dōm.
Of those we have excluded *sinoþdōm* from further consideration, since we regard it as a compound (*sinoþ* 'synod' + *dōm* 'law' = 'decree of a synod'). We also exclude compounds such as *sundorfrēodōm*, *woruldþēowdōm* and *woruldwīsdōm*. Those were created by combining existing derivatives with other nouns, and say nothing about the productivity of the suffix. By the same rationale, formations in which a prefix, such as negative *un-*, was added to a *dōm* derivative are also disregarded, since they may indicate the productivity of the prefix rather than that of the suffix. Thus, *unwīsdōm* will be excluded from our list.

'discipleship, allegiance, minority, subjection, obedience, service, vassalage', *hæftedōm* 'captivity, service', *hōrdōm* 'adultery', *martyrdōm* 'martyrdom', *þeowdōm* 'service, servitude, slavery, bondage, thraldom; a service of a church, divine service', *þēowotdōm* 'a service', *þrymdōm* 'glory', *wītegdōm* 'knowledge derived from a superhuman source, prophesy, foreknowledge; a statement of what is known through superhuman agency, a prophesy' (13 derivatives);

c. 'a quality': *gāstedōm* 'spirituality' (1 derivative);

d. 'an act, activity': *lārdōm* 'teaching, instruction', *lāreowdōm* 'the action of a teacher, instruction, guidance; what is taught by a teacher, a study', *lǣcedōm* 'healing', *swicdōm* 'deceit, fraud; treachery, failure in loyalty, treason; an offence', *wiccedome* 'witchcraft, sorcery, magic', *wiccungdōm* 'witchcraft, sorcery, magic' (6 derivatives);

e. 'a thing': *lǣcedōm* 'medicine, a medicine, remedy, cure' (1 derivative);

f. 'a group of people, collectivity': *campdōm* 'the army, the military', *cristendōm* 'body of persons under Christian rule', *eorldōm* 'the people/liegemen of an *earldom*' (3 derivatives);

g. 'territory, a place': *cristendōm* 'body of territories under Christian rule', *cynedōm* 'kingdom, realm', *eorldōm* 'the territory governed by an *eorl*' (3 derivatives);

h. 'time': *cynedōm* 'term during which kingship is held, reign' (1 derivative);

2. in adjectival derivatives:

a. 'state, condition': *dysigdōm* 'folly, ignorance', *ealddōm* 'age', *frēodōm/frīgdōm* 'the state of being free, freedom, liberty, release from slavery, servitude; freedom, release from constraint or restriction; freedom of will, thought, the quality of being free from the control of fate or necessity; freedom, release, deliverance from evil, misfortune, etc.; discharge, release from payment of a debt; (state of) exemption from a tax, rent, obligation, etc., from subjection to someone else's authority', *hǣðendōm* 'heathendom, paganism, the belief and practice of a heathen people', *mīndōm* 'the state of exile', *wīsdōm* 'a wisdom, discretion; knowledge, cognisance; wisdom, knowledge, learning' (6 derivatives);

b. 'a quality': *frēodōm/ frīgdōm* 'liberality, generosity', *hāligdōm* 'holiness, sanctity', *mīndōm* 'smallness, abjectness, pusillanimity' (3 derivatives);

c. 'an act, activity': *unrihtdōm* 'wrong, iniquity' (1 derivative);

d. 'a thing': *frēodōm/ frīgdōm* 'a grant or privilege, a charter which grants the right to freehold land, rent, income, etc.', *hāligdōm* 'holy things, relics, holy work, a sacrament' (2 derivatives);

e. 'a group of people, collectivity': *hǣðendōm* 'people among whom paganism prevails' (1 derivative);

f. 'territory, a place': *hǣðendōm* 'district in which paganism prevails', *hāligdōm* 'a holy place, place specially appointed for worship, sanctuary' (2 derivatives);

3. in a deverbal derivative:

'an act, activity, an event': *sceacdōm* 'flight, hurried departure' (1 derivative);

4. in a de-pronominal derivative:

'state, condition': *selfdōm* 'independence' (1 derivative).

Of these derivatives, 19 survived into Middle English.

3. Middle English *-dōm*

3.1 Previous studies

ME word-formation has received even less attention than Old English. A discussion of some selected issues related to derivation or a more succinct description of longer lists of suffixes can be found in Martin (1906), Dorskiy (1960), Fisiak (1965, 1968), Marchand (1969), Sauer (1992), Dalton-Puffer (1996) and the *MED* (1956-2001).

Martin (1906:47-49), who offers the most comprehensive approach to the ME suffix *-dōm*, provides a division into OE continuations and new formations. Additionally, he classifies words according to the part of speech from which they were derived. However, Martin's treatment of *-dōm* is semantically rather coarsely grained, with only one sense ascribed to all but three formations. Dorskiy (1960), who basically deals with OE abstract nominal suffixes, includes some remarks concerning Middle English. He indicates that since *-dōm* has become semantically unrelated to the independent word *dōm*, it can be regarded a proper suffix (Dorskiy 1960:128-129). He lists only a restricted number of ME *-dōm* formations, mostly due to his reliance on Stratmann (1891).

A more systematic treatment of whole derivation in Middle English, though brief, is presented in Fisiak (1965, 1968). In his *Morphemic structure of Chaucer's English*, Fisiak (1965:67) describes the *-dōm* suffix both as combinative and productive, forming abstract nouns from adjectives. He did not find any formations derived from nouns in his Chaucer corpus. Also in his *Short Grammar of Middle English* (1968 [2004]:109) Fisiak refers to denominal formations with *-dōm* and lists some more examples of its occurrence.

Marchand (1969:262) notes that the suffix *-dom* acquired additional senses in Middle English, i.e. 'territory' (see also Sauer 1992:229) and 'collectivity of...'. As illustrations of the meaning 'territory', he mentions words such as *Christendom*, *dukedom*, *earldom* and *kingdom*. However, as demonstrated above, these two senses had already appeared in Old English and were further developed in Middle English. Moreover, Marchand gives inaccurate dates of the first attestations of some *-dōm* derivatives (e.g., *sheriffdom*), which have to be revised in view of recent datings of manuscripts. Here, it should be remembered, however, that Marchand based his research on the first edition of the *OED*.

Burnley (1992: 1439-450) does not mention *-dom* at all in his treatment of ME word-formation. Indeed, his section on word-formation in *The Cambridge history of the English language* is not as systematic or comprehensive as Kastovsky's (1992) for Old English.

Sauer (1992), although concentrating on EME compounds, lists some *-dōm* derivatives as well (1992:229-231).

Dalton-Puffer (1996:75-77) devotes a short passage to *-dom*. She describes it as a moderate-frequency suffix forming denominal and deadjectival abstract nouns and provides some examples. Dalton-Puffer (1996:77) recognizes two meanings of *-dom* in words derived from nouns, i.e., 'condition (dominion, authority, state) of N' and 'collectivity of Ns in condition of N'. Deadjectival nouns had the sense 'quality of being A'.

Bongetta (2003:78-79) compares the definitions of *-dōm* provided by Bosworth and Toller (1898-1921) for Old English and by the *MED* for Middle English. Like Marchand (1969), she seems to accept the erroneous dates provided by the *OED*, even though she claims to use the *MED* as one of the sources of her data. Moreover, her semantic analysis is supported by only a few examples. Additionally, Bongetta (2003:88-89) erroneously claims that all nominal bases of the OE and ME derivatives in *-dōm* carried the meaning 'person'. According to her, the sense 'collectivity' was added in Middle English (Bongetta 2003:88). As we have shown above, however, it had developed already in Old English.

According to the *MED* (1956-2001: s.v. *-dōm*), the suffix *-dōm* could be attached to nouns to denote "office, rank, status, or state, but also the domain or realm of an office or institution", or to adjectives to denote "a state". However, within the denominal and adjectival groups the only distinction that is made is between nouns inherited from Old English and ME coinages. A classification of formations according to their meanings is missing, most disturbingly so within the former group. One noun listed in the *MED*, i.e., *thēdōm* 'activity; prosperity', is classified as derived from a verb, although according to P. Kitson (personal communication) the word could also have been derived from the noun *thē*.[7] Finally, words such as *hālīdōm* 'a sanctuary', *lēchedōm* 'a remedy' and *wīsdōm* 'a proverb or saying' had specialized senses.

---

[7] However, *thē* is attested for the first time only in 1450, i.e., later than *thēdōm* itself (1330; 1308 in personal names).

3.2 Semantics of -dōm in Middle English

3.2.1 The semantics of EME -*dōm* in formations inherited from Old English

19 of the OE words with the suffix -*dōm* survived into Middle English, and some new ones came into being. The ME continuations attested in the *MED* are: *alderdōm* < OE *ealdordōm*, *cristendōm*, *ērldōm* < OE *eorldōm*, *frēdōm* < OE *frēodōm*, *hālīdōm* < OE *hāligdōm*, *hēthendōm* < OE *hǣðendōm*, *kinedōm* < OE *cynedōm*, *kingdōm* < OE *cyningdōm*, *lāverddōm* < OE *hlāforddōm*, *lēchedōm* < OE *lǣcedōm*, *martirdōm*, *pōpedōm* < OE *pāpdōm*, *rīchedōm* < OE *rīcedōm*, *swīkedōm* < OE *swicdōm*, *theudōm* < OE *þēowdōm*, *wicchedōm* < OE *wiccedōm* and *wīsdōm*. In addition, *hōredōm* and *maisterdōm* belong to the group which the *MED* classifies as originating in Middle English. However, *hōredōm* (*Ormulum* 1200), which is labelled as being derived from OE *hōre*, is actually recorded already in Old English, namely in *Saints' Lives: Saint Nicholaus*, written about 1100. This occurrence is of course contained in the *Toronto Corpus*, but it is not mentioned in Bosworth and Toller (1898-1921), the *OED* or Hall (1894 [2000]). For *maisterdōm*, see below.

As regards the meaning of the suffix -*dōm* in this group of derivatives, a few developments can be observed. In six words, i.e., *alderdōm*, *lāverddōm*, *lēchedōm*, *maisterdōm*[8], *martirdōm* and *wicchedōm*, the OE senses of the suffix were preserved.

In ten derivatives -*dōm* did not only preserve its original senses but also developed additional ones. In *theudōm*, the suffix developed the sense 'status, a rank or an office'. At the lexical level, the new meaning was 'dominion, rule, the power to control' (1150). *Rīchedōm*, where -*dōm* had the sense 'state, condition', began to be lexicalised with meanings such as 'wealth, treasure, splendor, magnificence,

---

[8] According to the *MED*, *maisterdōm* was a new ME coinage from either a Germanic or French stem, and appeared first around 1400. However, the form *mægsterdōm* can be found twice in the *Toronto Corpus of Old English*, namely in *Defensor's 'Liber Scintillarum'* from the early 11th century, which is in fact also mentioned by Bosworth and Toller (1898-1921), the *OED* and Hall (2000).

abundance' (1225). In the ME words *wīsdōm*, *hōredōm* and *Cristendōm* the suffix developed the new sense 'an act, activity'. In the first derivative that sense was incorporated in the word's overall meaning 'an act displaying prudence or discretion, an act displaying spiritual insight' (1150), the second derivative referred to 'an act of illicit sexual indulgence' (1225) and the third to a 'baptism, or christening' (1300). In addition, if preceded by the possessive pronoun *your*, *wīsdōm* was a form of respectful address. Moreover, *hōredōm* acquired the sense 'a person' ('a prostitute, whore' (1382)), which is a rather idiosyncratic development.[9] ME *kinedōm* and *kingdōm* developed the additional senses 'a group of people/collectivity', specifically 'king's subjects' (1425), and 'a family, tribe, community; one of the twelve tribes of Israel' (1400). Moreover, in *kingdōm*, the suffix, which in Old English had had a more restricted sense, behaved similarly as in *kinedōm* in Middle English. Thus, *-dōm* seems to have developed the sense 'territory' ('a state or community governed by a king; a monarchy' (1330) and 'a state, republic' (1450)). Also, in *frēdōm* the suffix seems to have expressed these two senses, which is reflected in the word meanings 'a group of people/collectivity' and 'territory' represented by 'the body of citizens forming the corporation of a city or town' (1457), and 'the corporate limits of a city or town, the territory under the jurisdiction of the corporation' (1423) respectively. A further new sense of the suffix in *frēdōm* was 'status, a rank, an office' ('the king's authority in general, royal prerogative' (1397) and 'the status of a wife (among the gentry)' (?1409)). ME *swīkedōm* occurred once with the meaning 'sinfulness' (1150), hence the suffix seems to have acquired the sense 'a quality'. Finally, in *pōpedōm*, *-dōm* appears to have conveyed the sense 'time span' ('the tenure of a pope, pontificate' (1425)), but this is quite an exceptional use of the suffix.

In three words one or two senses of *-dōm* seem to have been lost. In ME *ērldōm*, the suffix dropped its LOE sense 'a group of people/collectivity'. *Hēthendōm*, which among others used to refer to

---

[9] The word appears in *The earlier version of the Wycliffite Bible,* MS Bodley 959. The later version replaces *hōredōm* with *hōre*.

'people among whom (or a district in which) paganism prevails' appeared in a collocation *hēthendōmes folk* meaning 'pagans' in Middle English. Thus, it seems that in *hēthendōm*, *-dōm* had lost the two senses 'territory' and 'a group of people/collectivity'. Similarly, ME *hālīdōm* no longer described 'a holy place, [a] place specially appointed for worship, sanctuary', so that the suffix does not seem to have designated a 'territory' anymore.

3.2.2 The semantics of *-dōm* in new ME coinages

As for ME coinages from native bases, the *MED* includes 14 words, eight derived from nouns, five from adjectives and one from a verb. Hybrids (3 from nouns, 2 from adjectives and 1 – namely *wrongdōm* – from either a noun or an adjective) will be treated separately below.

In the new denominal formations, the suffix assumes the following senses: 'status, a rank, an office' (2 derivatives), 'state, condition' (3 derivatives), 'a quality' (3 derivatives), 'a thing' (1 derivative) and 'an act, activity' (2 derivatives). The sense 'status, a rank, an office' first appears in *þraldōm* 'the power to enslave someone, domination' (lit. and fig. *Ayenbite of Inwyt* 1340) and then in *lōrdesdōm* 'lordship, rule' (1450). It is worth mentioning that *þraldōm*, with its OE stem *þræl* reinforced by a parallel ON word, developed a few new meanings at the lexical level. A further sense of *-dōm*, i.e., 'state, condition' is also present in *þraldōm* referring to different kinds of literal and figurative subjection, subjugation or confinement, as well as to advantage or benefit, with its earliest meaning being 'subservience, also, compliance, submission' (*Lambeth Homilies* 1225). In the first quarter of the 15th century there appear two further new coinages with *-dōm* carrying the sense 'state, condition', i.e., *waxdam* 'full growth, maturity' (1400) and *cherldōm* 'servitude' (1425). In 1330 ("Why werre...") the suffix acquires the sense 'a quality' in *shreuedōm* 'wickedness'. That sense also develops in *falsdōm*[10] 'deceitfulness,

---

[10] According to the *MED* the derivational base in *falsdōm* was of either Germanic or French origin. The word, however, existed in Old English as *fals* and was only reinforced by parallel but later French lexemes. Hence, *falsdōm* is treated here as a coinage from a native stem.

treachery, wrong-doing, wickedness' (1400-1500) and *willerdōm* 'willfulness, headstrongness' (1475). In *þraldōm* 'tax imposed on an inferior' (1450), *-dōm* seems to refer to 'a thing'. Finally, the sense 'an act, activity' appears in *wrākedōm* 'avenging, revenge' (*Laȝamon's Brut* 1275) and in *falsdōm* 'a falsehood or lie' (*Dame Sirith* 1300).

The senses which *-dōm* expressed in nouns formed from adjectives are: 'state, condition' (3 derivatives), 'a quality' (1 derivative) and 'an act, activity' (1 derivative). The suffix assumes the sense 'state, condition' in the chronologically first deadjectival coinage, *wrecchedōm* 'misery, suffering' (1225). The next two nouns in which *-dōm* carried the same sense were coined in Late Middle English. *Wreccheddōm* 'misery, hardship', which is formally and semantically related to *wrecchedōm* appears in 1390 (*Castle of Love*). The other derivative is *faindōm* 'gladness, joy' (1450). In *wercchedōm* 'vileness, baseness; moral reprehensibility' (1250) the suffix also carries the sense 'a quality'. In *wikkedōm* 'wickedness, evil; specifically treason, treachery' (1450), *-dōm* refers to 'an act, activity'.

There is also one formation derived from an OE verb, namely *thēdōm* 'activity, prosperity' (*The Seven Sages* 1330) from OE *þēon* (see also above and note 7). The sense of the suffix is 'a quality'.

As for hybrids, the *MED* lists three *-dōm* formations from French stems, i.e., *caitīfdōm* (AF&CF), *dūkdōm* (OF) and *victurdōm* (AF), and three from Scandinavian bases, i.e., *bondedōm, ūseldōm* and *wrongdōm*.[11] Although they are of Norse origin, however, *bonde* (n.), *ūsel* (adj.) and *wrong* (n./adj.) belong to the OE wordstock. In *bondedōm* 'bondage, servitude' and in the deadjectival *caitīfdōm* 'captivity' (1390) the suffix has the sense 'state, condition'. In denominal *dūkdōm*, *-dōm* has two senses: 'territory' ('a duchy' (1450) and 'a small kingdom' (1425-1500)), and 'status, a rank, an office' ('the status of a duke' (1500)). In denominal *victurdōm* 'a victory; a victory celebration, triumphal procession' (1500) the suffix can be

---

[11] Some hybrids have already been mentioned by Martin (1906), Wehrle (1935), Dorskiy (1960) and Sauer (1992). However, none of them has provided a complete list of the seven derivatives.

considered to have the sense 'an act, activity'. *Ūseldōm* 'a state characterized by deprivation, wretchedness' (*Ormulum* 1200) includes the suffix with the sense 'state, condition'. In *wrongdōm* 'harm' (1500) the suffix *-dōm* stands for 'an act, activity'. Thus, *-dōm* assumed the following senses in hybrids: 'state, condition' (in 3 derivatives), 'an act, activity' (in 2), 'a territory' (in 2) and 'status, a rank, an office' (in 1 derivative). All the hybrids first appeared in Late Middle English.[12]

The new ME derivatives in *-dōm* are attested for all dialect areas.

3.3 Productivity

As regards productivity, Martin (1906) provides the longest, however not an exhaustive, list of 11 new ME formations with *-dōm*.[13] Nevertheless, he concludes that "[d]as Suffix *-dom* ist eines der Suffixe, die im Mittelenglischen die größte Einbuße erlitten haben" (Martin 1906:49). Dorskiy (1960:128-129), who based his study on Stratmann (1891), lists 7 new constructions.[14] He argues that the suffix was hardly productive in Middle English. Sauer (1992:230-231) gives 10 new coinages in Early Middle English and one new formation, i.e. *dūkedōm* in later texts.[15] Dalton-Puffer (1996:75-77), while investigating *-dōm* only in the first three (1150-1420) of four ME subperiods in the *Helsinki Corpus*, claims that the suffix does not exhibit any distinct productivity. According to her, "[f]or both deadjectival and denominal formations the picture is one of stagnation and eventual decline" (Dalton-Puffer 1996:76). She has found 23

---

[12] In terms of *Helsinki-Corpus* periods in ME4 (1420-1500) or towards the end of ME3 (*caitifdōm* 1390). The only exception is *ūseldōm* (< ON *ūsel*), which is recorded already in ME1 in a North-Eastern text, i.e., in an area under strong Scandinavian influence.

[13] The word *hōredōm*, which Martin labels as a ME coinage, needs to be recategorized as a continuation of an OE lexeme. See also above.

[14] Two of them, i.e., *rīchedōm* and *pōpedōm* need to be reclassified as originating in Old English.

[15] Two words have been left out of our consideration here, i.e., *burh-dōmes* (EME) a compound meaning 'judgement in a city court' and *unwīsdōm*, which is *wīsdōm* with a prefix (see also Note 6).

types, but provides no distinction between inherited ones and new ones. Bongetta (2003) mentions only 19 coinages altogether.[16]

Our own view is that the suffix *-dōm* was productive in Middle English. When our data are projected on the temporal scale used in the *Helsinki Corpus*, a steady emergence of new formations in particular subperiods can be observed. Between 1150-1250 (ME1) three new coinages are attested, in ME2 (1250-1350) five new words appeared and in 1350-1420 (ME3) three more. In the last ME subperiod, i.e., 1420-1500, nine new derivatives can be found. Altogether, there are 20 new coinages with *-dōm* in Middle English with six of them being hybrids.[17] The *MED* records three *-dōm* derivatives from French bases and three from Scandinavian loans. For some of them the *MED* provides more than one token, e.g. *caitīfdōm* 3, *dūkedōm* 6 (with 2 senses).

4. Summary

As we hope to have demonstrated, the history of *-dōm* is by no means static. It gained the status of a suffix already in Old English. In OE derivatives the suffix had the following senses (ranked in order of type frequency):

1. 'state, condition' (20)
2. 'status, a rank, an office' (17)
3. 'an act, activity' (8)
4. 'territory, a place' (5)
5. 'a quality' (4)
6. 'a group of people/collectivity' (4)
7. 'a thing' (3)
8. 'time' (1).

Some words were lost when entering Middle English. Still, 19 derivatives survived. In six of them *-dōm* maintained its OE senses. In ten of them the suffix preserved its original senses and additionally developed new ones such as: 'an act, activity' (in 3 derivatives), 'a

---

[16] This suggests that she relied exclusively on the *OED*.
[17] Dalton-Puffer (1996:77) found no hybrids in her corpus.

group of people/ collectivity' (in 3), 'status, a rank, an office' (in 2), 'territory' (in 2) as well as 'state, condition', 'a quality', 'time' and 'a person' in one derivative each. In three other lexemes -*dōm* lost one or two of the senses it had expressed in Old English.

As regards new ME coinages, all OE senses are represented in them – except for 'a group of people/collectivity'. In Late Old English, denominal formations are clearly the prevailing type (37 from N : 9 from Adj), while new ME coinages do not display a similar proportion (11 from N : 7 from Adj). In LOE denominal derivatives -*dōm* chiefly has the meanings 'status, a rank, an office' (17 derivatives) and 'state, condition' (13 derivatives). In new ME formations, the following senses appear most frequently: 'state, condition' (4 times) and 'an act, activity' (4 (or 3) times),[18] 'status, a rank, an office' (3 times) and 'a quality' (3 times). In LOE deadjectival nouns 'state, condition' is the dominating sense (7 derivatives) followed by 'a quality' (3 derivatives). In new derivatives from adjectives -*dōm* still assumes most often the meaning 'state, condition' (5).

Finally, the examples we have collected suggest that the suffix -*dōm* was productive in Middle English, as it seems to have coined as many as 20 new transparent derivatives and not only from Germanic stems but also from French and Scandinavian ones.

References

Bauer, Laurie. 2001. *Morphological productivity*. Cambridge: CUP.
Blake, Norman (ed.). 1992. *The Cambridge history of the English language. Volume II: 1066-1476*. Cambridge: CUP.
Bongetta, Davide. 2003. "The development of the English Suffix '-dom'". *Linguistica e Filologia* 17: 57-92.
Borden, Arthur R. Jr. 1982. *A comprehensive Old English dictionary*. Lanham/New York: University of America.
Bosworth, Joseph and Thomas Northcote Toller. 1898-1921. *An Anglo-Saxon dictionary*. Glasgow: OUP.
Burnley, David. 1992. "Lexis and semantics". In: Blake, Norman (ed.): 409-499.

---

[18] *Wrongdōm* can be derived either from a noun, which means 4 derivatives, or an adjective, which means 3.

Cameron, Angus, Ashley Crandell Amos, Sharon Butler and Antonette diPaolo Healey (eds.). 1986-. *Dictionary of Old English*. (microfiche).
Carr, Charles Telford. 1939. *Nominal compounds in Germanic*. Oxford: OUP.
Ciszek, Ewa. 2004. "On some French elements in Early Middle English word derivation". *Studia Anglica Posnaniensia* 40: 111-119.
Dalton-Puffer, Christiane. 1996. *The French influence on Middle English morphology*. Berlin: de Gruyter.
-----. and Claire Cowie. 2002. "Diachronic word-formation and studying changes in productivity over time: theoretical and methodological considerations". In: Díaz Vera, Javier E. (ed.): 410-437.
Díaz Vera, Javier E. (ed.). 2002. *A changing world of words. Studies in English historical lexicography, lexicology and semantics*. Amsterdam and New York: Rodopi.
Dorskiy, S. L. 1960. *Slovoobrazovaniye otvlechennikh imyen sushchestvitelnikh v Drevnieangliyskom jazikie* [*The word-formation of abstract nouns in Old English*]. Minsk: Belgosuniversitet.
Faiss, Klaus. 1978. *Verdunkelte Compounds im Englischen: ein Beitrag zur Theorie und Praxis der Wortbildung*. Tübingen: Narr.
Fisiak, Jacek. 1965. *Morphemic structure of Chaucer's English*. University, Alabama: University of Alabama Press.
-----. 1968. *A short grammar of Middle English*. 8th ed. Warszawa: Państwowe Wydawnictwo Naukowe.
-----. 1985. *Historical semantics. Historical word-formation*. Berlin: de Gruyter.
Hall, J.R. Clark. 2000. *A concise Anglo-Saxon dictionary*. Toronto: University of Toronto Press.
Hogg, Richard M. (ed.). 1992. *The Cambridge history of the English language. Volume I: The beginnings to 1066*. Cambridge: CUP.
Holthausen, Ferdinand. 1934. *Altenglisches etymologisches Wörterbuch*. Heidelberg: Winter.
Jespersen, Otto. 1942. *A modern English grammar on historical principles. Voume VI: Morphology*. London: Allen and Unwin.
Kastovsky Dieter. 1986. "The problem of productivity in word formation". *Linguistics* 24: 585-600.
-----. 1992. "Semantics and vocabulary". In: Hogg, Richard M. (ed.): 290-408.
Kluge, Friedrich. 1926. *Nominale Stammbildungslehre der altgermanischen Dialekte*. Halle: Niemeyer.
Koziol, Herbert. 1937. *Handbuch der englischen Wortbildungslehre*. Heidelberg: Winter.
Marchand, Hans. 1969. *The categories and types of Present-day English word-formation. A synchronic-diachronic approach*. 2nd ed. München: Beck'sche Verlagsbuchhandlung.
Marckwardt, Albert Henry and James L. Rosier. 1972. *Old English language and literature*. New York: Norton.

Martin, Friedrich. 1906. *Die produktiven Abstraktsuffixe des Mittelenglischen.* Inaugural-Dissertation, Kaiser-Wilhelms-Universität Straßburg i. E. Straßburg: DuMont Schauberg.

MED = Kurath, Hans, Sherman M. Kuhn, John Reidy and Robert E. Lewis 1952-2001. *Middle English dictionary.* Ann Arbor: University of Michigan Press.

MED online – *Middle English Dictionary*: http://ets.umdl.umich.edu/m/med/ (2005)

Mossé, Fernand. 1945. *Manuel de l'Anglais du Moyen Âge, Tome 1, Vieil-Anglais.* Paris: Aubier Montaigne.

OED = Murray, J.A.H., H. Bradley, W.A. Fraigie and C.T. Onions 1928 [1989]. *The Oxford English dictionary.* 2nd ed. Oxford: Clarendon.

OED online = *The Oxford English dictionary online.* 2005. http://lib.amu.edu.pl/bazy/filologia.php

Quirk, Randolph and C. L. Wrenn. 1955. *A comprehensive grammar of the English language.* London: Longman.

Roberts, Jane and Christian Kay. 1995. *A thesaurus of Old English in two volumes.* Vol. II: *Index.* London: King's College London – Centre for Late Antique and Medieval Studies.

Sauer, Hans. 1992. *Nominalkomposita im Frühmittelenglischen, mit Ausblicken auf die Geschichte der englischen Nominalkomposition.* Tübingen: Niemeyer.

Stratmann, F. H. 1891. *A Middle English dictionary.* 3rd ed. Oxford: Clarendon.

Venezky, Richard J. and Antoinette di Paolo Healey. 1986. *A microfiche concordance to Old English.* Toronto: The Pontifical Institute of Medieval Studies.

Wehrle, Otto. 1935. *Die hybriden Wortbildungen des Mittelenglischen (1050-1400): Ein Beitrag zur englischen Wortgeschichte.* Inaugural Dissertation, University of Freiburg. Freiburg im Breisgau: Weis, Mühlhans and Räpple.

Wright, Joseph. 1914. *Old English grammar.* London: OUP.

Zbierska-Sawala, Anna. 1994. *Early Middle English word formation: semantic aspects of derivational affixation in the AB language.* Frankfurt/M: Peter Lang.

Ferdinand von Mengden
The peculiarities of the OE numeral system

1. Preliminaries

The cardinal numerals of Old English show a number of peculiarities which have often triggered speculations on the original character of the numeral system. It has been assumed that the numeral system of Old English – and in fact, that of all the Germanic languages – goes back to, or, according to more moderate versions, was once influenced by a duodecimal numeral system.[1] There are indeed some features of the OE numerals – their systematic arrangement and the morphological structure of particular expressions – which seem quite extraordinary both from a cross-linguistic perspective and compared with the numerals of Present-Day English. This is particularly true of the OE expressions for numbers from '70' to '129'. Not only do they have an unusual morpheme structure, the expressions for '100', '110', and '120' are also expressed as a continuation of the multiples of '10' (i.e. as *hund-teon-tig* 'ten-ty', *hund-endlef-tig* 'eleven-ty', *hund-twelf-tig* 'twelve-ty') and not – as e.g. in Present-Day English – as addends to the base '100'.

In the following, I should like to reassess traditional explanations involving a non-decimal numeral system, and raise the claim that any feature of the sequence of OE numerals is perfectly in accordance with decimal counting. Although I shall restrict myself to the data of

---

[1] It was Jacob Grimm (1819:265) who first suggested that a number of irregularities are due to an alleged duodecimal counting system of the ancient Germanic tribes. Other 19th century scholars followed him, sometimes developing additions or alterations to the general idea of non-decimal influence (e.g. sexagesimal system). Although in the course of the 20th century statements on a non-decimal numeral system have become less widespread and also more tentative and implicit, alternative explanations for the peculiarities of the numerals of the oldest Germanic languages cannot be found. The idea of a pre-historic duodecimal numeral system still gets a mention in numerous grammars, handbooks and other contributions on the numerals of the early Germanic languages. For a sketch of the history of the duodecimal theory see von Mengden (2005).

Old English, I am assuming that my suggestions will apply to any of the ancient Germanic languages, and, hence, to proto-Germanic, too. The Germanic sister languages – especially in their oldest attested stages – have either identical features or, at least, structural features comparable to those of Old English.[2] What I mean here by structural features will become more evident in the course of our discussion.

One reason why the idea of a historically underlying duodecimal system has been so attractive to many scholars may be that many historical-comparative linguists have focussed on the formation or the etymology of particular numeral expressions. However, to assume a certain *system* behind an etymology, or to explain a particular morphological feature by some alleged characteristics of the system, requires a preceding analysis of the system itself. It is essential to determine first of all which morphological or etymological features of an individual numeral expression may allow conclusions on the type of a numeral system (both cross-linguistically and in a particular language) and which may not. In other words, if we speak of a duodecimal system (or of any other type of numeral system), it is necessary to clarify what exactly the notion of a 'numeral system' implies. Intuitively, we might say that 'numeral system' refers to a systematic order and formation of the relevant numeral expressions. This, in turn, requires an assessment of how exactly the order (the arrangement of elements in a sequence) and the formation (the internal morphological structure of the individual expressions) constitute a linguistic numeral system.

Therefore, before going into the details of the relevant OE expressions, I should like to discuss some theoretical preliminaries (see 2.). These considerations, of course, cannot be comprehensive. I shall have to restrict myself to those aspects which will be relevant for the subsequent discussion of the peculiarities of the OE numerals (see 3.). The description in the following section will therefore necessarily be selective. For a broader theoretical framework on numerals and numeral systems cf. Hurford (1975, 1987), Greenberg (1978), Ifrah (1981), Seiler (1990), Wiese (2003), von Mengden (2004).

---

[2] I shall come back to the other Germanic languages at the end of this paper in 4.

2. General features of cardinal numerals

2.1 'Cardinal numerals' and 'cardinal numbers'

Cardinal numbers (cardinalities) are properties of sets. The property which a set of three cars and a set of three flowers have in common is that both consist of three elements. As such, numbers are abstract, logical categories. In order to operate with these properties of sets, i.e. in order to apply them for instance in trading, engineering, science, etc., these abstract categories need to be represented by signs of whatever type. The most common forms in which these number signs have developed are written (numerals as characters) or spoken (numerals as number words) systems. The most primitive type of such a representation is a set of arbitrary signs for each number value. Such a method meets difficulties, as soon as it becomes necessary to memorise a large number of arbitrary correspondences between the sign (the numeral) and the notion (the cardinality). Therefore, in whatever form numbers are represented, an efficient sign system for instantiating numbers – and, if applying them in a context, for assigning cardinalities to sets – employs recursive rules for combining a relatively small set of simple signs (written characters or monomorphemic expressions) with each other and thus forming more complex expressions. These combinations are based on arithmetical operations so that the structure of even the most complex numerals remains transparent and, thus, comprehensible. Recursivity and underlying arithmetical operations are necessary and, hence, universal properties of numeral systems of any kind.

The most successful of such sign systems is certainly the Indo-Arabic number notation. To my knowledge, this is the only numeral system in every-day use which contains a symbol for the non-significant digit, i.e. '0'. Most other numeral systems – written, spoken, or other – do not employ such an element. According to Greenberg (1978:255), a non-significant digit is not expressed in any linguistic numeral system of a natural language.[3] This requires that

---

[3] The fact that many modern languages have an expression for '0' is irrelevant here. What Greenberg's generalisation says is that these expressions are not part of the

simple expressions in linguistic numeral systems are of two kinds depending on the function they perform in the recursive system. The two types of simple numeral expressions, atoms and bases, will be discussed in more detail below in 2.3.

2.2 'Systemic' numerals vs. 'non-systemic' number expressions

Not every expression of a language that may be used to specify the cardinality of a set is a numeral in the sense that it is an element of the numeral system. Languages may have other expressions, like in English *dozen* or *score*, which may likewise assign cardinalities to sets, but which do not share some essential features of genuine, i.e. systemic, cardinal numerals. In contrast to expressions like *dozen* and *score*, genuine cardinal numerals constitute a particular system of expressions – the numeral system. This is irrespective of the fact that non-systemic expressions or phrases may have a similar meaning or may perform the same syntactic functions as 'systemic' numerals do.[4]

The distinction between systemic numerals and non-systemic number expressions which I suggest here is justified by a number of both linguistic and non-linguistic observations that cannot be treated in detail in this paper.[5] The strongest support, however, is only partly

---

numeral system (cf. the following section for the distinction between 'systemic' and 'non-systemic' number expressions). English *zero* does not occur in any complex numeral form and it is not used in pragmatically unmarked quantificational constructions; cf. *I bought three apples.* / *I bought no apples.* / *?I bought zero apples.*

[4] Cf. Greenberg (2000:772b): "As has been shown, the limits of the numeral system are narrower than those of numerical expressions in general." Greenberg also mentions that there are "extra-systemic resources, by which one can express numbers larger than the limit of the cardinal system proper". These resources would contain simple lexemes like *dozen* or *score*, but also morphologically complex expressions like e.g. *two fifties* or *nineteen hundred*, the latter of which, in contrast to the systemic *one thousand nine hundred* represents the same cardinality, but is limited in its recursive capability to form more complex number expressions (cf. e.g. *twelve thousand* vs. **a dozen thousand*, or *twenty-one thousand, nine hundred* vs. **twenty thousand, [and] nineteen hundred*).

[5] A more comprehensive discussion of the criteria for distinguishing between systemic and non-systemic number expressions is provided in von Mengden (2004:15-21).

from the domain of linguistics: basically, the systemic numerals are those expressions which occur in the conventionalised counting sequence of a language.

It may perhaps seem odd to claim that a rather trivial use of numerals should be their most essential characteristic. However, cognitively the abstract notion of a 'cardinality' can only be grasped by means of an ordered progression of well-distinguished elements. Counting, that is, the most primitive application of 'cardinality', is based on the ability to distinguish a higher valued cardinality from a lower valued one. This requires that cardinalities are perceived in a hierarchical order (Benacerraf 1965; Wiese 2003:60-67). As such, the existence of an ordered progression is a purely logical prerequisite for counting. Yet, cognitive psychological studies have shown that the acquisition of the counting sequence necessarily precedes the acquisition of numeracy during the development of an infant. In other words, the acquisition of the counting sequence (i.e. of an ordered progression of well-distinguished words) is a cognitive prerequisite for the ability to conceptualise the use of numbers, and, hence, for the (arithmetically adequate) use of numerals – irrespective of whether they are used in a spoken or in a written form (Wiese 2003:151-179). The expressions of the counting sequence are therefore the linguistic (or lexical) instances of 'number' (Wiese 2003:68-90) and the conventionalised counting sequence is, in turn, that particular set of expressions which constitutes the numeral system.

2.3 Atoms, bases, and complex numerals

Having thus distinguished what I refer to as 'numerals' from what I exclude from this class of lexemes, we shall look at what numerals are like, or rather, how the elements of a numeral system are shaped.

Leaving idiosyncrasies aside, numerals may be mono-morphemic or complex. As we said above, mono-morphemic numerals, in turn, can be 'atoms' or 'bases'. Complex forms are combinations of a base and a less complex numeral. Semantically, these combinations reflect arithmetical operations. These are the key features of any numeral system of a natural language. I shall illustrate these features briefly in the following.

The atoms of the numeral system of Present-Day English are the expressions from *one* to *nine*. The bases are the expressions *ten, hundred, thousand, million*, etc. Any other numeral of the counting sequence is formed as a combination of a base with another (simple or complex) numeral expression. Clearly, this is a rather approximate description and, at the moment, we are disregarding deviations from this general principle. However, this recursive principle – a potentially infinite set of expression is generated by a rather small set of primitive elements (atoms and bases) – generally applies cross-linguistically (cf. e.g. Greenberg 1978; Seiler 1990).

Atoms always occur in the numeral system as a paradigmatic set of expressions forming an ordered progression (sequence)[6]. This means that in any combination of an atom and a base, *any* of the nine atoms also occurs in that morphological combination and, hence, in the same arithmetical function. To illustrate this, *four-teen* represents an addition of '4' and '10'. The slot for the atom *four* in this combination may also be taken by any other atom, as in *fif-teen* '5 + 10', *six-teen* '6 + 10', etc.[7] Or, to give another example, all atoms may be used as multipliers to the second base *hundred*. Hence, the fact that the expression *two hundred* '2 × 100' exists in the numeral system of Present-Day English necessarily implies the existence of a parallel formation with any other atom, i.e. *three hundred* '3 × 100', *four hundred* '4 × 100' up until *nine hundred* '9 × 100'. The principle of the continuously recurring sequence of atoms implies that bases, in contrast to atoms, form the constants in the underlying arithmetical principle.

---

[6] In the following, I shall use the term *sequence* in the sense of an 'ordered, finite, progression of well-distinguished elements'. Note that this refers to a set of expressions with a paradigmatic distribution, not to a sequence in the sense of a syntactic sequence.

[7] Apparently, we have left the expressions *eleven* and *twelve* unconsidered and we have assumed that the numerical values '11' and '12' would regularly have to be expressed as **one-teen* '1 + 10' and **two-teen* '2 + 10', respectively. We shall come back to *eleven* and *twelve* below (3.6).

2.4 Variant forms

If we say that there are arithmetical operations underlying the structure of any complex numeral, we should add that the default forms of some numerals may undergo some variation if used in a particular combination. For instance, the numeral *thirty* consists of the constituents *thir-* and *-ty*. We can generally analyse *thir-* as an allomorph of the atomic numeral *three* and *-ty* as a suffix representing the base numeral *ten* (similarly to *-teen* in *thir-teen*). Arithmetically, this makes sense since the expression *thirty*, representing the numerical value '30', would thus, be based on the underlying arithmetical operation '3 × 10' (and, accordingly, *thir-teen* '13' on '3 + 10').

Having said that PDE *-teen* and *-ty* both represent the base *ten* in these forms, the question arises in which relation *-teen* and *-ty* stand to *ten*. All these elements represent the numerical value '10'. However, while *ten* is a free form, *-ty* and *-teen* are bound forms. '10' outside any arithmetical operation is always represented by the simple form *ten* and never by a complex form. In contrast, *-ty* and *-teen* are used only if the numerical value '10' is a component of an arithmetical operation, i.e. multiplication and addition, respectively. Therefore, in contrast to the compound numeral *two hundred* '2 × 100', both *thir-teen* '3 + 10' and *thir-ty* '3 × 10' are affixations. This analysis is not only justified by the purely formal criterion that *-teen* and *-ty* are bound forms. In addition they are also more specific than the simple (free) form *ten*. In any formation with *-teen*, the suffix does not only represent the numerical value '10', but it means '10, if (and only if) used as an augend'. Likewise, *-ty* does not only mean '10' but it generally means '10, if (and only if) used as a multiplicand'.[8] It

---

[8] Arithmetically, there is no need to distinguish between the two (or more) elements forming the operation because addition and multiplication are both commutative operations. However, complex linguistic numerals formed by addition (e.g. *four-teen* '4 + 10') or by multiplication (e.g. *for-ty* '4 × 10') are usually combinations of a sequence of atoms and a constant base, as e.g. in *thir-teen* '3 + 10', *four-teen* '4 + 10', *fif-teen* '5 + 10' etc. Here, a distinction between the two elements forming the operation can be drawn, that is, between the *addend* or *multiplier* (the variable) and the *augend* or *multiplicand* (the constant), respectively. Although arithmetically

follows from the recursive character of numeral system that this applies to any use of these elements in any higher valued numeral of a however complex structure: even in *thir-teen thousand* '(3 + 10) × 1,000' and *thir-ty thousand* '(3 × 10) × 1,000' our analysis is valid.

After having discussed some theoretical prerequisites, exemplified by the numerals of Present-Day English, we shall now turn to the numeral system of Old English.

3. The analysis and classification of the OE numeral system

3.1 The OE expressions for numbers from '70' to '120'

Table 1 shows those expressions of the numeral system of Old English which represent the multiples of '10'.

Table 1. Multiples of '10' in Old English

morphological structure	expression	underlying arithmetical operation	numerical value	section	typological status
	tyn		'10'		
	twen-tig	'2 × 10'	'20'	A	
	þri-tig	'3 × 10'	'30'		
	feower-tig	'4 × 10'	'40'		
⇧	*fif-tig*	'5 × 10'	'50'		
{X} + *tig*	*six-tig*	'6 × 10'	'60'		
hund + {X} + *tig*	*hund-seofon-tig*	'7 × 10'	'70'	B	
⇩	*hund-eahta-tig*	'8 × 10'	'80'		⇧
	hund-nigon-tig	'9 × 10'	'90'		common
	hund-teon-tig	'10 × 10'	'100'	C	rare
	hund-endlef-tig	'11 × 10'	'110'		⇩
	hund-twelf-tig	'12 × 10'	'120'		

---

irrelevant, the distinction becomes important in a linguistic context as the recursive principle underlying the combination of sequences (variables) and bases (constants) is the defining characteristic of numeral systems. To my knowledge, it was Joseph Greenberg (1978) who first used the terms 'addend' / 'augend' and 'multiplier' / 'multiplicand' in the context of linguistic numeral systems.

As can be seen in the table, the relevant expressions in sections B and C deviate morphologically from those in section A.[9] Furthermore, the table also shows a typologically very uncommon feature: the expressions for the multiples of '10' do not end with '90', but the sequence continues up until '120'. In other words, after 'ninety' the sequence of multiples of '10' continues using expressions that could best be rendered as 'ten-ty', 'eleven-ty', and 'twelve-ty'. Cross-linguistically section C represents a phenomenon extremely rare in natural languages.

Thus, while the difference between section A and section BC is a morphological one – the distinction between section AB and section C is motivated by typological considerations. Both phenomena indicated by the two dividing lines in Table 1 have played a role in the discussion of the alleged duodecimal system, and in the further course of this paper, I shall argue that they are both perfectly in line with decimal counting. I shall start with the analysis of the morphological structure of the multiples of '10' (3.2) and then proceed to discuss the section from '100' to '129' (3.3).

3.2 The morphological structure of the multiples of '10'

Without exception, the extant grammars of Old English analyse the expressions in sections B and C of Table 1 as tri-morphemic expressions (cf. e.g. Campbell 1959:284, § 684; Lass 1990:213). The structure of the corresponding expressions for the lower valued multiples of '10' might actually suggest this analysis: the numerals in section A all have a structure consisting of an atomic numeral plus the

---

[9] The numerals of sections B and C are the default forms in Old English. The remarks in the grammars of Old English are imprecise in this point. They all imply that there has been a free variation between circumfixed and suffixed forms from Early West Saxon onwards (cf. Campbell 1959:184, § 686, Brunner 1965:255, Lass 1994:214). Before the Norman Conquest, however, the forms *seofontig* '70' and *eahtatig* '80' occur only in the section between Book II.7. and Book V of the OE *Orosius*. There is no evidence for a systematic use of suffixed expressions for numerical values above '69' outside this passage – nor for a free variation between suffixed and circumfixed expressions. On this phenomenon see von Mengden (2006).

suffix *-tig*; i.e. *twen-tig* '2 × 10', *thri-tig* '3 × 10', *feower-tig* '4 × 10', *fif-tig* '5 × 10', *six-tig* '6 × 10'. Superficially, it looks as if the expressions in sections B and C are formed by attaching a prefix *hund-* to the structure of the lower valued expressions of section A.

However, if the structure {*hund-* + atom + *-tig*} consisted of three distinct morphological constituents, one would have to account for a function of the constituent *hund-* independent from that of *-tig*. Since the arithmetical operations underlying the expressions of sections B and C are obviously the same as those of the numerals in section A, I would argue that the multiplicand '× 10' in the higher valued expressions is represented by one discontinuous morpheme, i.e. by a circumfix. In other words: analysing *hund-* as an independent prefix would require an independent meaning or grammatical function for *each* of the three elements in the structure *hund-seofon-tig*. I can see no such meaning or function for *hund-* alone as *hund-seofon-tig* clearly means '70' and therefore parallels semantically (i.e. arithmetically) the lower valued expressions of section A. The structures of both expressions, *six-tig* and *hund-seofon-tig* represent a multiplication of an atom ('6', '7') with the base '10'. Accounting for an additional function of the element *hund-* is therefore not feasible – neither on arithmetic grounds nor by insinuating any other meaning or grammatical function of *hund-*.

Furthermore, since the suffix *-tig* and the circumfix *hund-__-tig* are distributed complementarily, we may say that *-tig* and *hund-__-tig* are two allomorphic variants of the same morpheme, both representing the base numeral *tyn* '10' in its arithmetical function as a multiplicand (cf. 2.4).[10] A mere allomorphic variation within the sequence of multiples of '10' is, however, no evidence for a different counting method.

---

[10] A similar distribution of two allomorphic variants – a suffix and a circumfix – can be found in OE verbal morphology: the past participle of verbs is generally marked by the circumfix *ge-__-ed* (for strong verbs: *ge-__-en*) while the past participle of prefixed verbs is marked by the suffix *-ed* (for strong verbs *-en*). The two forms, suffix and circumfix, show a complementary distribution which suggests their allomorphic relation. The lack of an independent function of the element *ge-* shows that the structure {*ge-* + verbal root + *-ed (-en)*} is composed of two rather than three morphemes.

Variations like this within a particular section of the counting sequence are not at all infrequent in numeral systems and have as such no evidential value. Therefore, the split between the expressions of section A in Table 1 and those in sections BC cannot be taken to reflect the influence of a different, that is, a non-decimal counting system, unless there is further evidence for such influence.

Admittedly, the homophony of the element *hund-* in the circumfix and the expression *hund(red)* '100' is confusing. It has encouraged the view that *hund-* is an element isolated from *-tig*. The question of the etymology of both expressions is too complex to be dealt with here. However, cross-linguistic evidence suggests that *hund(red)* is derived from an expression for '10' rather than the inverse, i.e. that the element *hund-* in the multiples of '10' originates from an expression for '100' (cf. e.g. proto-Gmc. **þus-hund-* 'strong hundred' > '1,000'; Italian *milli-one* 'great thousand' > 'million'), as has occasionally been conjectured.[11]

3.3 The overrunning of the base '100'

In the previous section our focus was on that constituent within the expressions for the multiples of '10' which represents the multiplicand '10'. We have disregarded so far the constituent representing the multiplier. As I have already indicated above in 3.1, the cross-linguistically common pattern is that the multiplier in these numerals is represented by members of the set of atoms. There is a strong tendency in numeral systems of natural languages that the numerical value of a multiplicand (the constant) in a complex expression always exceeds that of the multiplier (the sequence of usually atomic variables) (cf. Hurford 1975:67-80; Greenberg 1978:270-271). In a

---

[11] To take but one out of many examples, cf. the discussion in Lass (1994:213): "The real problem is the sense of *hund* in the OE numerals [from '70' to '129'] [...]. One interpretation might be something like '(special) hundred made of (groups) of sevens', etc. i.e. the higher decades are taken to be something more like lower hundreds (in our sense)." As I see it, such constructs are rather far-fetched and have no parallels in numeral systems of natural languages. If we accept the analysis of *hund-* forming one discontinuous morpheme together with *-tig*, which represents the multiplier '10', a "problem" like the one mentioned e.g. by Lass does not exist.

decimal system this sequence of atoms ends with '9'. The almost universal way to form expressions representing the numerical values from '100' onwards is the pattern we are used to from Present-Day English, where there is a sequence of nine multiples of the first base '10' and, once this sequence is used up, the second base '100' is employed as an augend as in (*one*) *hundred and ten* '100 + (1 × 10)' and (*one*) *hundred and twenty* '100 + (2 × 10)'.

However, Table 1 above reveals that in Old English the sequence of multipliers to the base '10' is larger than we would expect. In addition to the nine atoms, the sequence of multipliers also contains the expressions for '10', '11', and '12'.[12] The case of the numeral system of Old English shows that the constraint described above cannot be taken as an absolute universal. Albeit cross-linguistically extremely infrequent, it is, of course, not logically necessary that the series of multipliers ends with '9', i.e. that the series of multiples of '10' should not continue with '10 × 10', '11 × 10', up until '12 × 10'.

Thus, what we are dealing with in section C is an idiosyncrasy in the numeral system, and such a systemic idiosyncrasy, of course, calls for an explanation, especially if it is cross-linguistically such an exceptional phenomenon. This particularity has often been explained by the influence of a non-decimal counting system. However, as we shall see in the following, an analysis of particular features of the expressions that constitute our section C will suffice to rule out any non-decimal influence on these numerals.

3.4 Why not duodecimal?

As with every multiple of '10', the OE expressions *hund-teon-tig*, *hund-endlef-tig*, and *hund-twelf-tig* may serve as augends for the whole set of atoms. In other words, in order to express the numerical values in between the multiples of '10', the Anglo-Saxons counted accordingly 'ten-ty-one', 'ten-ty-two', etc., and 'eleven-ty-one',

---

[12] In the case of '10' and '11', in fact, the multipliers are represented by the allomorphic variants *-teon-* and *-endlef-*, representing the atoms *tyn* '10' and *endleofan* '11', respectively.

'eleven-ty-two', etc., up until eventually 'twelve-ty-nine'. Cf. the examples in (1):

(1)a Wintr-a   hæf-de   fif   and   hund-teon-tig
      winter-GEN.PL   have-3S.PRT   5   +   CIRC-10-×10
      'He was 105 years old.'
      (GenAB 1130; Krapp 1931:39)

(1)b he   hæf-de   ðreo   ond   hund-ændlef-tig   wintr-a
      he   have-3S.PRT   3   +   CIRC-11-×10   winter-GEN.PL
      "He was 113 years old."
      (Mart 5 (Ja 10, A.2); Kotzor 1981:16, 14, 2)

(1)c fif   &   hund-twelf-tig   byssceop-a
      5   +   CIRC-12-×10   bishop-GEN.PL
      "125 bishops"
      (Bede 5B 17.460.1; Miller 1890-91:460)

Only from '130' onwards are the numerals formed exactly like in Present-Day English, i.e. (an) hundred and þri-tig '100 + (3 × 10)'. But we will not focus on the base hund(red) in Old English here, since we are interested in what is behind the rather uncommon case of the section of multiples overrunning the base '100'.[13]

What matters, first of all, is that the sequences from '101' – '110', from '111' – '120' and from '121' – '130' are arranged as sets of ten elements, i.e. as decades and not as duodecads. A purely duodecimal system would require an arrangement in duodecads, i.e. in sequences of twelve recurring elements.[14] This alone shows that the general

---

[13] The principle described here is the default way for the formation of numerals from '100' to '129'. However, in Old English we do occasionally find additions to '100' which correspond to the pattern of Present-Day English, i.e. an hund and twa and twentig '122', or '100 + 2 + (2 × 10)'. For a more detailed discussion cf. von Mengden (2004:32-41).

[14] Speaking of 'pure' or 'regular' numeral systems (as I do here and in the following) is, of course, a theoretical consideration. There is hardly any natural language whose numeral system does not show idiosyncrasies in the arrangement of its counting sequence. At the same time, I am not aware of any numeral system of a natural language, where such an idiosyncrasy would be strong enough to defy the general arrangement of the system. Thus, the systematic (i.e. recursive and based on

order is decimal, even in the typologically unusual section C. Outside section C, the order of elements in the rest of the numeral system is also unambiguously decimal: before '100', the underlying arithmetical operations are the same as, say, in the PDE numeral system. Moreover, from '130' onwards the second decimal base *hund(red)* '100' is employed as augend, again just like in the English of today. We may conclude that the fundamental base of the numeral system of Old English is in any case '10'.

Yet, this fact alone does not rule out any secondary influence of a non-decimal numeral system. Moreover, it does not explain why the OE numeral system shows such a highly unusual feature by first ignoring the second decimal base '100' and then employing it from '130' onwards in a regular way. Indeed, the fact that the sequence overrunning '100' ends with the twelfth multiple, has often been taken as evidence for a historically underlying duodecimal system. Again, I would argue that the scope of the overrunning sequence (i.e. the fact that section C ends with the twelfth element) bears clear evidence *against* any possible duodecimal influence rather than in favour of it. In order to illustrate my point, let us see how serially recurring sequences in numeral systems are most likely to behave.

In a regular decimal system (again, let us take the example of the ModE system) it is the tenth element of any recurring subsequence which requires a change: any decade (that is, any subsequence of ten elements) consists of nine (!) serially recurring atoms plus a diverging final element. For instance, the sequence of teens goes *seven-teen* '7 + 10', *eight-teen* '8 + 10', *nine-teen* '9 + 10', but the tenth element of

---

serialized arithmetical operations) arrangement of a numeral system is a linguistic universal. What I do methodologically if I speak of a 'regular' system is to assume, for the sake of the argument, that a particular system is devoid of idiosyncrasies. For instance, I have been ignoring so far the idiosyncratic forms *eleven* and *twelve* and I have assumed that the numerical values '11' and '12' were expressed as '1 + 10' (*one-teen) and '2 + 12' (*two-teen), respectively, as they actually are in the vast majority of languages. This is justified by the remarkable uniformity of the recursive principles according to which numeral systems of natural languages are arranged. These general principles are independent of whether a system employs '10' or any other numerical value as base.

the sequence has a different structure: the expression for '20' is formed as a multiple of '10', *twen-ty* '2 × 10'. (Once more, we are momentarily leaving the irregular forms *eleven* and *twelve* out of consideration.) To take another example, the fourth decade of the PDE counting sequence begins with *thirty-one* '(3 × 10) + 1', then continues up to *thirty-eight* '(3 × 10) + 8', *thirty-nine* '(3 × 10) + 9', but ends with an expression that replaces the atom *thir-* with *for-* (and the resulting *for-ty* '4 × 10', in turn, serves as an augend in the next higher decade).

I would claim that the pattern described here is *the* defining feature of a decimal system. It does not only apply to the decades, but also to any other serially used sequence of atoms: for instance, the multiples of '100' are formed by the nine atomic numerals as multipliers, beginning with *one hundred* '1 × 100' and *two hundred* '2 × 100', continuing this way up to *nine hundred* '9 × 100', and the final element, the base *thousand*, is again structurally different. Thus, in a regularly arranged decimal system any sequence of ten elements consists of nine equally formed expressions and of a tenth element which deviates in its shape. In fact, we may say that the tenth element of each sequence anticipates the structure of the following sequence.[15]

If we now transfer this pattern to a duodecimal system, we would have to expect each sequence (each duodecad) to consist of eleven elements with parallel constituent structures and to be terminated by the twelfth, morphologically deviating element. In Old English, however, the twelfth element in the sequence of multiples of '10', i.e. *hundtwelftig* '12 × 10', corresponds in its morphological structure to the previous eleven multiples. In other words, the idiosyncrasy continues up until '129' and the new formation pattern begins with '130'. Therefore, if the irregularly overrunning sequence in the OE

---

[15] Strictly speaking, this does not apply to the very first decade of the counting sequence, as the tenth element – PDE *ten*, OE *tyn* – is a mono-morphemic and arbitrary form and as such not *morphologically* different from the nine atoms. However, the element '10' is *functionally* different from the atoms '1' – '9' in that it can re-occur in any later stage (i.e. in any higher valued subsequence) of the counting sequence as a constant (i.e. as a base) while the atoms always function as variables in the underlying arithmetical operations.

system were due to a non-decimal counting system, the only candidate for a model would be a 13-based system because the next possible turning point is the numerical value '130'. The possibility of a 13-based system, however, can be ruled out not only because the OE expression for '130' is formed with the second decimal base *hund(red)* '100', i.e. as (*an*) *hund(red) and þritig* '(1 × 100) + (3 × 10)', and hence, according to the pattern of an entirely regular decimal system. A 13-based system is also improbable on typological grounds, since a 13-based numeral system is cross-linguistically unattested (cf. Greenberg 2000:773).

3.5 How do we account for the overrunning sequence?

If we say that the overrunning of the second base '100' cannot be due to a non-decimal counting system, how else do we account for it? How do we account for the fact that the OE numeral system defies the very strong universal tendency to introduce a new base at that point in the counting sequence where the series of atoms is used up as multipliers to the base '10'?

The simple reason for the overrunning of the base '100' is another irregularity in the numeral systems of all Germanic languages: the irregular forms of the expressions for '11' and for '12'. In an entirely regular decimal system, the numerals for '11' and '12' would be expressed as an addition of the atoms and the base, hence as '1 + 10' and '2 + 10', respectively (the constituent order of addend and augend is irrelevant here); cf. Classical Latin *un-decim* '1 + 10', *duo-decim* '2 + 10', *tre-decim* '3 + 10'.[16] The expressions from '13' to '19' are formed exactly after this pattern (cf. PDE *thir-teen* '3 + 10' ... *nine-teen* '9 + 10'), but the expressions for '11' and '12' are idiosyncratic and (synchronically analysed) mono-morphemic. Such irregularities occur in most numeral systems of natural languages, but, in spite of their irregularity in shape, these forms do not defy the general

---

[16] Note that this applies to all linguistic numeral systems, but not necessarily to all non-linguistic number notation systems. Systems which employ a symbol for the non-significant digit, necessarily have complex bases of the shape ⟨10⟩. Cf. above 2.1 and note 3.

recursive principle of a system: they re-occur in more complex numerals like *two hundred and twelve* (instead of **two hundred and two-teen*).

Since, owing to this idiosyncrasy, the set of potential multipliers of the base '10' is mono-morphemic even beyond the base '10', it is less inconvenient in Germanic to continue the sequence of multipliers beyond '9' analogously to the lower valued expressions than it is in other languages, where the expressions for '11' and '12' are complex. This would not be the case if the numerical values '11' and '12' were expressed in Old English according to the other expressions in the sequence of teens, i.e. as **an-tyne* '1 + 10' and **twa-tyne* '2 + 10', respectively.

3.6 Are the idiosyncratic expressions for '11' and '12' due to a duodecimal system?

So far, we have rejected any non-decimal influence as an explanation for the overrunning section from '100' to '129'. Instead we have explained one deviation from the ideal decimal arrangement – the overrunning of the second base – by another deviation – the non-complex forms of the expressions for '11' and '12'. The obvious question now is whether the idiosyncratic shape of the expressions for '11' and '12' is the actual trace of a duodecimal system.

Again, I would argue, it cannot be. While explaining the overrunning section from '100' to '129' in 3.5, we needed to analyse the expressions for '11' and '12' synchronically, and hence as arbitrary and mono-morphemic expressions. To explain the idiosyncrasy of the expressions for '11' and '12', however, requires a diachronic analysis. Diachronically, the expressions for '11' and '12' are compounds: they go back to proto-Gmc. **aina-lif* 'one remaining' and **twa-lifa* 'two remaining' with the respective first elements of these formations being the elements '1' and '2' and the second part being interpreted as 'remaining, left'. Thus the expressions for '11' and '12' in proto-Germanic originally meant '1 remaining' and '2 remaining', respectively. We can see that their original structure is still idiosyncratic in that it deviates from that of the remaining forms in the second decade which is of the type OE *þreo-tyne*, PDE *thir-teen*

'3 + 10'. While still deviating from the overall system, their reconstructed proto-Germanic forms refer to the base '10', since 'one remaining' and 'two remaining' can arithmetically only mean 'remaining from 10'. Thus, the etymologies of the expressions for '11' and '12' in Germanic unambiguously reveal that the two expressions originate in a decimal counting method.

Moreover, *if* analysed etymologically, these expressions are complex numerals. In this case, again, the twelfth element of a duodecimal sequence would have to show a different morpheme structure than the eleventh element (cf. 3.4). However, this is not the case. The morpheme structures of the two proto-Germanic expressions are clearly parallel and therefore cannot have been generated by a duodecimal system.

4. Conclusion: the Germanic pre-history

The claim I have raised in this paper is that, even in the earliest stages of proto-Germanic, the numeral system was – in spite of its idiosyncrasies – entirely decimal. Methodologically, I suggest that statements on the numeral system cannot be inferred from etymological considerations alone. The key feature for determining the type of numeral system of a language is the arrangement of serially recurring progressions in the counting sequence (3.4). In Old English, as in any other Germanic language, any recurring sequence of elements consists of ten members (which implies the possibility of larger sets of hundred or thousand recurring elements). Hence, the numeral system of any Germanic language, at any stage in its history, has been decimal.

Having said this, I should mention that in Old Norse, there is indeed one feature of the numeral system based on the multiplicand '12'. The sequence of multiples of '10' in Old Norse ends with the expressions *nio tiger* '9 × 10', *tio tiger* '10 × 10', *ellefo tiger* '11 × 10' and is then – different from Old English – followed by the expression *hundraþ* '120'.[17] Thus, there is indeed a duodecimal element in the

---

[17] There are occasional instances where *hundraþ* does in fact represent '100'. We shall leave this out of consideration and treat '120' as the default numerical value of

numeral system of Old Norse, otherwise the second base at this point of the counting sequence could not be accounted for. This does not mean that the numeral system of Old Norse *is* a duodecimal one. That it is still generally decimal – in spite of this disturbance – can be seen first of all by the fact that the aforementioned expressions leading up to *hundraþ* in the counting sequence (*nio tiger, tio tiger, ellefo tiger*) are all multiples of '10' (and the corresponding subsequences are therefore decades and not duodecads). A duodecimal system proper would require a sequence of twelve duodecads terminated by a base representing '144' (as '12 × 12'). Moreover, the sequence of multipliers to the second base (*an hundraþ* '1 × 120', *tuau hundroþ* '2 × 120', *þriu hundroþ* '3 × 120', etc.) is again only a sequence of ten elements, as the third base *þusund* usually stands for '1,200', but never for '1,440'. Therefore, the use of the expression *hundraþ* for '120' in the numeral system of Old Norse is a (solitary) duodecimal feature within an otherwise decimal system.

As to the other ancient Germanic languages, they all correspond with Old English in so far as they show the morphological split after '60' (cf. Table 1, section A vs. B). I have not tried to explain this split and I doubt it is possible to substantiate a theory which will explain it fully. However, as I have tried to show in 3.2, the split in Old English (as well as in the other Germanic languages) – whatever its historical explanation – does not allow the conclusion that the underlying counting method was not decimal.

The extent to which the second base of the numeral system is overrun by the multiples of '10' differs among the Germanic sister languages, provided the expressions in question are attested at all. What is crucial is the following: all Germanic languages use an expression derived from proto-Gmc. **hund-* for the second base (cf. above, 3.2). In only one of these languages, in Old Norse, its numerical value is '120', in all other Germanic languages it is '100'. Employing the method of comparative reconstruction these data alone suffice to conclude the numerical value of proto-Gmc. **hund-* must

---

ON *hundraþ*. The significantly higher frequency of '120'-instances in contrast to the '100'-instances of *hundraþ* justifies this assumption.

have been '100' and not '120'. The evidence of the proto-Indo-European reconstruct of this numeral – *kṃtóm is well attested throughout the Indo-European family exclusively as '100' – is not even needed.

Whatever the reason for the deviation in the (generally decimal) numeral system of Old Norse may be – it is a particular phenomenon of Old Norse that must have developed after the disintegration of the Germanic languages. Outside Old Norse there has never been the slightest influence of a duodecimal numeral system at any stage in the (pre-)history of the Germanic languages.

Transferring the method employed here to the classification of other numeral systems, we may, as a final remark, mention the numeral system of Modern Danish. The Danish numeral system has often been labelled as vigesimal for one single reason: etymologically, the (synchronically opaque) expressions for the multiples of '10' represent multiplications by '20', i.e. *halv-treds* '50', or '(3 – ½) × 20', *tres* '60', or '3 × 20', *halvjerds* '70', or '(4 – ½) × 20', *firs* '80', or '4 × 20', and *halvfems* '90', or '(5 – ½) × 20'. The etymologies of these expressions suggest serially recurring sections of twenty elements, at least from '50' onwards. However, there is not one vigintiad in the counting sequence of Danish. It is arranged entirely in sequences of ten (nine atoms plus a final element). In spite of the idiosyncratic forms for the multiples of '10', Danish has a decimal numeral system. The example of Danish confirms our claim: we may ask for a historical explanation for deviations in the form of particular (sets of) numeral expressions as compared to the overall system. But the etymology of particular expressions cannot be taken as sufficient evidence for statements on the arrangement, and hence on the type of the numeral system.[18]

---

[18] Thanks to Florian Haas, Niki Ritt and to two anonymous reviewers for their critical comments and valuable suggestions on earlier versions of this paper.

References

Benacerraf, Paul. 1965. "What numbers could not be". *Philosophical Review* 74: 47-73.
Brunner, Karl. 1965. *Altenglische Grammatik. Nach der angelsächsischen Grammatik von Eduard Sievers*. Dritte, neu bearbeitete Auflage. Tübingen: Niemeyer.
Campbell, Alistair. 1959. *Old English grammar*. Oxford: Clarendon.
Greenberg, Joseph H. 1978. "Generalizations about numeral systems". In: Greenberg, Joseph H. (ed.). *Universals of human language. Volume III: Word structure*. Stanford: Stanford University Press: 249-295.
-----. 2000. "Numeral". In: Booij, Geert, Christian Lehmann, Joachim Mugdan in collaboration with Wolfgang Kesselheim, Stavros Skopeteas (eds.). *Morphology: an international handbook on inflection and word-formation*. Berlin: de Gruyter: 770-783.
Grimm, Jacob. 1819. *Deutsche Grammatik. Erster Teil*. Göttingen: Dieterich.
Hurford, James R. 1975. *The linguistic theory of numerals*. Cambridge: CUP.
-----. 1987. *Language and number: the emergence of a cognitive system*. Oxford: Blackwell.
Ifrah, Georges. 1981. *Histoire universelle des chiffres*. Paris: Seghers.
Kotzor, Günter (ed.). 1981. *Das altenglische Martyrologium. Band II: Edition, Anmerkungen und Indices*. München: Bayerische Akademie der Wissenschaften.
Krapp, George Philip (ed.). 1931. *The Junius Manuscript*. (= Anglo-Saxon Poetic Records 1). New York: Columbia University Press.
Lass, Roger. 1994. *Old English: a historical linguistic companion*. Cambridge: CUP.
von Mengden, Ferdinand. 2004. *Cardinal numerals in Old English*. Ph.D. Dissertation, Freie Universität Berlin.
-----. 2005. "How myths persist: Jacob Grimm, the long hundred and duodecimal counting". In: Knappe, Gabriele (ed.). *English linguistics and medieval studies: positions – perspectives – new approaches*. Frankfurt: Lang: 201-221.
von Mengden, Ferdinand. 2006. "Modern English Numerals in the Old English *Orosius*". In: Johnston, Andrew James, Ferdinand von Mengden and Stefan Thim (eds.). *Language and texts: current perspectives on English and Germanic historical linguistics*. Heidelberg: Winter.
Miller, Thomas (ed.). 1890-1891. *The Old English version of Bede's Ecclesiastical History of the English People*. Part I. (= Early English Text Society, Original Series 95, 96). London: OUP.
Seiler, Hansjakob. 1990. "A dimensional view on numeral systems". In: Croft, William, Keith Denning and Suzanne Kemmer (eds.). *Studies in typology and diachrony: papers presented to Joseph H. Greenberg on his 75th birthday* Amsterdam: Benjamins: 187-208.
Wiese, Heike. 2003. *Numbers, language and the human mind*. Cambridge: CUP.

Letizia Vezzosi
From *agen* to *own*

> Lady Monica Carmoyle: "We Towcesters aren't easy to place. The Towcester men have all been lilies of the field. Why, Uncle George didn't even put on his own boots."
>
> Sir Roderick, her husband: "Whose boots did he put on?"
> [Wodehouse RJ 4]

0. Introduction[1]

Clearly, and despite its traditional categorization in most dictionaries and grammars, the semantic contribution of *own* to the introductory quote above goes beyond emphasising the possessive meaning of the pronoun *his*.[2] In fact, the very humour of the passage hinges on the ambiguity of the verb phrase *to put on his own boots*, which allows for different readings. Thus, the crucial sentence can either mean that uncle George did not put on the boots belonging to him (this is what Sir Roderick appears to have understood), or that he did not put on his boots by himself, but needed help (this is what Lady Monica Carmoyle most probably meant).

The widespread assumption that *own* is linked to the notion of possession is partly based on its etymology, as *own* derives from OE *agen*, i.e. the past participle of OE *agan* 'possess, own'. At the same time, *agen* is often glossed as 'own' in OE dictionaries and grammars, and is also considered as a possessive emphatic in most of the

---

[1] I am grateful to Ekkehard König, Anette Rosenbach and two anonymous reviewers for their useful comments and to Gregory Conti who very kindly revised the English version of this paper. I also deeply thank the Alexander von Humboldt Foundation which supported the research project on the results of which this paper is based.

[2] 'Belonging' is the paraphrase given in the *Cambridge international dictionary of English* (PONS) and the *Dictionary of contemporary English* (DCE) regards the implication of "adding force to the idea of possession" as the essential semantic ingredient of *own*. Similarly traditional grammars describe the combination of *own* with a possessive pronoun as a means of "giv[ing] emphasis to the idea of personal possession" (ALD), "emphasiz[ing] ownership" (Zandvoort 1957:142) or "the idea of possession" (Curme 1931:529).

literature (Ingersoll 1978, Mitchell 1985). Nevertheless, given the ambiguity of PDE *own*, the question arises whether that ambiguity is an innovation, or whether it may not already have characterised the ways in which OE *agen* could be used.

In this paper I will try to answer that question. To do so, I shall first determine the semantic value of OE *agen* within the group of words related to the same lexical stem (sections 1 and 1.1), and then compare the meaning and usage of OE *agen* (1.2 and 1.3) to those of ME *own* and ModE *own* (sections 2 and 2.2). Necessarily, this has to be done on the basis of corpus evidence. The specific corpora used for this study are the *Dictionary of Old English corpus in electronic form* (*DOEC*) for the Old English period and on the *Helsinki Corpus* and the *Oxford English Dictionary* (*OED*) for Middle and Modern English.[3] The periodization used in this paper follows that of the *Helsinki Corpus*, but makes no further subdivisions within the three main periods. Occurrences of *agen-own* in Old, Middle and Modern English will be compared, and differences and overlaps between usages in each of the three periods pointed out. Specifically, it will be shown how and when *agen-own* became a functional word, that is to say, an identity marker (or phoric marker), whose function and occurrence is closely linked to the focussed identity marker or intensifier[4] *himself* (2.1 and 3.).

---

[3] The examples quoted in the paper have been checked in the relevant complete texts, but are quoted according to the conventions used in the *Dictionary* of *Old English corpus in electronic form* on-line and in the *Helsinki Corpus*. My translations are intended to be as literal as possible, and mirror the syntactic structure of the source sentences, as long as this does not completely disrupt the syntactic structure of the PDE translation.

[4] With the term 'intensifier' I refer to expressions which have a specific lexical meaning, i.e. they denote an identity function, and which are invariably in focus and are thereby related to specific types of alternative expressions. The asserted value must be topical, either on extra-contextual or contextual grounds. And the alternative values always stand in some specific relation to the referent of the head NP (cf. König 2001). When there is no such relation, an intensifier is inappropriate.

(1) *The president himself opened the meeting* (implying *not his secretary* vs. **not the pope*)

[$_{NP}$ the president himself] = ID (the president) = the president

1. *Agan* and *agen* in Old English

The OE word *agen* is formally the past participle[5] of a Germanic preterite-present verb which is also attested in Goth. *aih* 'to possess', in OHG *eiga*, in OE *agan*. Together with verbs like like OE *habban* 'have', or OE *healdan* 'hold', OE *agan* belongs to the sub-class of possession predicates characterised by the feature [-movement] (cf. Schendl 1992), which express a state of possession – not a change of possession like verbs such as OE *sellan* 'to give', OE *onfon* 'to receive' and so on. OE *agan* and *habban*, however, do not appear to be synonyms, since there are patterns where one occurs to the exclusion of the other as in (1)a vs. (1)b: *habban* can express more abstract notions of possession, while *agan* only occurs with concrete objects that can be somebody's property.

(1)a Gif hit ðonne sie dead butan fulwihte, gebete he hit mid eallum ðam ðe he **age** (*hæbbe). (*LawIne* 2.1.)
'If, however, it dies without baptism, he shall compensate it with all he possesses'

(1)b Gif hwa sie deaðes scyldig and he cirican geierne, **hæbbe** (*age) his feorh. (*LawIne* 5.)
'If anyone is liable to death [penalty] and flees to a church, he will have his life'

It is not easy, however, to reconstruct what *agan* means and, in what respects it differs from *habban* as a verb of possession. Some help is provided by a comparison of *agan* with lexemes derived from the same stem: deverbal nouns, such as *agnung* 'ownership and declaration or proof of ownership', secondary verbal derivations, such as the weak verb *agnian* or *ægnian*[6] 'to possess and to prove or claim as one's own', or its past participle *geagenud* 'adopted and what is

---

SECRETARY.OF ([[the president]]) = [[the secretary of the president]]
PROXY.OF ([[the president]]) = [[the vice-president]]
[5] The past participle is formed by a suffix *-*an*- as in English *open* or in German *offen*.
[6] The weak verb *agnian*, derived from OE *agen*, developed into the ModE verb *to own*.

owned, possessed by law', all imply a notion of legal or rightful possession.

This semantic nuance is also evident in the noun *agend*, which refers to 'the one who possesses, the possessor', and 'the one who rightfully owns everything, i.e. the Lord', or in its compound *agendfrea* (or *agendfrigea*) 'the proprietor, i.e. the lord or the master who legally possesses', but also in the meaning of *agen*, as in (2), where *agen* does not refer to something that is actually possessed, but to something that ought to be owned, or to the ownership of which there exists a right'.[7]

(2) *Forðæm, ðonne ðonne we ðæm ðearfum hiera neidðearfe sellað,* **hiera ægen** *we him sellað, nalles ure* (CP 45.337.23)
 'Therefore, whenever we give the poor what they need, we give them but their due, not at all ours'

1.1 Semantic content of agen in Old English

The meanings which *agen* expressed when it occurred as an attributive modifier seem difficult to account for exclusively in terms of its being the old past participle of the verb *agan*. Indicatively, this aspect is completely neglected by traditional grammars and the relevant literature, which describe *agen* as the OE correspondent of PDE *own* (Campbell 1959, Ingersoll 1978) at best. Also Ælfric does not behave much differently, and pays no attention to the connection between *agen* and *agan* in his *Grammar*. Interestingly, however, he relates *agen* to Lat. *proprius* (< *pro privo*) which denotes 'what belongs or

---

[7] *Agan* thus expresses a normative component, in addition to the notion of possession. This semantic component is the prevailing one in the development of OE *agen* into ModE *owe* and plays a significant role in the rise of *ought to* to a modal auxiliary. A similar combination of normative and possessive components can be observed in the German verb *gehören* (lit. 'belong to, to be s.o.'s property'), which contrasts with *besitzen* exactly in this respect. In certain constructions the possessive component has weakened and the normative one is clearly dominant: *Pauls Haare gehören geschnitten* 'Paul's hair ought to be cut', *das gehört sich nicht* 'that is not to be done'; *du gehörst ins Bett / in die Arbeit /in die Schule* 'you should be in bed – at work – at school'.

pertains to the sphere of the single', often in opposition to Lat. *communis*.

A close textual analysis shows that in most occurrences *agen* contrastively re-asserts the possessive relationship encoded by the preceding genitive NP or pronoun: the occurrence of *agen* marks the possessor as the only rightful or legitimate one (thus ruling out potential alternatives). Specifically, the relation between the head NP and the referent of the possessive often corresponds either to prototypical dimensions of possession (62%) – property, kinship terms, part-whole relationships as in (3)a – or to less prototypical ones (31%), including psychological or physical properties as in (3)b. Much less frequently (7%), *agen* expresses a more vague notion of possession as 'appurtenance'[8] (Seiler 1983), often with abstract nouns, see (3)c.

What is worth mentioning is a correlation between certain modal verbs and the occurrence vs. absence of *agen*, as in (3)d, where the normative meaning of *agen* is reinforced by the modal *sculan*: one earns the status of a model through what one has done, i.e. to the deeds that are rightfully related to oneself, and not through somebody else's actions.

(3)a   Demetrius ... gefeaht on scipum wið Ptholomeus, & hiene bedraf on **his agen** lond (*Or* 3 11.150.4)
'Demetrius... fought on ships against Ptholomeus and drove him on his own land'

(3)b   <He> byð swiðe dysig, se þe getruwað on his horses swiftnesse, for þæm hit is swiðe leas tohopa; for þæm nawþer ðam horse ne þæm rædmen ne wyrð geboren of **his agnum** cræftum. (*PPs* (prose) 32.15)
'he is very foolish, who trusts his horse's speed, because there is very little hope; because neither to the horse nor to the horseman it is given by their own strength.'

---

[8] The notion of possession has long been theme of debate: possession has been defined in terms of sphere of influence (Langacker 1987), or of interest and involvement (Brugman 1988) between the *possessor* and the *possessum*. Seiler speaks of binary relations between two entities in terms of 'appurtenance', namely "the relationship between a human being and his kinsmen, his body parts, his material belongings, his cultural and intellectual products" (1983:4-7).

(3)c Her Herodes aswalt. se þe Iacobum ofslog ane geare ær **his agnum** deaþe. (*ChronA* 46.1)
'Here Herod died, he who killed Jacob one year before his own death.'

(3)d Ærest hi sculon eowian on **hiora agnum** weorcum eall ðæt hi eft læran willað mid hiora wordum ... (*CP* 64.461.24)
'First they shall show in their own works all that they afterwards will teach with their words...'

Quite frequently, *agen* seems to establish coreference with the subject. This is, however, a side effect of a contrast which the emphasis on (rightful) possession implies in certain situations: rightful possession makes it more plausible, or pragmatically more salient, to interpret the referent of the possessive and the subject as coreferential.

In some contexts, the double function of indicating both possession and contrast, helps to express an unexpected co-reference relation (27% of all occurrences). In other words, *agen* appears in those contexts where the simple possessive NP or pronoun would otherwise be interpreted as disjoint from the subject (cf. Comrie 1997). A case in point is example (4):

(4) Æfter þæm Xersis wearþ **his agenre** þeode swiþe unweorþ ... (*Or* 2.5.84.23)
'After that Xerses became very contemptible even to his own people ...'

That a king should become contemptible in the eyes of his own people seems to have been something unexpected at the time.

In spite of the natural variety among occurrences, it is fair to make the generalisation that *agen* conveys an implication of 'rightful or legitimate possession'. As a consequence, it appears to underline more prototypical notions of possession more often than less prototypical ones, such as what Seiler calls 'appurtenance'. OE *agen* is still preferred in those contexts where some kind of possessive relationship is implied, and when it modifies abstract nouns they are always characterised by a high degree of nouniness⁹. In this respect *agen* differs from *his selfes*.

1.2 Syntactic properties of agen in Old English

In spite of its etymological origin in a past participle, it is not plausible to consider *agen* as a verbal form at all in Old English. Unlike other past participles, *agen* never occurs as part of a predicate (**hit is agen*) nor after an auxiliary (**ic habbe ær feoh agen*).

It is always used attributively. When it occurs within an overtly headed NP, *agen* may or may not[10] be preceded by a determiner (possessive pronouns, NPs,[11] or the definite article) or modifier (a beneficiary dative). In NPs without overt heads, *agen* must be modified by a possessive pronoun or NP. Like OE adjectives, *agen* agrees in number, case and gender with its head NP, and is both strongly and weakly inflected (Fischer 2000).

However, *agen* is also special among OE adjectives.[12] If the head noun is also modified by a determiner, a possessive or a genitive NP, *agen* occupies a fixed position in the phrase, namely a rigid post-determiner[13] position: exceptions are invariably due to Latin

---

[9] For the concept of 'nouniness' and 'verbiness' see Rosenbach and Vezzosi (2000).

[10] When *agen* occurs without a modifier or determiner, it generally triggers a non-referential reading of its head NP, or refers to a generic possessor, but not necessarily so (e.g. *ÆCHom* I, 19. 330.142 *Is hwæðere getæht æfter godes gesetnysse. þæt wise men sceolon settan steore dysegum mannum. swa þæt hi ðæt dysig. & þa unþeawas alecgon. & þeah ðone man lufian swa swa **agenne** broðor* 'It is however taught according to God's law, that wise men shall determine punishment for stupid men, so that they abandon foolishness and sins and though love that man so as their own brother'). Also, such exceptional uses are marginal: Fischer (2000) has no instances of *agen* without a possessive.

[11] Although it has been argued that Old English is not a DG language (Wood 2004), I agree with Koike (2004) since, in the case of *agen*, possessive pronouns and genitive NPs behave as determiners (cf. Rosenbach 2002 for the determiner function of the *s*-genitive in Present-Day English).

[12] Fischer (2000) noticed that *agen* is one of the few OE adjectives which occur in the type 'det-adj₁-adj₂-noun', where *agen* would coincide with adj₁.

[13] One exception could be the following example found in the *DOEC*: *GDPref.* 11.275.9 *Of ðære wisan mæg beon ongyten, þæt þa, þam her byþ forgifen seo rummodnes and < arfæstnes > þara ælmæssylena and godra weorca, þa ylcan beoð*

influence.[14] The only other adjectives that resemble *agen* in this respect are: *ylc*, *self* and *same*, which, to use Fischer's words, "seem to form a unit with the determiner" (Fischer 2000:173). All of them have an identifying function, broadly speaking, and restrict the scope of reference.

The similarity between *self* and *agen* goes far beyond the position within the NP, and involves structural constraints of occurrence. Like *self*, *agen* (32% of occurrences) is favoured by contrastive patterns, such as coordination or comparative constructions, inclusion and exclusion structures (Keenan 2001). Here, *agen* contrastively picks out the referent of the possessive against textually given alternative possessors. In (5) *hira agen lif* is opposed to *Porsennes lif*. Its semantic contribution in these contexts is equivalent to that of *self*.

(5)   hie oþer forleosan woldon, oþþe **hira agen** lif, oþþe Porsennes
      þæs cyninges. (*Or* 2 3.68.26)
      'they would destroy either their own life or that one of the king
      Porsenna.'

1.3 Self *and* agen *in attributive patterns*

Here the similarity with *self* is even deeper. When preceded by a possessive pronoun or a genitive NP *agen* often alternates with the

---

þær wyrhtan þæs æpellican and þæs wundorlican **agnes** *huses*. 'In this way it may be understood that those to whom here will be granted the liberality and virtue of the almsgivings and good works, the same ones will be there makers of the noble and wonderful own house.' This example is dubious: given the strong inflection of *agnes*, *agnes huses* could be interpreted as a genitive modifying its head *þæs æpellican and þæs wundorlican*, i.e. the phrase has to be interpreted as 'the nobleness and the wonder of [his] own house'.

[14] Very occasionally, *agen* can even precede the determiner or occupy a postnominal position: *PPs* 78.11 *Wrec* **agen** *blod ena þinra, þæt wæs sarlice agoten* 'Avenge your own blood that was painfully spilled ...'; *ÆLet* 5 8 *þæt me is lað to tælenne* **agenne** *Godes freond* 'It is loathful to me to slander God's own friend'. Both word orders are definitely marginal and not proper to Old English but due to Latin influence: every instance of unusual word order is found in texts which are either heavily influenced by Latin texts or even interlinear translations from Latin originals, as evident in *LibSc* 16.2 *Qui a semetipso loquitur gloriam propriam querit / se þe fram him sylfum spycð wuldor* **agenne** *he secgð*, an interlinear translation.

genitive form of *self* as in (6)a vs. (6)b. Just as *self* is undoubtedly considered as an emphatic, or intensifying element (cf. Keenan 2001), also *agen* is often described as an emphatic adjective (Mitchell 1985, Campbell 1959): "rather than describing the degree of a quantity, or action, the emphatic adjectives intensify the noun or the pronoun they modify by redundancy: that is, they restate a concept which is already expressed elsewhere" (Ingersoll 1978:204).

(6)a and þa Maurus ongæn hine cwæð, þæt hit wære geworden for **his sylfes** bebode, & sæde ... þæt dyde þæt he dyde swa he hit nyste. (*GD* 2 (C) 7.116.1)
'and then Maurus told him that it had happened by command of himself [God] and said ... that he did what he did so as he did not know (was not aware of) it.'

(6)b ... man þananforð aa wile on ænne God æfre gelyfan and ... æfre his larum geornlice fylgean and **his agene** beboda rihtlice healdan. (*HC*/coinspol)
'... one will therefore always believe in one God ... and always follow his [God's] teaching earnestly and keep to his [God's] own commands firmly.'

Semantically, however, the two patterns do not completely overlap. In (6)a *his selfes* is an intensifier, which contrasts the referent of *his* to potential or actual alternatives: here its occurrence is justified by the very fact that it refers to God, who ranks most highly in the chain of being (König 2001). The *agen* in (6)b, on the other hand, intensifies the relationship between God and his 'commands' – in contrast to commands not given by God. However, that subtle difference may be neutralised in some contexts – such as in (7)a and (7)b –, where the *possessor* of the intensified *possessum* is also the discourse topic and the sentence subject, as well as with so-called 'relational' nouns (Löbner 1985), which can only be interpreted in relation to another noun.

(7)a ...he ridan scolde ... efne æt nehstan mid **his seolfes** hondum on hors hof. (<*R* 3.262.1>)
'... he should also ride at last with his own hands on the horse home.'

(7)b Æðelnoð biscop for to Rome ... & mid **his agenum** handum him his pallium onsette. (*HC*/cochroe 4)
'Athelnoth bishop left for Rome ...and with his own hands put his pallium on him.'

(7)c þu ... þurh ðinne hercyme, hælende Crist, ... þa gyldan geatu ... hat ontynan, ond usic þonne gesece þurh **þin sylfes** gong eaðmod to eorþan. (*HC*/cochrist 1518)
'You, Christ the Saviour, through your advent ordered to open the golden gates and then seek us benevolently through your own journey to the earth.'

Unlike *agen*, *self* must always be modified by a possessive pronoun or a genitive NP, on which it depends, as it agrees with it in number, gender, and case, see (7)a. Moreover, given that it is an intensified pronominal form, it can have the same semantic and functional use as any other genitive form, including the encoding of subjective and objective genitives, see (7)c.

2. *Own*[15] in Middle English

During the ME period *own* was affected by two major changes. First, and in structural terms, the cluster possessive + *own* became fixed, while other possible modifiers or determiners disappeared.[16] Thus, what had been optional – albeit highly preferred – in Old English became obligatory. Secondly, *his selfes* disappeared and was replaced by *his own*[17]. As a consequence, *his own* was more and more frequently added to NPs denoting actions, endeavours etc., even in those clusters which had originally had *his selfes* (see (8)a). More significantly, *his own* started modifying gerunds, i.e. nominalizations

---

[15] *Own* represents all spelling variants in which the word appeared in Middle English.
[16] To be precise, in Middle English there were still sporadic occurrences of unmodified *own* within non-referential NPs (e.g. *Ayenb*. 48/25 *Mid oȝen zuorde man may himzelue sle* 'With [one's] own sword one may kill oneself'). Moreover, *own* could still be modified by a definite article, but with the meaning of 'proper, appropriate, exact, very' in competition with the French loan word *proper*. *Own* was never completely replaced by *proper* as suggested by sentences like "the own meaning of *substitute*" (David Denison during his talk at the ICHEL 13 in Vienna 2004).
[17] Here and elsewhere *his own* is shorthand for the pattern 'POSS + *own*'.

characterised by a high-level of verbiness, as in (8)b: OE *agen* had been banned from such contexts.

(8)a þat þou wilt **þyn awen** nye nyme to þy-seluen ... (*Gawain* 2141)
'that you will bring your own harm to yourself...'

(8)b The Chief Justice ... is right sory of þe matier þat is cause of **your noun** [= own] comyng hedir ([1444] *Paston* 2.13)

In these latter contexts, *own* does of course not express any idea of possession in the strict sense of the term. Instead, it relates the referent of the possessive to the *possessum* in the abstract manner, as is characteristic of the genitive case.

2.1 The grammaticalization of his own

The major changes that took place in Middle English can be easily interpreted as effects of a grammaticalization process. Already in the OE period, *agen* was not invariably used in the purely possessive sense (stage I). In fact, OE *agen* also served to determine the referential identification of its head NP (Y) more extensively in terms of relatedness, 'appurtenance', or appropriateness and rightfulness (stage II). Thus, *agen* reasserted the identity (stage III) of both the *possessum* (Y) and the *possessor* (X). *Agen* was also used to assert a possessive relation in marked contexts ("X killed the servant that belonged to X"), thus signalling co-reference between a possessive pronoun and a noun phrase, typically the subject if no other salient referent was available. At the same time, *agen* was decategorised (Heine 2003) or, rather, lost some of the characteristics of independent words, such as mobility within the NP, and became a pre-modifier determiner[18], as it formed a unit with the preceding possessive.

---

[18] *Agen* acquired a function very similar to the identity function of pre-determiners in Teyssier's terminology, and a textual, cohesive meaning in the sense of Traugott (1988), similar to that of *same*. Its semantic change resembles the grammaticalization cline observed for (attributive vs. postdeterminer) comparative adjectives in the study of Breban and Davidse (2003). Also cf. Adamson (2000).

stage I : X's *agen* Y 'Y possessed by X' >

stage II: 'Y related to X' >

stage III: as a means of identifying Y
as a means of identifying X

This change made the alternation between *his agen* and *his selfes* possible in specific contexts, as, for example, in (7)a and (7)b. Double marking constructions as in (9) are clear signs of change in progress: *agen* and *self* can be assumed to be near-synonyms at that stage. Such combinations are exactly what one would expect in the first stages of a grammaticalization process, when the old pattern is maintained and overlaps with the new one (Hopper 1991).

(9) Se Hælend ... is gehaten Word ... and he sylf cwæð forði þæt seo spræc nære þe he þa spræc to him **his sylfes agen** spræc, ac his Fæder spræc (*ÆHom* 10.67)
'The Saviour... is called Word ... and he himself said henceforth that the language that he then spoke to them was not his own language, but his Father's language'

The change also paved the way for the replacement of *his selfes* by *his own*, when the 'unsettled' *his selfes* (Farr 1905,22-23) was affected by the changes in the English morphology, i.e. from stem-based morphology to word-based morphology. Essentially, *self* transparently agrees with the φ-features of the possessive pronoun only in the 3rd pers. sg., for which the possessive is identical with the genitive of the personal pronoun (*his selfes*): here the pattern can easily be interpreted as NP_{gen} [*his selfes*] + NP, with NP as the nucleus and NP_{gen} as an expansion. However, the genitive case of *self* was less motivated (*þurh þinne sylfes gong*) for the other persons, whose possessive is encoded by a special adjectival form. On the other hand, OE *self* can also show agreement in number, gender and case with the following NP (*þin sylfe bearn*):[19] in this case *self* is an attributive modifier of the

---

[19] This pattern seemed to continue in Middle English: *HM* 154.388 & *loki we hwuch wunne ariseð prefter I burþerne of bearne. hwen þt streon in þe awakeneð & waxeð. & hu monie earmðen anan awakeneð þerwið. þe wurcheð þe wa inoh; fehteð **þi seolue** flesch* 'and let us look what joy arises afterwards in the carrying of children,

head noun and the only possible interpretation of the NP is ₙₚ[*þin* ₐₚ[*sylfe bearn*]].

However, the structural unsettledness of *his selves* is not the only cause of its disappearance. The existence of two structures for the same function is uneconomical and semiotically disfavoured. As noted by Fischer in several publications (e.g. Fischer 1999 and 2000) iconicity plays an important role in syntactic change and in particular in processes of grammaticalization. In this case it is plausible to assume that the asymmetric situation in Late Old English and early Middle English – i.e. two strategies for the same function (contrastive identity marker) – may have accelerated the grammaticalization of *his agen*. At the same time it may have speeded up the development in which *his agen* replaced the less transparent and stable *his selfes*, so that the original bi-uniqueness was re-established.

The disappearance of *his selfes* allowed *his own*, which was a marker of relatedness, to extend its distribution to nominalizations, where it came to encode the least prototypical possession relationship, i.e. the objective and the subjective genitive. It was probably in such contexts that the contrastive quality originally associated with the notion of possession in certain contexts came to be more and more generally associated with all uses of *own* – as a result of a metonymic change (X betrayed the people belonging to him > X betrayed his own people, not somebody else's people):

> Stage IV: *agen* as means of identifying X > *own* as a means of evoking alternatives to X.

What seems to have become grammaticalized is not the single lexeme, but the entire construction POSS+*agen* (cf. Bybee 2003): the sequence POSS + [*agen*] was re-segmented in analogy to the pattern POSS + *selfes*, and thus re-analysed as [POSS *agen*].

If this hypothesis is right, it also entails: (a) the insertion of [POSS *agen*] into the intensifying paradigm [PRON+*self*]; (b) its

---

when the child in you quickens and grows, and how many troubles at once arise with it, which do you harm enough, attack your own flesch'.

development into a real intensifier;[20] and (c) an increasing degree of independence from the nominal head. Of course, this is exactly what one observes in Modern English, where *his own* can usually be interpreted as the genitive form of *himself*, as in (10), and thus in complex predicates it interacts with the relevant coreferent in the sentence and not with the NP on which it syntactically depends.

(10) She continued the research of him down to the day of **her own** mysterious disappearance = when she herself mysteriously disappeared. (Seppänen 1975)

2.2 His own *in Modern English*

In Modern English, *own* forms a stable cluster together with possessive NPs or pronouns and acquires a certain independence from its head NP, as it semantically modifies the referent it interacts with, namely the subject of the sentence. Its semantic contribution to the sentence is therefore very similar to that of the intensifier *himself*. This is evident in complex predicates, where the behaviour of *his own* is analogous to the use of intensifying *self*-forms. In (11)a, for example, *their own butchers and poulters* are not just opposed to somebody else's butchers, but *his own* opposes 'gentlemen' to somebody else and the meaning of the entire sentence is paraphrasable as "Gentlemen who, in the game season, become themselves butchers and poulters". In (11)b the semantic independence of *his own* from its noun phrase is even more evident, since *his own* focuses not only on the subject but also on its semantic role as an agent. As a consequence, the semantic contribution of *own* is not to contrast two or more chocolates (our

---

[20] If one considers *his own* as an intensifier in attributive position, *own* also expresses an identity function. In a phrase such as *Mary's own children* all that *own* appears to do is to map the referent of Mary onto itself once again. Since *own* is focused and therefore stressed, alternatives to the identity function are evoked through implicature. Applied to the value of the co-constituent of *own*, i.e. *Mary*, such alternatives are other potential '*possessors*' (i.e. parents) of the children. Since these alternatives are a function of 'Mary' they must also be defined with the help of the value 'Mary'. In this case plausible alternatives to the value the constituent which *own* interacts with (i.e. *Mary*'s) are '[the children] of Mary's neighbours' or '[the children] Mary was asked to look after'.

chocolate vs. somebody else's chocolate), but to exclude other possible agents, namely the cook. Accordingly, the sentence means something like "we boiled (our) chocolate ourselves, without anybody else's help, the cook being ill".

(11)a Gentlemen, who in the game-season ... become **their own** butchers and poulteres ([1800] WINDHAM *Sp.Parl.* 18 Apr.)

(11)b Cherishing it into a small fire, we boiled **our own** chocolate, the cook being ill. ([1848] tr. Hoffmeister's *Trav. Ceylon & India*)

In such contexts, *own* has totally lost most implications of possession. It interacts semantically with the rest of the sentence in a way that is not predictable from its syntactic position, and establishes a contrast within the whole predication.

3. Conclusion

The diachronic development of *own* is particularly significant because it sheds light on its present usage in the English language. More and more contributions have recently pointed out that *own* can be considered as an identity emphatic or intensifier (Moyne 1971; Cantrall 1973; Quirk *et al.* 1985; Baker 1995; König and Vezzosi 2001), given the "functional identity of the emphatic pronoun and the adjective *own*" and the semantic equivalence of 'his own X' to 'the X of [himself]'. For example, *Fred's own car* is equivalent to the *car of Fred himself* and contrasts with the *car of Fred's brother* etc. (König and Vezzosi forthcoming). However, the status of PDE *own* is not retraceable to its etymological meaning. Rather, it is an innovation, and the result of a grammaticalization process.

The development of *agen* into *his own* does not follow the typical phases of grammaticalization as described by Lehmann (1995). However, it resembles the development of sentence adverbials, discourse markers etc., in that semantic bleaching and partial structural decategorisation are associated with an increase in pragmatic meaning, i.e. discourse contrastiveness (König and Traugott 1991), and in scope (Tabor and Traugott 1997, Traugott 2003). In the course of the OE period *agen* changed from an attributive adjective that re-asserted the possession relationship between the *possessor* and the *possessum* into a type of pre-modifier/determiner which re-established the identity of either the possessor or the possessum. Due to the coalescence of two patterns (i.e. POSS + *selfes* and POSS + *agen*) during Early Middle English, *his own* came to function as a means of evoking alternative values to the possessor. That in turn allowed it to become functionally equivalent to *himself* (cf. 10)a and b).[21] Finally, in Modern English the primary meaning of *his own* has become definable as a contrastive identity function: it is an element which contrastively identifies the nominal it interacts with, and is similar in this respect to English intensifiers used as adjuncts.

References

Adamson, Sylvia. 2000. "A lovely little example". In: Fischer, Olga, Anette Rosenbach and Dieter Stein (eds.). *Pathways of change*. Amsterdam: Benjamins: 39-66.

Baker, Carl Leroy. 1995. "Contrast, discourse prominence, and intensification, with special reference to locally free reflexives in British English". *Language* 71: 63-101.

Breban, Tine and Kristin Davidse. 2003. "Adjectives of comparison: the grammaticalization of their attributive uses into postdeterminer and classifier uses". *Folia Linguistica* 37: 3-4; 269-318.

Brugman, Claudia Marlea. 1988. *The syntax and semantics of HAVE and its complements*. Unpubl. Ph.D. Dissertation. University of California, Berkeley.

Bybee, Joan. 2003. "Mechanisms of change in grammaticization: the role of frequency". In: Janda, Richard and Brian Joseph (eds.). *Handbook of historical linguistics*. Berlin: de Gruyter: 602-623.

Campbell, Alistar. 1959. *Old English grammar*. Oxford: Clarendon.

---

[21] The ambiguous interpretation of *his own* as in (10)a-b depends on the predicate. In (10)a-b there are two the possible structures, which are only apparently identical: in one case (a) we have an activity, i.e. a verb with two arguments, an actor (we) and an undergoer (chocolate); in the other case (b), we have an active accomplishment, i.e. a verb (to boil chocolate) with only one argument, the actor (we), or what Van Valin and LaPolla (1997) define as S-transitivity. In the latter case, *his own* cannot modify the NP on which it is syntactically dependent, because it is only a specification of the verb and thus can only contrastively identify the nominal it interacts with, namely the subject/agent, against alternative values.

Cantrall, William R. 1973. "Why I would relate *own*, emphatic reflexives, and intensive pronouns, my own self". *Current Linguistic Studies* 9: 57-67.
Comrie, Bernhard. 1997. "Reference-tracking and competing constraints". Paper given at the *XVIth International Congress of Linguists* (Paris, July 1997).
Curme, George Oliver. 1931. *A grammar of the English language*. Boston: Heath.
DCE = *Longman Dictionary of contemporary English*.2003. 4th ed. London: Pearson.
DOEC = Healey, Antoniette diPaolo, Joan Holland, Ian McDougall and Peter Mielke. 2000. *The dictionary of Old English corpus in electronic form*. TEI-P3 conformant version. Toronto.
Farr, James M. 1905. *Intensives and reflexives in Anglo-Saxon and early Middle English*. Baltimore: J.H. Furst.
Fischer, Olga C.M. 1999. "On the role played by iconicity in grammaticalization processes". In: Nänny, Max and Olga C.M. Fischer (eds.). *Form miming meaning: iconicity in language and literature*. Amsterdam: Benjamins: 345-373.
-----. 2000. "The position of the adjective in Old English". In: Bermúdez-Otero, Ricardo et al. (eds.). *Generative theory and corpus studies*. Amsterdam: Benjamins: 153-181.
Heine, Bernd. 2003. "Grammaticalization". In: Janda, Richard and Brian Joseph (eds.). *A handbook of historical linguistics*. Berlin: de Gruyter: 575-601.
Hopper, Paul. 1991. "On some principles of grammaticalization". In: Traugott, Elizabeth C. and Bernd Heine (eds.). *Approaches to grammaticalization*. Vol. I. Amsterdam: Benjamins: 17-35.
Ingersoll, Sheila Most. 1978. *Intensive and restrictive modification in Old English*. Heidelberg: Winter.
Keenan, Edward L. 2001. "Explaining the creation of reflexive pronouns in English". Online: http://www.linguistics.ucla.edu/people/keenan/shelpaper.pdf.
Koike, Takeshi. 2004. "The grammaticalisation of the determinative function of a genitive nominal after the end of the OE period". Paper given at the *ICHEL 13* (Vienna, 2004).
König, Ekkehard. 2001. "Intensifiers and reflexive pronouns". In: Haspelmath, Martin, Ekkehard König, Wulf Österreicher and Wolfgang Reible (eds.). *Language typology and language universals*. Berlin: de Gruyter: 747-760.
König, Ekkehard and Peter Siemund. 1996. "*Selbst*-Reflektionen". In: Harras, G. (ed.). *Wenn die Semantik arbeitet. Festschrift für Klaus Baumgärtner*. Tübingen: Niemeyer: 277-302.
König, Ekkehard and Elizabeth C. Traugott. 1991. "The semantics-pragmatics of grammaticalization revisited". In: Traugott, Elizabeth C. and Bernd Heine (eds.). *Approaches to grammaticalization. Vol. I*. Amsterdam: Benjamins: 189-218.
König, Ekkehard and Letizia Vezzosi. 2001. "Languages on Mediterranean area". In: Ramat, Paolo and Thomas Stolz (eds.). *Mediterranean languages. Papers from the MEDTYP workshop, Tirrenia, June* 2000. Bochum: Brockmeyer: 191-208.
-----. forthcoming. "On the historical development of attributive intensifiers". In: von Mengden, Ferdinand et al. (eds.). *Festschrift für Prof. Dietz*.

Langacker, Ronald W. 1987. *Foundations of cognitive grammar*. Vol. I. Bloomington: Indiana University Linguistics Club.
Lehmann, Christian. 1995. *Thoughts on grammaticalization. A programmatic sketch*. Revised and expanded version. München and Newcastle: Lincom.
Löbner, Sebastien. 1985. "Definites". *Journal of Semantics* 4: 279-326.
Mitchell, Bruce. 1985. *Old English syntax. 2 vols*. Oxford: Clarendon.
Moyne, J.A. 1971. "Reflexive and emphatic". *Language* 47: 141-163.
OED = *The Oxford English dictionary on CD-Rom. 1999*. Oxford: OUP.
PONS = Procter, Paul (ed.). 2000. *The Cambridge international dictionary of English*. Cambridge: CUP.
Quirk, Randolph, Sidney Greenbaum, Geoffrey Leech and Jan Svartvik (eds.). 1985. *A comprehensive grammar of the English language*. London: Longman.
Rosenbach, Anette and Letizia Vezzosi. 2000. "Genitive constructions in Early Modern English: new evidence from a corpus analysis". In: Sornicola, Rosanna, Erich Poppe and Ariel Shisha-Halevy (eds.). *Stability, variation and change of word-order patterns over time*. Amsterdam: Benjamins: 285-307.
Rosenbach, Anette. 2002. *Genitive variation in English*. Berlin: de Gruyter.
Schendl, Herbert. 1992. "A valency description of Old English possessive verbs". In: Rissanen, Matti *et al.* (eds.). *History of Englishes: new methods and interpretations in historical linguistics*. Berlin: de Gruyter : 418-436.
Seiler, Hansjakob. 1983. *Possession as an operational dimension of language*. Tübingen: Narr.
Seppänen, Aimo. 1975. "On the Modern English 'adjective' *own*". *Anglia* 93: 293-306.
Tabor, Wh. and Elizabeth C. Traugott. 1998. "Structural scope expansion and grammaticalization". In: Giacalone Ramat, Anna and Paul Hopper (eds.). *The limits of grammaticalization*. Amsterdam: Benjamins: 229-272.
Traugott, Elizabeth Closs. 2003. "Constructions in grammaticalization". In: Janda, Richard and Brian Joseph (eds.). *Handbook of historical linguistics*. Berlin: de Gruyter: 624-647.
Van Valin, Robert D. and Randy Jr. LaPolla. 1997. *Syntax. Structure, meaning and function*. Cambridge: CUP.
Wood, Johanna. 2004. "Demonstratives and possessives: from Old English to present-day English?". Paper given at the *ICEHL 13* (Vienna, 2004).
Wodehouse, Pelham Grenville. 1923. *The inimitable Jeeves. Sir Roderick comes to lunch*. London: Herbert Jenkins.
Zandvoort, R.W. 1957. *A handbook of English grammar*. London: Longman.

Ilse Wischer
Grammaticalisation and language contact in the history of English: the evolution of the progressive form[1]

1. Introduction: the notion of grammaticalisation

Although grammaticalisation studies have a long tradition, in recent years critical voices have appeared that question its status as a theory of language change, considering it an epiphenomenon or a cover term for a combination of changes that can be explained otherwise. The following paper is meant as a survey of current grammaticalisation research, providing arguments for the existence of a theory of grammaticalisation. This theory will then be applied to the evolution of the progressive form in the history of English in section 3. A possible grammaticalisation path from Old English on is developed, suggesting a double scenario with regard to the establishment of a periphrastic construction and the subsequent emergence of a new grammatical category. Finally, the role of language contact in this process of grammaticalisation is discussed in 3.3.

Grammaticalisation (also 'grammaticisation') is commonly understood as a process by which linguistic elements (lexical, pragmatic, sometimes even phonetic) change into constituents of grammar, or by which grammatical items become more grammatical in time. Hopper and Traugott (2003:xv) define it as "the process whereby lexical items and constructions come in certain linguistic contexts to serve grammatical functions and, once grammaticalized, continue to develop new grammatical functions". Here it is important to have a clear concept of grammar in mind. This grammatical character is further specified in Lehmann's (2004:155) most recent definition of grammaticalisation: "Grammaticalization of a linguistic sign is a process in which it loses in autonomy by becoming more subject to constraints of the linguistic system".

---

[1] This paper is dedicated to Günter Rohdenburg on the occasion of his 65th birthday.

The process of grammaticalisation is seen as a gradual, directed development that combines a number of mechanisms: it begins in the speaker-hearer interaction with certain pragmatic inferences in particular contexts. This is accompanied by semantic bleaching of the linguistic item which is being grammaticalised. Then a morpho-syntactic reanalysis takes place and the item is de-categorialised. Analogical extension leads to a spread to new contexts. These mechanisms constitute the process whereby a lexical item or construction turns into a grammatical item. Further, phonological attrition and coalescence can lead to agglutination and finally to inflectional morphology. In the course of this development grammatical items become more grammatical.

Similar ideas about the origin of grammar have a very long tradition (cf. Heine, Claudi and Hünnemeyer 1991). As early as 1746, Étienne Bonnot de Condillac in his *Essai sur l'origine des connaissances humaines* claimed that personal endings of the verb are the result of agglutination of personal pronouns, or that verbal tense results from the coalescence of a temporal adverb with the stem of a verb. Similarly, John Horne Tooke in *The diversions of Purley* (vol. I: 1786, vol. II: 1805) saw the origin of prepositions in former nouns or verbs.

A more detailed description is given by Wilhelm von Humboldt (1994 [1822]). He points out that grammatical forms derive through four stages by loss of meaning and attrition of sounds through frequent use. At stage I, a state-of-affairs is described by phrases or sentences. In a next step (stage II), a fixed word order and words with conceptual or functional meanings develop. In stage III, agglutination of former function words takes place and finally (stage IV) real grammatical words and inflections emerge. Although this is somewhat simplified and too much generalised, it nevertheless includes the idea of a gradual change and considers a number of essential constitutive mechanisms of the process of grammaticalisation.

William Dwight Whitney (1970 [1875]) described the genesis of grammatical forms in a similar way, referring for instance to the origin of the past tense inflection *-ed* in English and the French future inflection *-ai*, as in *donner-ai*. Also Georg von der Gabelentz (1891) proposed that the source of inflectional endings is to be found in the lexicon, whereby lexical words gradually lose their independent character, their lexical meaning and original sound structure before they turn into affixes. Gabelentz saw two driving forces behind such changes, a tendency towards distinctness and a tendency towards ease.

While the scholars of the 18th and 19th centuries more or less sporadically deal with the origin of grammar, systematic and empirically founded studies on grammaticalisation begin to appear in the early 20th century. It was Antoine Meillet (1912) who first used the term 'grammaticalisation' and described it as one important principle of grammatical change besides analogy. Like von der Gabelentz, he mentioned two driving factors, which he called 'expressivité' and 'usage'.[2]

When structuralism came up, studies in grammaticalisation declined since, on the one hand, diachronic processes were no longer in the centre of interest, and, more importantly, synchronically the concept of grammaticalisation challenged the fundamental theoretical constructs of structuralism and later also of generativism, such as the discreteness of categories and the autonomy of syntax. Outside structuralism the Indo-Europeanist tradition of grammaticalisation theory remained uninterrupted. Authors such as Jerzy Kuryłowicz or Emile Benveniste studied the inflectional categories of Indo-European languages.

Since the 1970s a renewed interest in grammaticalisation studies has emerged. Inspiration came, especially in the United States, from Talmy Givón and his famous slogan "today's morphology is yesterday's syntax" (1971:413), and in the 1980s in Germany from the Cologne Project for the Study of Language Universals, where authors such as Christian Lehmann or Bernd Heine studied the manifestations of grammaticalisation in a wide range of languages and their consequences with regard to typological aspects and language universals.

---

[2] They correspond to von der Gabelentz's tendencies towards distinctness and towards ease.

In the last two decades, the amount of research within the framework of grammaticalisation has increased enormously. Numerous books and articles have been published and conferences are held regularly on the topic. Several collective works and conference volumes, and even a *World lexicon of grammaticalization* (Heine and Kuteva 2002) have appeared.[3]

Important topics today are the relationship between grammaticalisation and lexicalisation, the problem of unidirectionality, the status of a theory of grammaticalisation in relation to other theories of language change (cf. Roberts and Roussou 2003), empirical works based on large text corpora (cf. Rissanen, Kytö and Heikkonen 1997), the role of contexts in the process of grammaticalisation, the emergence of more peripheral grammatical items such as discourse markers, honorifics, or classifiers, and finally, the description of particular paths of grammaticalisation of individual linguistic items.

2. Critical voices and arguments for the existence of a theory of grammaticalisation

Recently critical voices have been raised that question the status of a theory of grammaticalisation.[4] As stated above, grammaticalisation is considered an epiphenomenon, a cover term for a combination of changes that can be explained otherwise.

Campbell (2001:124) claims that "unidirectionality is built into the definition of grammaticalisation ... *lexical > grammatical,* or *grammatical > more grammatical*" and he provides a list of alleged examples of degrammaticalisation, thus attempting to deconstruct the general framework of grammaticalisation. Similarly, Janda (2001) claims that language transmission is discontinuous, and grammaticalisation is counterable. Here it can be argued that the

---

[3] Cf. Pagliuca (1994); Rissanen, Kytö and Heikkonen (1997); Giacalone Ramat and Hopper (1998); Wischer and Diewald (2002); Fischer, Norde and Perridon (2004).
[4] Cf. Campbell (2001); Newmeyer (2001); Janda (2001); Joseph (2001); a special edition of *Language Sciences* (23, 2001) has been devoted to criticism of grammaticalisation as a theoretical framework.

concept of unidirectionality is of course built into the definition, because it is the result of empirical observation, the result of generalisations made on the basis of empirical analyses of historical data in a wide range of languages, while the opposite is simply not clearly attested, or, indeed, extremely rare. The concept of unidirectionality is not only based on extensive empirical evidence, but also on a number of theoretical considerations:

(1) The process of grammaticalisation includes a generalisation of meaning. This allows the use of the grammaticalised item in more and more contexts.[5] A reversal of this generalisation would restrict the number of contexts and gradually increase the constraints on the environments of a form, which is very unlikely for a linguistic item that has reached a certain degree of abstractness and general use.

(2) Alleged counterexamples to the unidirectionality claim are often simple instances of conversion (*the ups and downs*) or secretion (*an ism*), which are the result of rather conscious, spontaneous word formations, and not of gradual degrammaticalisation processes. Degrammaticalisation is virtually impossible because speakers have only limited conscious access to functional elements. Thus it is very unlikely that they should use them in place of less grammaticalised ones (cf. Haspelmath 1999), i.e. it is very unlikely that speakers undo automatisation (Lehmann 2004:184).

(3) Other so-called counterexamples to the unidirectionality claim are simply the result of the principle of divergence (cf. Hopper 1991). Let us take, for instance, the ModE examples *dare* and *need*.[6] Here we can see that the original lexical verb and the new auxiliary-like form can co-exist for quite a long time. In such a situation it is possible that the innovative use cannot get hold in a language

---

[5] *Go* meaning 'to move' can only combine with agent nouns and directional complements; *be going to* with a future meaning can take all kinds of subjects and verb phrases.

[6] For the development of *dare* and *need* as potential counterexamples to the unidirectionality hypothesis cf. e.g. Warner (1993:202f.), Taeymans (2004) or – for *dare* – particularly Beths (1999); for a critical assessment of Beths's findings see Traugott (2001).

community and is finally given up. What looks like a reversal is just an incomplete change.

(4) Most of the scholars, however, acknowledge that exceptions to the unidirectionality hypothesis exist. One well-known potential example is the English possessive -'s morpheme (cf. Plank 1995; Janda 1980 and 2001; and particularly Norde 2002). It seems to have developed from an inflection in Old English to a clitic in Modern English. If this was the case, it must indeed have gained in syntactic freedom, and we would have a clear counterexample to the grammaticalisation cline. However, there remain doubts about what really happened after the decay of the inflectional case system in English. One possible explanation could be that in the functional renewal process the former genitive inflection -s was reinterpreted as a possessive marker and, supported by pronominal possessive constructions like *the king his castle,* was exapted into the function of a possessive clitic.[7]

There might of course be instances of language change that run counter to the general grammaticalisation cline; since almost nothing is exceptionless, however, such occurrences are extremely rare compared to the large number of cases that support the unidirectionality claim.

Another criticism of grammaticalisation has been raised by Campbell (2001:141ff.). He reduces grammaticalisation to reanalysis and analogical extension and argues that the other mechanisms involved are not essential for the evolution of grammar. However, reanalysis taken alone is not restricted to grammaticalisation processes. There are, for instance, examples of reanalysis that affect solely the lexicon (*an adder* < *a nadder*). A grammatical item emerges only if reanalysis occurs in combination with other mechanisms, such as loss of autonomy, loss in weight and variability, gain in cohesion, desemanticisation and phonological reduction. Furthermore, grammaticalisation is gradual and directional, whereas

---

[7] This does not mean that the clitic -s developed from *his* (cf. also Allen 1997), but that the *his*-construction may have supported this development (a similar view is shared by Plank 1995:218). The process of *exaptation* is described by Lass 1990.

reanalysis alone is abrupt and non-directional. Hence, reanalysis is only part of the categorial change (lexical > grammatical), not of the further grammaticalisation, when an item becomes more grammatical. Reanalysis alone has no explanatory power but is in need of explanation itself, which can be found in a framework of grammaticalisation.

Opponents of grammaticalisation even claim that "grammaticalization is derivative, epiphenomenal, and has no independent status of its own" (Campbell 2001:151), and thus declare that "there is no such thing as grammaticalization" (Newmeyer 2001:188).

However, the data which have been examined constitute convincing evidence that the mechanisms and principles involved in grammaticalisation constitute a complex process of coding and organisation of language. It is not enough to know the individual mechanisms, because none of them is confined to grammaticalisation. They can all be involved in other processes of language change. It is only in their interaction that they make up a gradual and directed path that leads to the evolution of grammatical forms. Only "jointly they are responsible for grammaticalization taking place. They can be said to constitute different components of one and the same general process" (Heine 2003:579).

Finally, Lehmann (2004) has pointed out that there is no language that can do without grammar.[8] Thus, the evolution and maintenance of grammar in a language is absolutely necessary and it cannot develop by accidence. There is a need for language activity to produce grammars. And finally he concludes: "If there are universal principles determining the form of grammars, then there are universal principles of linguistic change that produce such grammars" (Lehmann 2004:183). And this is what grammaticalisation theory tries to find out.

---

[8] This has also been observed in the development of creoles.

3. The evolution of the progressive form in the history of English

3.1 Grammaticalisation

Numerous scholars have approached the evolution of the progressive form in the history of English from diverse angles.[9] Parallel formal constructions in Old English (*beon/wesan* + V-*ende*) have been discussed as influenced by medieval Latin (Mustanoja 1960; Kisbye 1971) or as inherently Germanic developments. Some scholars argue for a decline of the OE constructions in Middle English and favour a new development of the progressive based on verbal noun constructions, such as *be on* V-*ing*. Sometimes French influence is made responsible (Visser 1963-73) or even a Celtic substrate (Dal 1952; Preusler 1956; Mittendorf and Poppe 2000).

The grammaticalisation of the progressive is usually located not earlier than in the EMod. period. Bauer (1970:150) proposed that it had not even started in the time of Chaucer and Gower. Similarly Strang (1982:429) claims that only after 1700 do we find a "systematic or grammatically required use". Similarly Denison (1993:407) dates the grammaticalisation of the progressive at the end of the 18th century.

It becomes obvious that most scholars associate the grammaticalisation of the progressive with the completion of its establishment as an aspectual gram. However, if we analyse the occurrences of the expanded form before the 17th century as periphrastic verb constructions, we must acknowledge that they are already elements of grammar, albeit less systematic and not yet obligatory, thus reflecting a lower degree of grammaticalisation.[10] If we further assume a continuous development of the construction in Middle English, which most scholars seem to do today (cf. Denison

---

[9] For the most comprehensive and influential studies cf. Jespersen (1931), Mossé (1938), Visser (1963-73), Nickel (1966), Nehls (1974), Scheffer (1975), Strang (1982), Mitchell (1985).

[10] Since the early occurrences of *be* + V-*ende/-ing* in Old and Middle English had not been used yet to mark a progressive aspect we prefer the term 'expanded form' to denote this particular periphrastic construction.

1993:400), we must conclude that its grammaticalisation began in Old English.

In the following, a scenario of a possible path of grammaticalisation from Old English on will be proposed, and within this scenario the role of language contact will be considered. It has to be taken into account that we are dealing with the grammaticalisation of a construction containing an element of grammar (an auxiliary) and constituting itself an element of grammar (an aspectual marker). So we are faced with a 'double scenario' of grammaticalisation: (1) the auxiliarisation of the copula *be* resulting in a periphrastic construction, and (2) the assignment of a grammatical function to this construction together with the establishment of a new grammatical category ASPECT.

We know today that grammaticalisation has its origin in the speaker-hearer interaction. New grammatical meanings or constructions arise out of pragmatic inferences in particular linguistic contexts. The role of contexts in these early stages of grammaticalisation has become an important topic of linguistic studies recently.

Various syntactic constructions may have served as such 'critical contexts' for the evolution of the expanded form in Old English:[11]

(1) Predicative participial adjective constructions:
oþ him þa biscepas sædon þæt ealle godas him irre **wæren** & **wiðwinnende** (*Orosius*, R 7.112.35)
'till the bishops told him that all gods **were** angry with him and **fighting** against him'

(2) Appositive participial constructions:
& þy ilcan geare ferde to Rome ..., & þær **was** xii monaþ **wuniende** (*Chronicle MS A Early (O2)*, R. 855.4)
'and in the same year he went to Rome ..., and **stayed** there for 12 months'

---

[11] For the various types of context in grammaticalisation cf. Diewald (2002). – Examples are taken from the *Helsinki Corpus*.

(3) Agent noun constructions:
Hie þær ða **winnende wæron** oþ hie ða burg abræcon, (*Orosius*, R 2.66.21)
'There they had been fighters/fighting till they broke into the town,'

It can be assumed that the agent noun constructions must have been most dominant in providing such an ambiguous context. Agent nouns with the suffix *-end* (pl.*-ende*), in the North with *-and,* were quite frequent in Old English, more than in the other Germanic languages, whereas participial adjectives and appositive participial constructions occurred with a similar frequency in the other Germanic languages (Kisbye 1971:29, fn.3; Nickel 1966:283ff.; Nehls 1974:122).

Although agent noun constructions are not listed as possible source structures by Bybee, Perkins and Pagliuca (1994) in their cross linguistic study on the evolution of tense, aspect and modality grams, Heine (1997) claims that progressives can also be derived from equational sentences of the form 'X is a Y' as in *'he is (an) eating (one)'*. It will be shown how this may indeed have happened in Old English.

Equational sentences with agent noun constructions as in (3) may have served as 'critical contexts' for the reanalysis (cf. Figure 1).

Figure 1. The reanalysis of agent-noun-constructions

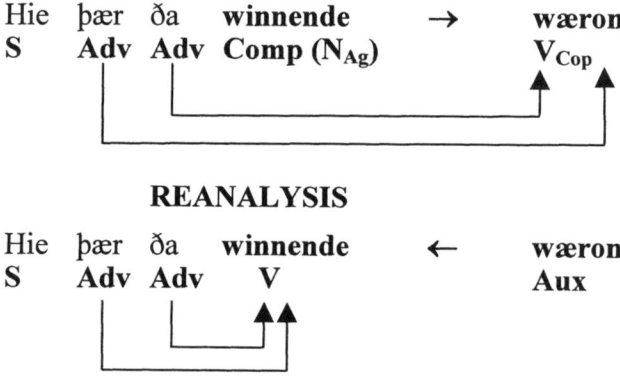

The predicate refers to a stative situation type. But since an agent noun is involved, there is an activity implied in the situation. If this activity is foregrounded, the hearer may reinterpret the agent noun as verbal participle since both are formally identical. The adverbials in the clause *(þær, ða)* are now seen as modifying this activity. They are reinterpreted as adjuncts to the participle. The former copula gets restricted in its scope to function as auxiliary to the verb *winnende*.[12] A meaning change of *beon/wesan* in terms of semantic bleaching is irrelevant here since the copula *be* is already semantically empty.[13]

This reanalysis might have been supported by language contact with speakers of Celtic languages, who had parallel syntactic constructions. Another supporting factor may have been translations of Latin participial and deponens constructions.[14]

Real agent noun constructions, however, seem to be quite rare in Old English. In the *Orosius* sample in the *Helsinki Corpus* only 9 out of 66 instances of expanded forms might be considered agent noun constructions. The others either have a singular subject that does not agree with the suffix *-ende*, but would require *–end* (4), they control a direct object (5),[15] or they have an adverbial modifier (6). Sometimes they cannot be identified semantically as agent nouns (7). Often even more than one criterion apply.

(4)   & him **Cirus wæs æfterfylgende**, (*Orosius*, R 4.74.33)

(5)   hie ... wæron biddende **ðæt Metellus to Rome moste**. (*Orosius*, R 9.232.21)

---

[12] *Beon/wesan* auxiliarises of course only in the respective constructions. In other contexts, it was still used as copula. This is what Hopper (1991) calls the principle of 'split'.

[13] Hence many languages do not formally realise it (cf. Latin, Russian, Arabic, etc.).

[14] For parallel syntactic constructions in Middle Welsh and their possible influence on the origin of the progressive in English cf. e.g. Mittendorf and Poppe (2000). For translations from Latin as a supporting factor cf. Nickel (1966) and similarly Scheffer (1975).

[15] If a real agent noun has a complement, it is used in the genitive case, as in *Hie wæron ehtende cristenra manna.* (Denison 1993:372).

(6) & **raðe** ('hastily') eft wæs cirrende wiþ Rome weard (*Orosius*, R 11.236.12)

(7) him ða siððan **se feondscipe** wæs betweonum **weaxende**, (*Orosius*, R 9.232.25)

If the agent noun construction is the major source for the evolution of the expanded form in Old English (cf. also Nickel 1966), the data in the *Orosius* would be a clear indicator for a beginning grammaticalisation by that time. The new construction had already spread from 'critical contexts', in which the reading as agent noun or verbal participle was still ambiguous, to so-called 'isolating contexts' (Diewald 2002), i.e., contexts that favour the new periphrastic reading and exclude the old agent noun reading.

Although the auxiliarisation of *beon/wesan* had taken place, the new periphrastic verb construction had not yet acquired an aspectual meaning.[16] Most authors that have studied the expanded form in Old English point out that its major function was to make the utterance more vivid, more descriptive or emphatic.[17] My own analyses of the expanded forms in the *Orosius*, where they are often used with adverbs like *swiþe, longe,* or with superlatives of adjectives, have confirmed this view.

The next step, in which the whole construction acquires a grammatical meaning, namely to code the progressive aspect, lies again in the speaker-hearer interaction. The speaker uses this

---

[16] This is to be presupposed if the construction is recognised as a periphrasis. With regard to agent noun origin, there is no doubt about this. However, it could be argued that a fusion of participial (adjectival and appositional) and agent noun constructions led to the expanded form (Mitchell 1985:279f.) and that what we consider periphrases are rather stative copula constructions. This is indeed very difficult to decide, particularly as Brinton (1988:268) points out that the progressive and the corresponding stative can have identical syntax. But when Jespersen's (1931:229f.) or Visser's (1963-73:1931ff.) tests are applied, it becomes obvious that real periphrastic constructions exist (probably parallel with the older stative constructions). The very existence of periphrastic constructions is evidence enough that *beon/wesan* had been auxiliarised.

[17] Cf. Mossé (1938); a number of various functions is listed in Nickel (1966) and in Nehls (1974).

construction for emphatic reasons, or to catch the attention of the hearer, according to the speech act maxim of extravagance (cf. Haspelmath 1999).

In the – frequent – contexts with durative verbs this focus on vividness, emphasis, or intensity implied a focus on duration as a conversational implicature. This was obviously the status of the expanded form in Old English, where the aspectual meaning was not yet conventionalized. It was basically a stylistic device, which, however, was not fully unconstrained. It was never used with perfective verbs, that is, it did not occur with the prefixed verbs with *ge-, a-, for-, be-, of-*. Mossé (1938) remarks that *be* + V*-ende* could remain peripheral in Old English because verbs were durative anyway unless a prefix marked them as non-durative.[18] So the periphrastic construction had an association with the imperfective aspect in contrast to the perfective aspect from Old English on.

The conventionalisation of the conversational implicature of the aspectual meaning can only have happened in Late Middle English, or even in Early Modern English, when a considerable increase in frequency can be observed.[19]

3.2 The direct descendent hypothesis

Before the role of language contact in this grammaticalisation process, especially in Middle English, shall be discussed, I will provide some arguments for the direct descendent hypothesis, i.e. for the view that the ModE progressive form directly derives from the OE construction, and does not have its roots in a new development in Middle English.

Firstly, the OE *beon/wesan* + V$_{ende}$ construction was never given up in Middle English. An analysis of the occurrences of this construction in the first two sub-periods of Middle English in the *Helsinki Corpus* yielded the following results (cf. Table 1). In the first sub-period (1150-1250), 19 examples are attested in Southern texts, 12 in East

---

[18] On the use of prefixed verbs as markers of aspect or aktionsart in Old English cf. Wischer and Habermann (2004).

[19] For the increasing use and the dialectal distribution of the progressive in Middle English cf. Mustanoja (1960:585f.).

Midland texts, 14 in West Midland, and 3 in Kentish texts. In the second sub-period (1250-1350), no examples occur in Southern texts, but 21 in East Midland ones, 1 in West Midland, and 7 in Kentish texts. Unfortunately, the *Helsinki Corpus* does not contain any Northern texts in the first and second sub-periods of Middle English. But Mossé states in his survey of the dialectal distribution of the progressive form in Middle English that the North is the area with the most extensive use of that construction.[20]

Table 1. Occurrences of the expanded form (EF) in the first two sub-periods of Middle English in the *Helsinki Corpus*

	1150-1250			1250-1350		
	words	EF	per 1,000 words	words	EF	per 1,000 words
South	21,000	19	0.9	32,000	0	0
Kent	6,000	3	0.5	14,000	7	0.5
West Midland	62,000	14	0.2	5,000	1	0.2
East Midland	29,000	12	0.4	49,000	21	0.4
North	---	---	---	---	---	---
Total	**118,000**	**48**	**0.4**	**100,000**	**29**	**0.3**

I also checked the occurrences of expanded forms in the *English Prose Treatises of Richard Rolle de Hampole*, a Northern text of about 19,000 words, which would fall into the second sub-period of the *Helsinki Corpus*. It contains 7 expanded forms, i.e., it shows an average of 0.4 per 1,000 words. This does not support Mossé's findings, but of course one text is not sufficient for the falsification of his theory.

Thus, I would argue that the expanded form continued to be used in Middle English in the same functions and in a similar quantity as in Old English, cf. (8) – (12).

(8)   swa swa þᵗ godspel cyþ þᵗ ðe Hælend **wære** nihterne on bedum **wacende**. (*Bodley Homilies*, 44; 12th c., South)

---

[20] Similarly Mustanoja (1960:585) maintains that in Middle English the dialectal distribution of the construction is very uneven, but that it is common in late 13th century texts north of the Humber.

(9) 'Hlauerd, opene mine eiene ... þat ich **naure ne bie slapinde** on ðare saule deaðe, ... (*Vices and Virtues*, 127; 12th c., East Midland)

(10) and forði heo **bið wuniende** inne þisse pine. (*Lambeth Homilies*, 43; 12th c., West Midland)

(11) & wæs, þt sum man **wæs farende** of Judea lande, þæs name wæs Natan. (*Vespasian Homilies*, 88; 12th c., Kentish)

(12) bot if þay be ay criande ... (*Richard Rolle de Hampole*, 37; 14th c., North)

In the Northern and East Midland texts, there are also a lot of agent nouns with the suffix *-and*.[21] Especially in the ME *Prose Psalter*, an East Midland text from the second sub-period, they are frequently used with a direct object, as in (13) and (14).[22]

(13) þat he made me sauf fram **þe pursuand my soule** (*Prose Psalter*: 138)
'that he made me safe from **the pursuers (of) my soule**'

(14) Ich am partener of **alle þe dredand þe** & **kepand þy comaundement** (*Prose Psalter*: 149)
'I am partner of all the "fearers" (people who fear) (of) you and "keepers" (of) your commandments'

Some of these constructions are again ambiguous, so that they can be reanalysed as periphrastic constructions:

(15) for-soþe God **is iugeand hem** in erþe (*Prose Psalter*: 68)
'truly God **is (a) judge (of) them** on earth'
[... is judging them ...]

---

[21] When we consider that real agent noun constructions with *–end* were quite rare in Old English since reanalysis and extension had already taken place, their renewed occurrence in ME Northern and East Midland texts may seem surprising. But the new agent noun constructions with *–and* are obviously of Scandinavian origin.

[22] Since this text is a translation from Latin or French, one has to be cautious with any generalisations. But even if these constructions are based on the particular syntax of the original, their very existence in English texts is an interesting phenomenon.

A second argument for the direct descendent hypothesis is that a phonological change from [-endə] to [-ɪŋ] is possible. Kisbye (1971:31) states that the weakened vowel of *-and, -end* and *-ind* must have been of indistinct quality since scribes use these spellings variously even in the same manuscript. As an example he gives *Havelok the Dane*, an East Midland text from 1280, where forms like *gangande, driuende* and *fastinde* can be found. Even if the change of final [nd] to [ŋ] remains puzzling, it may be argued that here an amalgamation with the function of the gerund or the verbal noun may have played a role.

In Layamon's *Brut*, an East Midland text from the first ME sub-period, we find:

(16)   ... ich æm wald**inge** ... (LAYBR, I, 80)

(17)   ... ich nes weld**inde** ... (LAYBR, I, 90)

Mustanoja also gives an example from a different passage in the same text where various forms of the participle occur even side by side:

(18)   *ne go**inde** ne rid**ingge** (Lawman* B 1582; in Mustanoja 1960:547)

The data from the *Helsinki Corpus* suggest that the change from *-inde* to *-ing* must have occurred in the mid 14th century, between sub-periods 2 and 3, and probably had its origin in the Midlands. In the North the participle ending *-and* and the ending of the verbal noun, or gerund *-ing* were largely kept distinct till the end of the ME period. In Richard Rolle de Hampole's text there are 74 participles and agent nouns with the ending *-and(e)* and 281 verbal nouns and gerunds ending in *-yng(e)*, while only 4 participles and one agent noun end in *-ynge*, and one participle in *-ende* (cf. Table 2). One verbal noun has the ending *-enge* instead of *-ynge*. It is interesting that three of the participles and the agent noun in *-ynge* occur in a passage that is not based on the Thornton, but on the British Museum Manuscript, which is thought to be of Midland dialect.

Table 2. Endings of participle, agent noun and verbal noun in the 'English Prose Treatises of Richard Rolle de Hampole'

Participle	-and(e)	69
	-ende	1
	-ynge	4
Agent Noun	-ande	5
	-ynge	1
Verbal Noun / Gerund	-ynge	281
	-enge	1

A third argument for the direct descendent hypothesis is that the locative construction (*he was on hunting*) was comparatively rare in Middle English (cf. also Denison 1993:387). In the first two ME subsections of the Helsinki Corpus (1150-1350) not a single instance of that construction has been found.

3.3 The role of language contact

Grammaticalisation, like any other process of language change, is not deterministic. Changes of that kind cannot be predicted, they do not have to occur or do not have to go to completion. It may happen that particularly sociolinguistic factors stop or accelerate an ongoing change. Haase and Nau (1996), and recently Heine and Kuteva (2005) have shown how grammaticalisation can be influenced by external factors, particularly by language contact.

It would have been possible that the use of the expanded form might have declined in the course of Middle English, and that the construction would have finally disappeared, as it happened in Old High German; instead we can observe a considerable increase in frequency in the second half of the ME period. How can this be accounted for?

In Middle English, non-finite constructions (i.e., infinitive, participial and verbal noun constructions) became more productive generally, and the style as a whole, at least in the written language, seems to have become more nominal in character.[23] It is very likely that the phonetic instability of the endings [ən/ənd(ə)/ɪnd(ə)/ɪŋ]

---

[23] Remember that in Richard Rolle de Hampole's text 282 verbal nouns and gerunds are attested.

promoted a functional confusion between participle, infinitive, and gerund, which in turn led to the merger of the endings and finally to an increasing number of *ing*-forms. This confusion between notionally and formally related non-finite forms is to be expected particularly in contact situations where many non-native speakers are involved.

Furthermore, in contact situations more transparent constructions are preferred for an easier understanding (cf. Barber 1993:157), so the periphrastic construction, composed of the auxiliary *be*, a high frequency item marking person, number, mood and tense, and the invariable participle, allowed the speaker to avoid the more complicated and less transparent inflected verb forms.[24] This may be the reason why this construction was so dominant already in early Middle English in the North and the North East Midlands (cf. Mossé 1938), the area with many mixed Scandinavian – Anglo-Saxon communities.

The period around 1400, when the use of the periphrastic construction grew steadily throughout the whole of England, is also the time when the French nobility had shifted to English, i.e., when the consequences of the contact situation with French become obvious, especially in the vocabulary. But also some grammatical structures may have been reinforced in their use on the basis of parallel structures in Old French, such as the verb-participle constructions. French forms like *aler chantant* probably contributed to an increasing use of such ME forms as *com ridinge, lay sleeping, goth disputing*, which in turn may have strengthened the position of *be + -ing*-constructions (cf. also Mustanoja 1960:558).

The increase in use of the periphrastic construction was an important factor for the conventionalisation of the implied aspectual meaning. Another factor may have contributed to that development: while, as mentioned before, in Old English the construction could remain peripheral, by the end of Middle English it became more important as a marker of duration. By that time most verbal prefixes

---

[24] This applies especially to the past tense; note that the system of strong and weak verbs was restructured in Middle English, which must have led to a great deal of insecurity in the use of the past tense forms.

had been lost, and so the lexical contrast, or aktionsart contrast, between durative and non-durative verbs had been largely destroyed. The periphrasis, as a durative marker, may have filled this vacuum (cf. also Mossé 1938). It would also explain why in early Middle English the expanded form was far more frequent in the North than in the South: in Northern dialects the verbal prefixes disappeared much earlier than in the South due to Old Norse influence (cf. Mustanoja 1960:447).

The conventionalisation of the aspectual meaning in the periphrastic construction led finally to its obligatorification in the appropriate contexts and thus to the establishment of a grammatical category of aspect in English. This took place only in the late 18th or even in the course of the 19th century. The grammarians of the 18th century were aware of that construction and its function as marker of imperfectivity, but they still considered it a rather optional device.

4. Summary

The English progressive form has its origin in language internal developments. It can be explained as the result of a grammaticalisation process. Its evolution began in particular contexts through speaker-hearer interaction. Cognitive processes, such as pragmatic inferencing, led to a syntactic reanalysis and the auxiliarisation of the copula *be*. Only then analogical extension to other contexts took place. This had already happened in Old English, though the choice of the expanded form was still optional then. It took a long time until it was firmly established as an aspectual marker and finally became obligatory in Modern English. In such a development, it can even happen that an incipient change is stopped, as it obviously was in German. On the other hand, it is possible that a change is accelerated by external factors. This was noticeably the case in the history of English. A survey of the relevant factors in the grammaticalisation of the progressive form in English is given in Table 3.

Table 3. Summary of the relevant factors in the grammaticalisation of the progressive form in English

Time	Grammaticalisation	Language contact
Pre-OE	'critical contexts': Agent noun constructions (copula + agent noun -*ende*) (Participial adjective constructions) (Appositive participial constructions)	
OE	Reanalysis → Auxiliarisation Extension to 'isolating contexts' Periphrastic verb construction (*beon/wesan* + V-*ende*) Optional use: emphasis, vividness, descriptive force	Celtic substrate Latin participial and deponens constructions
ME	[ənd]/[ɪnd] – [ən] – [ɪŋ] → [ɪŋ] Increase in frequency	Scandinavian – Anglo-Saxon language contact French participial constructions
EModE	Conventionalisation of aspectual meaning	
PDE	Obligatorification	

References

Allen, Cynthia. 1997. "The origins of the 'group genitive' in English". *Transactions of the Philological Society* 95(1): 111-131.

Barber, Charles. 1993. *The English language: a historical introduction.* Cambridge: CUP.

Bauer, Gero. 1970. *Studien zum System und Gebrauch der 'Tempora' in der Sprache Chaucers and Gowers.* Wien: Braumüller.

Beths, Frank. 1999. "The history of *dare* and the status of unidirectionality". *Linguistics* 37(6): 1067-1110.

Brinton, Laurel J. 1988. *The development of English aspectual systems: aspectualizers and post-verbal particles.* Cambridge: CUP.

Bybee, Joan L., Revere D. Perkins and William Pagliuca. 1994. *The evolution of grammar: tense, aspect and modality in the languages of the world.* Chicago: University of Chicago Press.

Campbell, Lyle. 2001. "What's wrong with grammaticalization?" *Language Sciences* 23: 113-161.

Dal, Ingerid. 1952. "Zur Entstehung des englischen Participium Praesentis auf -*ing*". *Norsk Tidsskrift for Sprogvidenskap* 16: 5-116.

Denison, David. 1993. *English historical syntax.* London: Longman.

Diewald, Gabriele. 2002. "A model for relevant types of context in grammaticalization". In: Wischer, Ilse and Gabriele Diewald (eds.): 103-120.
Fischer, Olga, Muriel Norde and Harry Perridon (eds.). 2004. *Up and down the cline – the nature of grammaticalization.* Amsterdam: Benjamins.
Gabelentz, Georg von der. 1891. *Die Sprachwissenschaft. Ihre Aufgaben, Methoden und bisherigen Ergebnisse.* 2nd ed. Leipzig: Tauchnitz.
Giacalone Ramat, Anna and Paul J. Hopper (eds.). 1998. *The limits of grammaticalization.* Amsterdam: Benjamins.
Givón, Talmy. 1971. "Historical syntax and synchronic morphology: an archaeologist's field trip". *Chicago Linguistic Society* 7: 394-415.
Haase, Martin and Nicole Nau. 1996. "Einleitung: Sprachkontakt und Grammatikalisierung". *Sprachtypologie und Universalienforschung* 49(1): 3-8.
Haspelmath, Martin. 1999. "Why is grammaticalization irreversible?" *Linguistics* 37(6): 1043-1068.
Heine, Bernd, Ulrike Claudi and Friederike Hünnemeyer. 1991. *Grammaticalization: a conceptual framework.* Chicago: University of Chicago Press.
Heine, Bernd. 1997. *Possession: cognitive source, forces, and grammaticalization.* Cambridge: CUP.
Heine, Bernd and Tania Kuteva. 2002. *World lexicon of grammaticalization.* Cambridge: CUP.
Heine, Bernd. 2003. "Grammaticalization". In: Joseph, Brian and Richard D. Janda (eds.). *The handbook of historical linguistics.* Oxford: Blackwell: 575-601.
Heine, Bernd and Tania Kuteva. 2005. *Language contact and grammatical change.* Cambridge: CUP.
Hopper, Paul J. 1991. "On some principles of grammaticalization". In: Traugott, Elizabeth C. and Bernd Heine (eds.). *Approaches to grammaticalization.* Vol. I. Amsterdam: Benjamins: 17-35.
Hopper, Paul J. and Elizabeth C. Traugott. 2003. *Grammaticalization.* 2nd ed.. Cambridge: CUP.
Humboldt, Wilhelm von. 1994 [1822]. "Über das Entstehen der grammatischen Formen und ihren Einfluß auf die Ideeenentwicklung". *Abhandlungen der Akademie der Wissenschaften zu Berlin.* Reprint: Humboldt, Wilhelm von, *Über die Sprache.* Tübingen: Francke: 52-81.
Janda, Richard D. 1980. "On the decline of declensional systems: the overall loss of OE nominal case inflections and the ME reanalysis of *-es* as *his*". In: Traugott, Elizabeth C., R. Labrum and S. Shepherd (eds.). *Papers from the 4th International Conference on Historical Linguistics [1979]* Amsterdam: Benjamins: 243-252.
Janda, Richard D. 2001. "Beyond 'pathways' and 'unidirectionality': on the discontinuity of language transmission and the counterability of grammaticalization". *Language Sciences* 23: 265-340.

Jespersen, Otto. 1931. *A modern English grammar on historical principles. Part IV: Syntax, Vol. III.* Heidelberg: Winter.
Joseph, Brian. 2001. "Is there such a thing as 'grammaticalization'?" *Language Sciences* 23: 163-186.
Kisbye, Torben. 1971. *An historical outline of English syntax.* Tryk: Akademisk Boghandel.
Kuryłowicz, Jerzy. 1965. "The evolution of grammatical categories". *Diogenes* 51: 55-71.
Lass, Roger. 1990. "How to do things with junk: exaptation in language evolution". *Journal of Linguistics* 26: 79-102.
Lehmann, Christian. 2004. "Theory and method in grammaticalization". *Zeitschrift für Germanistische Linguistik* 32(2): 152-187.
Meillet, Antoine. 1912. "L'évolution des formes grammaticales". In: Meillet, Antoine (ed.). *Linguistique générale et linguistique historique.* Paris: Champion: 130-148.
Mitchell, Bruce. 1985. *Old English syntax. Vol. I.* Oxford: Clarendon.
Mittendorf, Ingo and Erich Poppe. 2000. "Celtic contacts of the English progressive?" In: Tristram, Hildegard C. (ed.). *Celtic Englishes II.* Heidelberg: Winter: 117-145.
Mossé, Fernand. 1938. *Histoire de la forme périphrastique 'être' + participe présent en Germanique.* Paris: Klincksieck.
Mustanoja, Tauno F. 1960. *A Middle English syntax.* Helsinki: Société Néophilologique.
Nehls, Dietrich. 1974. *Synchron-diachrone Untersuchungen zur expanded form im Englischen. Eine struktural-funktionale Analyse.* München: Max Hueber.
Newmeyer, Frederick J. 1998. *Language form and language function.* Cambridge, Mass.: MIT Press.
Newmeyer, Frederick J. 2001. "Deconstructing grammaticalization". *Language Sciences* 23: 187-220.
Nickel, Gerhard. 1966. *Die Expanded Form im Altenglischen: Vorkommen, Funktion und Herkunft der Umschreibung 'beon/wesan' und Partizip Präsens.* Neumünster: Karl Wachholtz.
Norde, Muriel. 2002. "The final stages of grammaticalization: affixhood and beyond". In: Wischer, Ilse and Gabriele Diewald (eds.): 45-65.
Pagliuca, William (ed.). 1994. *Perspectives on grammaticalization.* Amsterdam: Benjamins.
Perry, George G. (ed.). 1987. *English prose treatises of Richard Rolle de Hampole.* 2nd revised ed (Early English Text Society, Original Series, 20, 1866). Millwood, N.Y.: Kraus Reprint.
Plank, Frans. 1995. "Entgrammatikalisierung – Spiegelbild der Grammatikalisierung?" In: Boretzky, Norbert *et al.* (eds.). *Natürlichkeitstheorie und Sprachwandel.* Bochum: Brockmeyer: 199-219.

Preusler, Walther. 1956. "Keltischer Einfluss im Englischen". *Revue des Langues Vivantes* 22 : 322-350.
Rissanen, Matti, Merja Kytö and Kirsi Heikkonen (eds.). 1997. *Grammaticalization at work: studies of long-term developments in English.* Berlin: Mouton.
Roberts, Ian and Anna Roussou. 2003. *Syntactic change: a minimalist approach to grammaticalization.* Cambridge: CUP.
Scheffer, Johannes. 1975. *The progressive in English.* Amsterdam: North-Holland.
Strang, Barbara. 1982. "Some aspects of the history of the *be* + *ing* construction". In: Anderson, John (ed.). *Language form and linguistic variation: papers dedicated to Angus McIntosh.* Amsterdam: Benjamins: 427-474.
Taeymans, Martine. 2004. "*Dare* and *need* in British and American Present-Day English". In: Kay, Christian, Simon Horobin and Jeremy Smith (eds.). *New perspectives on English historical linguistics. Vol. I.* Amsterdam: Benjamins: 215-227.
Traugott, Elizabeth C. 2001. "Legitimate counterexamples to unidirectionality". Paper presented at Freiburg University, October 17th 2001: www.stanford.edu/~traugott/papers/Freiburg.Unidirect.pdf.
Visser, Frederic Theodor. 1963-73. *An historical syntax of the English language.* 4 vols. Leiden: E.J. Brill.
Whitney, William Dwight. 1970 [1875]. *The life and growth of language.* Hildesheim: Olms.
Warner, Anthony R. 1993. *English auxiliaries: structure and history.* Cambridge: CUP.
Wischer, Ilse and Gabriele Diewald (eds.). 2002. *New reflections on grammaticalization.* Amsterdam: Benjamins.
Wischer, Ilse and Mechthild Habermann. 2004. "Der Gebrauch von Präfixverben zum Ausdruck von Aspekt/Aktionsart im Altenglischen und Althochdeutschen". *Zeitschrift für Germanistische Linguistik* 32(2): 262-285.

W. Garrett Mitchener
A mathematical model of the loss of verb-second in Middle English

1. Introduction

The first step toward understanding syntactic change is to describe the language before, during, and after the transition. Important features of the initial and final grammars must be identified and expressed formally. The rise of new sentence types and the decline of obsolete types must be understood. Once these descriptive questions are answered, the next step is to address more difficult questions: why did this change occur? Why did it spread? Why did it happen at the time it did rather than earlier or later? Why did a potential change in slightly different circumstances fail to happen? In particular, how well do chance and internal factors explain the change, and to what extent should external factors, such as contact, be invoked to explain the change? This paper illustrates how mathematical models may be used to precisely express and test hypothetical explanations for syntactic change, using the example of the loss of verb-second in Middle English. Specifically, the model presented here is compatible with the hypothesis that the loss of verb-second may be attributed to contact between regional dialects, and that the timing of the change is related to the timing and amount of contact.

The basis for the model is a framework proposed by Lightfoot (1999) for explaining syntactic change: a shift in speech patterns weakens the evidence for the old grammar in the primary linguistic data (PLD) available to children, and the resulting ambiguous PLD leads children to acquire a new grammar. Their speech further dilutes the PLD for the next generation, resulting in the spread of the new grammar. In the case of Middle English, there is broad agreement in the literature that there were two regional dialects with different verb-second rules, and an increase in contact between them caused the initial shift in speech patterns that ultimately led to the decline of verb-second (Fischer *et al.* 2000; Kroch 1989; Kroch *et al.* 2000). The mathematical model is a representation of this process as a continuous dynamical system.

The grammar acquisition process is crucial to the spread of the change. Lightfoot (1999) also proposes a mechanism for the acquisition of verb-second: children listen for sentences in the PLD that can only be parsed by a grammar with a particular feature, sentences which Lightfoot calls *cues*. Children incorporate that feature into their native language only if the proportion of cue sentences they hear exceeds some threshold. Children learning the northern and southern dialects of Middle English would have been listening for slightly different cues because of the differences in how their native languages treat subject pronouns. At the boundary between the two dialects, the PLD would have been a confusing mixture of the two, and, Lightfoot asserts, the lack of compelling evidence caused children to acquire a grammar without verb-second. Lightfoot's proposed learning process may be expressed easily in mathematical notation, and the model shows that with reasonable numerical parameter settings it produces the correct result.

Other learning processes have been suggested in the language modelling literature. For example, the memoryless learner (Niyogi and Berwick 1996) is a simple, mathematically convenient learning model; however, it produces the puzzling result that in simulations, verb-second languages are extremely stable and in fact all languages eventually become verb-second. Clearly this does not reflect the current state of the world's languages. The model in this paper shows that grammar acquisition must strike the proper balance between matching the PLD and ignoring noise if it is to correctly predict that Middle English could lose verb-second, and this is precisely where simple memoryless learners fail.

Section 2 gives some background on the word order of Middle English and the differences between the regional dialects. Section 3 describes the mathematical model and its behaviour as the two regions mix. In particular, a phenomenon known as a *bifurcation* takes place, resulting in the loss of one language. Section 4 discusses what goes wrong if a memoryless learner is used instead of Lightfoot's cue-based learner. Finally, section 5 draws conclusions and describes some of the author's ongoing research on mathematical models of language change.

2. Verb-second in Middle English

Middle English had underlying subject-verb-object (SVO) word order, and like most Germanic languages, also had a rule known as verb-second in which top-level sentences are re-organized such that a topic and the finite verb always appear at the front of the sentence. Example 1 comes from the northern dialect, which was heavily influenced by Old Norse in its grammar and vocabulary. This word order will be abbreviated SVO+CPv2.

(1) $[_{CP} [_{DP}$ Oþir labur$]_j$ $_V$sal$_i$ $[_{IP}$ t$_i$ þai do t$_j]$]
other labour shall they do
'They must do other labour.'
(*The Rule of St. Benet,* Fischer *et al.* 2000, p.131)

Since embedded sentences do not show this reorganization, the formal description of verb-second word order in this case is that the finite verb is raised to C and a topic, which can be any DP or a sentential adverb, is raised to Spec-CP. Such reorganization is not possible in an embedded sentence because C is already occupied by a complementizer.

Lightfoot (1999) proposes that sentences of the form

(2) $[_{CP}$ XP$_{Topic}$ V$_{Finite}$ $[_{IP}$ DP$_{Subject}$ ...]]

are the cues for verb-second. Assuming that children have determined that the underlying ME word order should be SVO, sentences of the form in (2) have clearly been reorganized from the underlying order, indicating to children that a verb-second rule is required.

Southern Middle English had a slightly different form of verb-second. Pronominal subjects behave differently from full noun phrases, and can appear between the fronted finite verb and the fronted topic, as in (3):

(3) [$_{CP}$ [$_{DP}$ alle þese bebodes]$_j$ $_{PRO}$ic $_v$habbe$_i$ [$_{IP}$ t$_i$ ihealde t$_j$ fram childhade]]
all these commandments I have kept from childhood
'I have kept all of these commandments from childhood.'
(*Vices & Virtues,* Fischer *et al.* 2000, p. 130)

Furthermore, Old English allowed for verb-second effects in embedded sentences under some circumstances, leading to the suggestion that the finite verb does not raise all the way to C, but stops at some intermediate position between C and I. Fischer *et al.* (2000) name this position F, so the southern word order will be abbreviated SVO+FPv2+pro.

Since pronominal subjects are common in speech, sentences where the finite verb appears third as in (3) would have been frequent. Northern children at the boundary between the dialects would have heard such sentences and failed to recognize them as cues for verb-second. The resulting shortage of cues then led them to use the modern SVO word order by default.

3. The dynamical system

The proposed mechanism behind the loss of verb-second in Middle English may be expressed mathematically as follows. We first make the simplification of working with two grammars, G_1 and G_2, and assume that people speak either one or the other, but not both. G_1 is analogous to the northern SVO+CPv2 dialect, and G_2 may be interpreted as being analogous to either the southern SVO+FPv2+pro or the emerging SVO dialect. Some comments on these simplifying assumptions are called for. The historical situation seems to have involved at least three grammars, namely SVO+CPv2, SVO+FPv2+pro, and SVO. However, a model with two grammars suffices to illustrate how one grammar might displace another, and the resulting dynamical system is much simpler, requiring only two dimensions rather than the four required to express the model for three grammars. Manuscripts also suggest that speakers were diglossic, that is, they used mixtures of verb-second and non-verb-second grammars. The decline in sentences of the forms (1) and (3) seems to be due to a smooth shift among all speakers from using all verb-second to using no verb-second, rather than a decline of exclusively verb-second speakers in favour of exclusively SVO speakers. The model can be reformulated to include diglossia, but the mathematics is significantly more complicated and the overall behaviour is essentially the same. So for now, we will ignore diglossia in formulating the model.

To model learning, we assume that the sentences accepted by G_1 form a superset of those accepted by G_2. Sentences not accepted by G_2 are therefore cues for G_1. Children hear n sentences total, and if m or more of them are cues, they acquire G_1, else they acquire G_2. Cue sentences are produced frequently by speakers of G_1 at a rate $p_1 \approx$ 30%, and rarely by speakers of G_2 at a rate $p_2 \approx$ 5%. The choice of 30% is based on a figure cited in Lightfoot (1999). The choice of 5% is arbitrary, and was made to represent a reasonably large amount of noise in the PLD, due for example to exceptional phrases such as "Never before has such-and-such been attempted". The behaviour of the model is essentially unchanged for a range of values of p_1 and p_2; the only requirement is that p_2 should be much smaller than p_1. Mathematically, acquisition is modelled by the function $q(x)$ as defined in equation (4), which represents the probability a child will acquire G_1 given that a fraction x of the surrounding population uses G_1 and a fraction $1 - x$ use G_2:

$$(4) \quad q(x) = \sum_{j=m}^{n} \binom{n}{j} \gamma^j (1-\gamma)^{n-j} \text{ where } \gamma = p_1 x + p_2 (1-x)$$

The number γ is the probability that a cue sentence is spoken if a speaker is selected at random and asked to produce a sentence. With the choices $n = 100$ and $m = 20$, the function $q(x)$ has the shape shown in Figure 1.

Figure 1. A graph of the learning function $q(x)$ for Lightfoot's cue-based learning algorithm. The line $q(x) = x$ and the three points of intersection are drawn for reference.

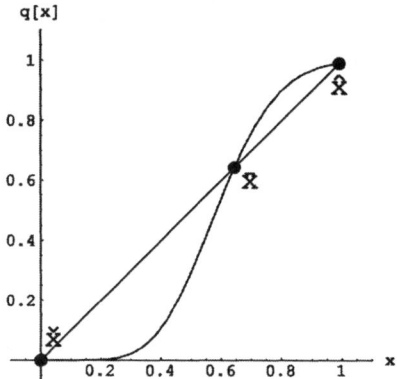

Figure 2. Phase portrait for the dynamical system, with no migration between regions, that is $\alpha = \beta = 0$

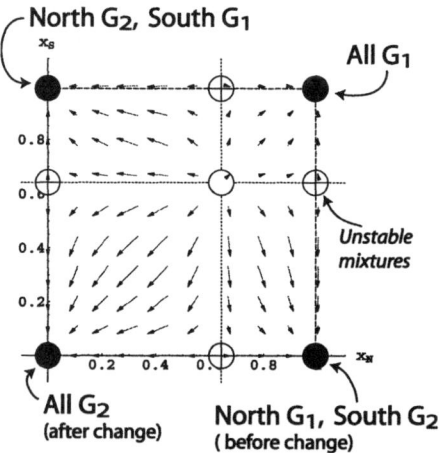

The model population is divided into two regions, north and south. The state of the population consists of two functions of time, $x_N(t)$ and $x_S(t)$, representing the fraction of the population in the two regions that speaks G_1 at time t. Both are between 0 and 1. A pair of differential equations defines how they change in time:

(5) $\dot{x}_N = q(x_N) - x_N + \alpha(x_S - x_N)$
$\dot{x}_S = q(x_S) - x_S + \beta(x_N - x_S)$

The dot represents the derivative with respect to time. For this formulation, the units of time have been scaled so that the birth and death rates are both 1. The $q(x)$ terms represent the fraction of births that yield a child who learns G_1. The $-x$ terms represent the death of speakers of G_1. The letters α and β represent constant migration or mixing rates between the two regions. A system of differential equations such as (5) is known as a *dynamical system,* and is studied with techniques such as linear stability analysis and Lyapunov functions (Strogatz 1994). A picture called a *phase portrait* describes the behaviour of the system (see Figure 2). The arrows are called a *vector field* and represent the direction in which population states flow, as given by equation (5). There are nine singularities called *fixed points* in the vector field where $\dot{x}_N$ and $\dot{x}_S$ are both zero; these are denoted by dots and represent equilibrium states of the population, that is, states for which there is no tendency to flow. Some are stable, and the population will return to such a state if disturbed. These stable fixed points are called *sinks* and are drawn as black dots. The others are unstable, and come in two types. A *source* is the reverse of a sink, and a population near but not exactly on top of a source will move away. Sources are denoted by white dots. A *saddle* repels most nearby populations, but they follow a path that initially brings them near the saddle, then swerve. Saddles are denoted by circles with crosses. Dotted lines (called *stable manifolds*) separate trajectories that swerve in different directions upon approaching a saddle point. Dashed lines (called *unstable manifolds*) are drawn along trajectories that flow most directly away from a saddle and attract those swerving trajectories. The locations and stabilities of the nine fixed points are determined by the shape of the $q(x)$ graph, specifically, where it crosses the line $q(x) = x$, and by the mixing parameters α and β.

In Figure 2, there are four sinks, one in each corner, representing the extreme states of the population where each region uses one grammar exclusively. This is the scenario when there is no mixing between the regions. The bottom right sink is analogous to the situation before the extinction of northern Middle English, where the population is split: the northern region speaks exclusively G_1, and the southern speaks exclusively G_2. Any population using a similar mixture of the two grammars will flow along the vector field and converge to the sink in the lower right. It will remain there indefinitely even in the presence of small perturbations. The sink in the lower left represents a population in which both regions speak exclusively G_2, and attracts populations where G_1 is used by fewer than about 60% of northerners.

Figure 3. Phase portraits for different values of the mixing parameters. As mixing increases, the sinks in the upper left and lower right corners collide in a pair of saddle-node bifurcations. The square in picture (d) shows where the collision takes place.

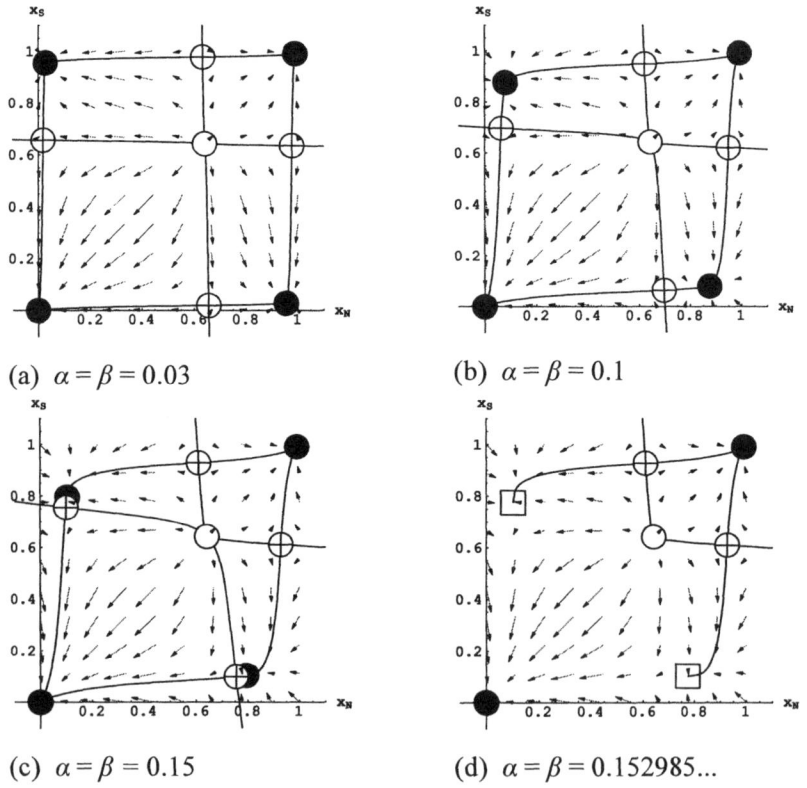

(a) $\alpha = \beta = 0.03$

(b) $\alpha = \beta = 0.1$

(c) $\alpha = \beta = 0.15$

(d) $\alpha = \beta = 0.152985...$

Now consider what happens when the mixing parameters are stepped up to allow more interaction between the regions (see Figure 3). As α and β increase, the vector field changes, and the fixed points shift. Initially, the population can remain in a split state with most northerners speaking G_1 and most southerners speaking G_2. Eventually, the lower right sink collides with a nearby saddle in an event called a *saddle-node bifurcation*. The term *bifurcation* refers to the fact that two features of the phase portrait have collided and annihilated one another, and the name *saddle-node* refers to the fact that one of the features was a saddle and the other was a nodal sink (as opposed to a spiral sink, which does not occur in this model). After the bifurcation, there is no longer a stable split state for populations to converge to, so they are attracted to the sink in the bottom left corner, resulting in the extinction of G_1.

Figure 4. Time traces of the population when the mixing parameters increase smoothly: $\alpha = \beta =$ a linear function of time τ. The time axis is in rescaled units, not years. As the mixing parameters increase, the bifurcation takes place and x_N converges rapidly to 0.

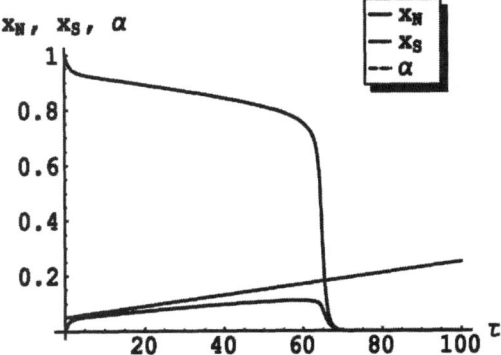

We may also set the mixing parameters into continuous motion, as in Figure 4. The population is initially placed in a split state, with exclusively G_1 in the north and exclusively G_2 in the south. As the mixing parameters slowly increase, the population tracks the bottom right sink as it shifts, maintaining a split state. When the bifurcation occurs, that sink vanishes, and the population flows to the bottom left sink and G_1 disappears. Thus, the timing of the loss of G_1 is determined by the timing and strength of the mixing between the two regions.

4. Comparison to memoryless learner

Niyogi and Berwick (1996) studied a simple learning algorithm called *memoryless learner,* which searches a universal grammar (UG) consisting of a finite set of grammars $U = \{G_1, G_2,...,G_n\}$ as follows. It starts with a randomly selected hypothesis grammar $H \in U$. Given a sentence from the environment, if H can parse the sentence, the learner stays there, otherwise it switches to another randomly selected hypothesis, possibly one it has already visited, hence the term *memoryless.* The process ends after a fixed number of sentences, and the hypothesis at that point is the output of the algorithm. In one of their simulations, also discussed in Lightfoot (1999), a model UG consisting of eight grammars determined by three binary parameters is studied under memoryless learning. Oddly, all verb-second languages are stable in this simulation and non-verb-second languages tend to extinction in favour of their verb-second counterparts. (A similar phenomenon was observed by Briscoe (2000) under certain circumstances in his more complex simulation.)

Figure 5. A graph of $q(x)$ for the memoryless learner. The line $q(x) = x$ is included for reference.

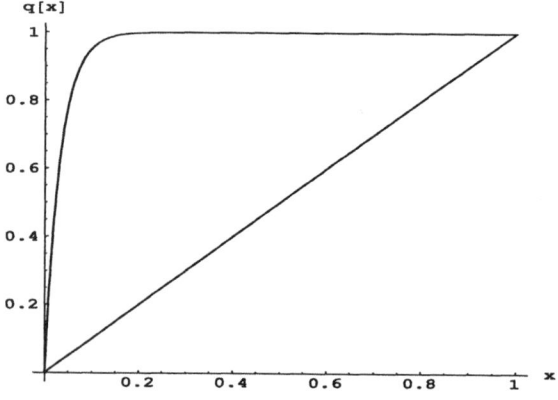

The model (5) yields a mathematical explanation for this unexpected behaviour. If we replace the cue-based learning algorithm with memoryless learning on $U = \{G_1 = \text{SVO+v2}, G_2 = \text{SVO}\}$, then the function $q(x)$ changes shape dramatically, as in Figure 5. A single cue sentence is enough to cause a memoryless learner to choose SVO+v2 over SVO, and it will never have reason to switch hypotheses again. Because of this hypersensitivity, memoryless learners are unlikely to acquire G_2 even if the presence of G_1 in the population is minimal. This skews $q(x)$ and causes the phase portrait of (5) to appear as in Figure 6, where the only sink is in the upper right and represents a population where both regions speak exclusively G_1. There is no way for the bifurcation from Section 3 to take place, and there is no way for G_1 to disappear.

Figure 6. Phase portrait for the memoryless learner and no mixing between regions. All populations tend to the sink in the upper right.

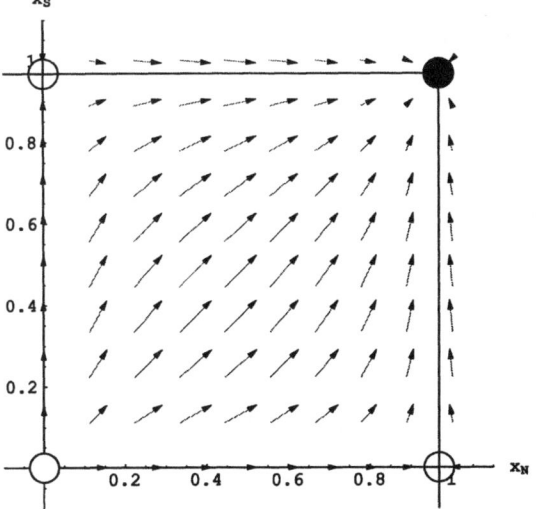

In summary, the dynamical system presented here shows that memoryless learning is overly sensitive to noise, and cue-based learning provides a more historically accurate alternative.

5. Conclusion and future work

The dynamical system model presented in this paper shows that mathematical modelling techniques can help linguists to express hypotheses about language change precisely, and to then use mathematics to understand how these models behave. Specifically, we have seen how the loss of a regional dialect of Middle English may be understood as a consequence of a saddle-node bifurcation. The model is compatible with the hypothesis that contact between regional dialects caused the loss of verb-second in Middle English. Furthermore, Lightfoot's cue-base acquisition algorithm provides a mechanism by which such a change might spread, but only when contact is sufficiently high. The time course of the change is directly tied to the strength and timing of the contact.

The model makes a number of simplifying assumptions that should be relaxed in future work. In particular, manuscript data suggests that speakers of Middle English used varying mixtures of verb-second and non-verb-second grammars. The model can be extended to allow for such speakers at the expense of additional complexity: regions must now be represented as densities where $u(z,t)$ is the probability at time t that a speaker selected at random from the region uses G_1 a fraction z of the time. The result is an infinite dimensional differential equation, which could potentially have much more complex behaviour than the two dimensional model discussed here. However, for reasonable choices of the learning process, the means of the regional densities obey the same dynamics as given in section 3, so this simplified model still gives useful results.

An alternative question is to study in more detail what learning processes generate the correct behaviour in the infinite dimensional model. Currently, much less is known about how children acquire usage frequencies than how they might acquire particular syntactic structures, and the infinite dimensional model might shed some light on this subject.

The current model splits the population into two compartments, which is a fairly crude approximation to the spatial structure of medieval England. The model could be improved by adding additional spatial structure, for example, a network of discrete communities or a continuous population density. A network of discrete communities requires a higher dimensional dynamical system. A continuous population density requires a system of partial differential equations, which are generally much more difficult to understand than dynamical systems.

The dynamical system model is deterministic, so it requires an external event (the increase in contact between regional dialects) to initiate the syntactic change. It does not allow for the possibility that the loss of verb-second might have happened purely spontaneously. To remedy this situation, the model may be altered to include random events by reformulating it as a set of stochastic differential equations. Such an improvement would allow further investigation into how much of the change should be attributed to contact and how much to random chance, but at the expense of substantially increasing the mathematical complexity of the model.

Other future work includes detailed simulations of individual agents that may speak many more possible grammars. The plan is to use the minimalist framework to construct grammars, and use ideas from Yang (2002) as the basis of a learning algorithm. The population will include social and spatial structure as well as simulated literacy. Eventually, the results of the simulation will be compared to manuscript data from the *Pennsylvania Parsed Corpus of Middle English*, and simplified mathematical models will be constructed to better understand the essential details.

References

Briscoe, Ted. 2000. "Evolutionary perspectives on diachronic syntax". In: Pintzuk, Susan, George Tsoulas and Anthony Warner (eds.). *Diachronic syntax: models and mechanisms*. Oxford: OUP: 75-105.

Fischer, Olga, Ans van Kemenade, Willem Koopman and Wim van der Wurff. 2000. *The syntax of Early English*. Cambridge: CUP.

Kroch, Anthony. 1989. "Reflexes of grammar in patterns of language change". *Language Variation and Change* 1/3: 199-244.

Kroch, Anthony, Ann Taylor and Donald Ringe. 2000. "The Middle English verb-second constraint: a case study in language contact and language change". In:

Herring, Susan, Pieter van Reenen and Lene Schløsler (eds.). *Textual parameters in older languages*. Philadelphia: Benjamins.
Lightfoot, David. 1999. *The development of language: acquisition, changes and evolution*. Malden, MA: Blackwell.
Niyogi, P. and Robert C. Berwick. 1996. "A language learning model for finite parameter spaces". *Cognition* 61: 161-193.
Strogatz, Steven H. 1994. *Nonlinear dynamics and chaos*. Reading, MA: Perseus Books.
Yang, Charles D. 2002. *Knowledge and learning in natural language*. Oxford: OUP.

Päivi Pahta and Arja Nurmi
Code-switching in the *Helsinki Corpus*: a thousand years of multilingual practices*

1. Introduction

Code-switching, the co-occurrence of two or more languages in a single communicative event, is a well-attested discourse practice in present-day multilingual communities.[1] While it is commonly considered a feature of informal spoken language, it also occurs in written texts, including those of the past. Like other language contact phenomena, code-switching has lately received increasing attention in linguistic and more philologically oriented research related to the history of English.[2] The focus of interest has been on the medieval period: numerous studies have analysed structures or functions of switching in texts representing different genres, including mixed-language business accounts, administrative and legal texts, medical and scientific writings, letters, sermons, drama and other literary materials. Less is known about code-switching in other periods in the history of English, while studies by e.g. Wright (1994, 1998), Schendl (2004), Dossena (2002), Pahta (forthcoming), Nurmi and Pahta (2004), and Pahta and Nurmi (forthcoming) show that there is potential for further enquiry.

---

* The research reported here was supported by the Academy of Finland Centre of Excellence funding for the Research Unit for Variation and Change in English at the Department of English, University of Helsinki, and by the Helsinki Collegium for Advanced Studies. We would like to thank Professor Outi Merisalo, Dr Klaus Karttunen and Dr Harry Halén for sharing their expertise in Classical, Romance, Asian and African languages with us in the course of analysing the data.
[1] For recent extensive studies of code-switching, see e.g. Sharp (2001), Myers-Scotton (2002), Clyne (2003) and Callahan (2004).
[2] For recent information on historical code-switching research related to English, see Schendl (2002), Pahta (2003, 2004a, 2004b), Nurmi and Pahta (2004). For other languages, see e.g. Argenter (2001), Adams *et al.* (2002) and Adams (2003). For studies on code-switching in present-day writing, see e.g. Graedler (1999) and Callahan (2004).

In this paper we examine code-switching between English and other languages in a long diachronic perspective. As our material we use the *Helsinki Corpus of English Texts*, a diachronic multi-genre corpus containing over 1.5 million words of running text from c. 700 to 1710.[3] It is worth noting that the corpus was compiled of texts representative of the English language, and thus any evidence of multilingual practices in the texts may be considered incidental.[4] Our study provides a quantitative and qualitative analysis of code-switching in the entire *Helsinki Corpus*, focusing on the relationship of switching practices with the language-external background information that has been coded into the corpus in the form of textual parameters. We shall first provide an overview of switching in a diachronic perspective, then discuss the most prominent findings in terms of the textual parameters of the corpus, and finally examine switching as a discursive practice in different types of text.

2. Overview: languages, structures and density of code-switching across time

The code-switching data was retrieved from the *Helsinki Corpus* using the text-level annotation indicating foreign language as the search parameter (see Kytö 1996:30-31). In addition, the foreign language passages that have been omitted from the texts during corpus compilation were retrieved from the editions and included in the analysis.[5]

A quantitative overview of switching in the *Helsinki Corpus* from Old English to Early Modern English is presented in Table 1. Since we are more concerned with textual and discursive aspects of

---

[3] For information on the *Helsinki Corpus*, see e.g. Rissanen *et al.* (1993), Kytö (1996).
[4] This means e.g. that samples of some text types where switching is endemic, such as early mixed-language business documents (Wright 1994, 1998) or macaronic verse (Schendl 2001), are not represented in the material.
[5] The omitted passages consist of some longer stretches of Latin and of Greek, which has not been transliterated. We have not added the word counts of the omitted passages to the total word count, but their length is not sufficient to influence the overall results.

switching than with structural features, we have counted foreign language passages instead of individual switches from one language to another. The total of code-switched passages in the corpus is 2,641. In order to make valid comparisons, we have used normalised frequencies of switches per 1,000 words. Another measure of the density of switching is the average length of switches: for this the length of each switch in orthographic words was counted, and related to the number of switches.

Table 1. Code-switching in the *Helsinki Corpus* (N = number of switched passages, ASL = average switch length in words)

Subperiod	Words	N	/1,000	ASL
Old English	413,250	752	1.8	4.7
Middle English	608,570	1,338	2.2	5.2
Early Modern English	551,000	551	1.0	5.1
Total	1,572,800	2,641	1.7	5.0

Table 1 shows that during the OE and ME periods there were approximately two switched passages for every 1,000 words; in the EModE period, one per 1,000 words. The average switch length is around five words during the whole time period studied. The shortest switches consist of a single word, while the longest Latin switched passage comprises 205 words and the longest French switch 98 words.[6] The structural range in each period contains both intrasentential and intersentential switches, including various kinds of phrases, clauses, sentences and sequences of sentences.

Table 2 shows languages other than English used in the *Helsinki Corpus* as well as their frequencies in the three periods. By far the most frequently occurring language in each period is Latin (see example (1)), with instances to be counted in hundreds in each case. In view of the strong presence of French in medieval England, the

---

[6] While single word switches (possible single borrowed lexemes) are quite frequent, excluding them from the figures in Table 1 does not dramatically change the frequency patterns. The overall number of switches longer than 1 word is 2,003; the frequency of switched passages in Old English is 1.2, in Middle English 1.8 and in Early Modern English 0.8. The average switch length is 6.3 for Middle English and Early Modern English, 6.4 for Old English. This clearly indicates that the pattern observed does not change even if single word switches are omitted.

amount of French in the material is surprisingly small (only 21 French passages in the ME period and 5 in the EModE period; see example (2)).[7] In the early subperiods the role of Greek is negligible. During the EModE period, the number of Greek passages increases slightly (34 instances); the increase is, however, mostly due to one sermon, illustrated in example (3).[8]

Table 2. Languages other than English used in the *Helsinki Corpus* (N = number of switches, ASL = average switch length in words)

	Old English			Middle English			Early Modern English		
	N	/1,000	ASL	N	/1,000	ASL	N	/1,000	ASL
Arabic	--	--	--	--	--	--	3	0.01	1.0
French	--	--	--	21	0.03	14.1	5	0.01	2.2
Greek	7	0.02	1.9	2	0.00	1.0	34	0.06	8.1
Italian	--	--	--	--	--	--	2	0.00	2.5
Latin	744	1.80	4.7	1,315	2.16	5.1	500	0.91	5.0
Spanish	--	--	--	--	--	--	5	0.01	1.4
Unknown	1	0.00	13.0	--	--	--	2	0.00	1.0

(1) Drihten herede & þus cwæð: **Qui facit angelos suos spiritus et ministros suos ignem urentem**; Hwilum se ilca God sendeþ his engla gastas to ærendwrecum, hwilum he sendeþ þurh fyres leg. (O2/3 950-1050, *Homily, Blickling Homilies* 17, R 111)

(2) Þo he sei þat he ne moste . habbe churche peis . / **Par crist** he sede sir tomas . **tu es Maveis** . / **Meint ben te ay fet** . vor he adde muche god . / Þer biuore him ido .& he it vuele vnderstod . (M2 1250-1350, *History*, Robert of Gloucester, 738)

(3) S. *Ignatius* when he had spoken of *Elias*, and *Titus*, and *Clement*, [...] gives this testimony, they were τοῖς γάμοις προσομιλήσαντες οὐχ ὑπό προθυμίας τῆς περὶ τὸ πρᾶγμα ἀλλ' ἐπ' ἐννοίας ἑαυτῶν τοῦ γένους ἔσχον ἐκείνους, that they might not be disparaged in their great names of holiness and severity, they were secured by not marrying to satisfie their

---

[7] Cf. e.g. Rothwell (1991) and Nurmi and Pahta (2004).
[8] Discounting single word switches does not greatly affect the overall picture in Table 2. Greek disappears from Middle English, and Arabic and the unknown language from Early Modern English. Otherwise, each category shows a slight decline in frequency and a slight rise in average switch length.

lower appetites, but out of desire of children. (E3 1640-1710, Sermon, Jeremy Taylor, 13)

Other languages found in the corpus, though only in the EModE period, are Arabic, Italian and Spanish; most instances occur in Samuel Pepys's diary, illustrated in example (4).

(4) Mrs. Martin ... doth tell me that this child did come **la meme jour** that it ought to **hazer** after my **avoir ete con elle** before her **marido** did **venir** home. And she would now have done anything **cum ego**; and did endeavour, but **su cosa stava mala**, which did **empescar**. Thence to the Swan, and there I sent for Sarah and mighty merry we were, but **contra** my will were very far from **hazer algo**. (E3 1640-1710, Diary, Samuel Pepys, VII, 413)

Three passages are classified as 'unknown language'. Example (5) is an OE incantation in a procedure of turning butter into a holy salve. While the charm is probably based on a real language, it has become a garbled rendering of the original.[9]

(5) Styre þonne mid ðy sticcan ða buteran, eal þæt fæt, ðu sing ofer ðas sealmas, **Beati immaculati**, ælcne ðriwa ofer, & **gloria in excelsis deo**, & **Credo in deum patrem**, & letanias arime ofer, þæt is ðara haligra naman & **deus meus et pater, et in principio**, & þæt wyrmgealdor, & þis gealdor singe ofer: *Acre arcre arnem nona ærnem beoðor ærnem / nidren arcun cunað ele harassan fidine* (O2/3 950-1050, Handbook Medicine, *Lacnunga*, R 63.9)

The unknown language in the EModE period is the word *otan*, referring to a harem (example (6)). It may be based on the Turkish word *oda* 'room' (cf. Turkish *odalïk* 'concubine, odalisk').

(6) and that if he cou'd circumvent him, and redeem her from the **otan**, which is the Palace of the King's Women (E3 1640-1710, Fiction, Aphra Behn, *Oroonoko*, 160)

---

[9] The editors of the text point out that while the incantation is probably based on a real language, this is a garbled form of the original, "gibberish" (Grattan and Singer 1972:125).

Table 2 also shows the average switch length for each language in each period. Latin switches average steadily at around five words, while French in Middle English reaches 14.1, and Greek in Early Modern English 8.1 words. We assume that average switch length reflects at least to some extent the writer's competence in the language of the switches.

3. Code-switching in relation to textual parameters in the *Helsinki Corpus*

In order to obtain knowledge about the possible language-external factors affecting multilingual practices in the periods covered by the *Helsinki Corpus*, we have analysed code-switching in relation to the textual parameters that have been coded into the corpus to provide extralinguistic background information about the texts. Twenty-five different textual parameters are used in the *Helsinki Corpus* (Kytö 1996:43-44). While some of them are not relevant for our research (e.g. 'name of text file', 'sample' and 'page'), others, such as 'text type', 'audience description' or 'relationship to spoken language', provide a fruitful starting point for the study of extralinguistic features connected to switching. For the sake of completeness, we have studied all 18 relevant textual parameters coded in the *Helsinki Corpus*, but in this paper we mainly focus on the two which showed the clearest trends and patterns: 'prototypical text category' and 'text type'.

3.1 Prototypical text category

The parameter 'prototypical text category' has seven possible values: expository, religious instruction, secular instruction, imaginative narration, non-imaginative narration, statutory and other (Kytö 1996: 55). As Table 3 shows, there is great variation in the frequency of switches between the values, as well as chronological variation within some values. Average frequencies (2 per 1,000 words in Old English and Middle English, 1 per 1,000 words in Early Modern English) are most clearly surpassed in most periods in expository texts, secular instruction and religious instruction. Of these, expository texts (typically scientific or educational) show a declining trend across time, as do secular instructive texts. Religious instruction, however, remains consistently above the average.

Table 3. Code-switching and prototypical text category (N = number of switches, ASL = average switch length in words)

Prototypical text category	Old English			Middle English			Early Modern English		
	N	/1,000	ASL	N	/1,000	ASL	N	/1,000	ASL
Expository	82	15.3	2.1	36	5.6	2.6	201	3.7	3.9
Religious instruction	329	3.3	5.4	746	3.5	6.6	114	3.5	8.9
Secular instruction	161	6.0	3.8	205	3.9	4.5	36	0.7	8.0
Imaginative narration	13	0.8	2.3	29	0.3	4.8	11	0.3	1.6
Non-imaginative narration	110	1.3	3.5	72	0.7	3.8	114	0.8	3.9
Statutory	8	0.5	4.8	13	1.0	4.2	10	0.3	2.4
Other	48	0.3	6.2	237	1.8	2.4	65	0.3	3.4

A different pattern emerges when the length of switched passages is considered: expository and instructive texts (both religious and secular) demonstrate a marked increase in average switch length during the thousand years studied. Statutory texts on the other hand show a declining trend, and imaginative narration peaks during Middle English only to decline again.

3.2 Text type

The *Helsinki Corpus* has material from a number of genres, or text types, as they are called in the corpus parameters. The inventory of categories varies slightly from subperiod to subperiod, according to the availability of texts in each genre (Kytö 1996:51-52). The number of text types ranges from 16 to 21 in the different subperiods; some text types, e.g. science and handbooks, have been broken down into further subcategories. For our study, all subcategories have been collapsed under their main category. Table 4 shows instances of code-switching according to text type.

Table 4. Code-switching and text type (N = number of switches, ASL = average switch length in words)

Text type	Old English			Middle English			Early Modern English		
	N	/1,000	ASL	N	/1,000	ASL	N	/1,000	ASL
Bible	4	0.1	2.0	1	0.0	1.0	0	0	0
Biography	35	1.0	3.7	10	0.4	6.1	10	0.3	6.7
Diary	--	--	--	--	--	--	31	0.8	2.0
Document	19	1.3	12.8	11	0.4	5.3	--	--	--
Drama	--	--	--	195	9.7	2.2	28	0.8	2.0
Educational treatise	--	--	--	--	--	--	43	1.3	4.9
Fiction	2	0.3	8.0	22	0.7	5.6	11	0.3	1.6
Geography	9	5.3	1.0	--	--	--	--	--	--
Handbook	21	1.0	9.8	195	4.2	4.7	30	0.9	9.1
History	75	1.4	3.4	59	0.9	3.4	21	0.6	3.5
Homily	53	1.9	7.1	210	4.4	9.2	--	--	--
Law	8	0.5	4.8	10	0.9	3.1	10	0.3	2.4
Letter (nonprivate)	--	--	--	12	1.5	3.8	4	0.2	2.8
Letter (private)	--	--	--	9	0.5	3.1	13	0.4	5.8
Philosophy	0	0	0	6	0.4	3.2	5	0.2	3.4
Preface/ Epilogue	5	1.3	44.6	6	1.0	3.2	--	--	--
Proceeding, deposition	--	--	--	0	0	0	--	--	--
Proceeding, trial	--	--	--	--	--	--	15	0.3	4.0
Religious treatise	185	4.2	5.6	263	2.0	5.7	--	--	--
Romance	--	--	--	7	0.1	2.3	--	--	--
Rule	90	3.6	3.9	51	7.1	4.4	--	--	--
Science	222	23.5	2.6	46	4.6	2.3	164	4.4	3.6
Sermon	--	--	--	225	5.9	5.8	114	3.5	8.9
Travelogue	2	0.3	2.5	0	0	0	52	1.3	4.6
Other	20	0.3	1.6	0	0	0	--	--	--

The most striking feature in Table 4 is the frequency of switches in OE scientific treatises. Also ME and EModE scientific texts clearly have more switches than the average of 1-2 per 1,000 words.[10] This is largely due to the frequency of code-switched technical terminology, a special category that is traditionally often regarded as a subtype of borrowing (see section 4.1 below). During Middle English, handbooks and homilies also show higher than average frequencies, while in Early Modern English, sermons peak above most other categories. The frequency of switching remains fairly constant in many text types across time. The text types bible, biography, fiction, history, law, philosophy and travelogue stay mostly well below the average throughout the whole timespan of the corpus, although in Early Modern English, the text type travelogue comes slightly above the average for the subperiod.

Some text types are not represented in all three periods of the corpus so that long-term diachronic patterns cannot be perceived for the whole timespan. Of these, code-switching is frequent in OE geographical texts, ME drama, ME homilies, OE and ME religious treatises and rules, and ME and EModE sermons.[11]

The average switch length for text types manifests clear trends. Compared to the average of five words, OE fiction, handbooks and homilies clearly stand out. In Middle English, the switch length of biography shows an increase, and homilies/sermons stay clearly above average, while switches in handbooks shorten. In Early Modern English, handbooks and sermons again lead, and biography has continued to gain switch length. The shortest switches in all

---

[10] When single word switches are discounted, the frequency in science in the OE period is halved, but still remains clearly above most other text types. In the case of Early Modern English, also, removing one-word switches leaves science clearly above the average frequency. In Middle English, there is no dramatic decline in numbers.

[11] Of the text types where code-switching is frequent, OE geography, ME drama and OE and ME religious treatises and rules show a decline in frequency when single word switches are discounted. In the case of OE geography, code-switching disappears entirely, whereas the other text types continue to show above average frequencies of switching.

subperiods can be found in the categories bible, geography and 'other'.

3.3 Other parameters

When analysing switching with regard to the textual parameters coded into the *Helsinki Corpus*, it became clear that the domain of texts was the most decisive factor. Texts connected with religion or science seem to favour switching. As noted above, the prototypical text categories which lead in frequency of switching are expository and religious instruction. Similarly, the text types where switching most frequently occurs are science, homily and sermon. Further evidence for the importance of domain is seen in the patterning of switching with some other parameters in the *Helsinki Corpus*.

Relationship to spoken language is a parameter only coded for Middle and Early Modern English (Kytö 1996:53). In the *Helsinki Corpus* switches show most frequently in scripted texts, i.e. texts written to be spoken. These are mostly homilies and sermons, where the frequency of switching may, however, be due to the religious content rather than the relationship to spoken language. Switch length shows a rising trend in scripted texts across time.

Intended audiences of texts have been coded as non-professional, professional or unknown (Kytö 1996:54). In Middle English, rather surprisingly, texts targeted at non-professional audiences show the most frequent switching. This is on account of handbooks, which deal mostly with scientific matters. Sermons and homilies have been coded 'unknown' (X) with regard to this parameter. In Early Modern English, however, it is texts aimed at professional audiences that contain more switching: the texts in question are mainly scientific and educational, hence the domain of science is once more relevant.

Looking at average switch length and audience description, we see that in Middle English average-length switches occur in texts targeted at non-professional audiences, while texts aimed at professionals contain clearly shorter switches. In Early Modern English, texts for non-professional audiences show greater than average switch length, whereas texts for professionals approach the average.

4. Discourse functions

In terms of discourse features, the code-switched segments in the *Helsinki Corpus* can be classified into distinct though partly overlapping categories that occur with varying frequency in the different text types and individual texts in the different periods. Much of the switching consists of prefabricated or formulaic chunks or conventionalised textual practices, whereas the kind of 'free' switching common in present-day spoken bilingual discourse is rare. An illustration of this latter type in our data is given in example (4) above, showing Samuel Pepys's use of multilingual resources. In this overview, we shall concentrate on the most frequent discourse functions in which switching is found in the data, commenting on the occurrence of code-switched segments in technical terminology, text-organising functions, quotations, references and dates, as well as on the occurrence of various kinds of conventionalised chunks. Most types are particularly characteristic of texts belonging to the scientific and religious domains. In many cases the switched segments simultaneously serve multiple discourse functions.

4.1 Terminology

Code-switched technical terms are common in the *Helsinki Corpus* throughout the whole timespan and in many text types. They are an important feature of special-language discourse, and particularly frequent in scientific treatises, handbooks, and religious texts, but also in legal documents; examples are given under (7) and (8). Some culture-specific items occurring e.g. in travelogues or in fiction (see example (6) above) can be included in this category. The same applies to professional or culture-specific designations (example (9)). Many of the items in this category belong to the controversial cline between code-switching and borrowing – one of the most challenging theoretical and practical issues in code-switching research in general.[12] In this study we have chosen to include these items,

---

[12] For discussions of code-switching vs. borrowing in historical code-switching research, see Schendl (2000), Pahta (2004a), or Nurmi and Pahta (2004).

consisting of single nouns or multi-word noun phrases, among code-switches, being aware that their exclusion would somewhat change the frequency patterns of code-switching in the data.

(7) The fift sorte doth containe all other fashions of foure cornered figurs, and ar called of the Grekes **trapezia**, of Latin mē **mensulae** and of Arabitians, **helmuariphe**, they may be called in englishe *borde formes* (E1 1500-1570, Science Other, Robert Record, B4R)

(8) Giet is an oðer derne senne ðe me and maniȝe oðre saule hafð beswiken. Hie hatte **tristicia**, þat is, sarinesse. Þes is an of ðe heued-sennes, ðeih hie dierne bie. Hie is icleped sarinesse, **tristicia mortem operante**, 'sarinesse deað wurchende,' for ðan hire ofþingþ of alle gode ðe aȝunnen bieð for godes luue te donne. (M1 1150-1250, Religious Treatise, *Vices and Virtues* 1, 3)

(9) Ic ðonne Wlfred mid Godes gaefe **archiepiscopus** ðas forecuaedenan word fulliae, & bebeode ... (O1-850, Document, Harmer 1 R 12)

4.2 Textual organisation

Switched segments frequently serve text-organising functions in many text types throughout the whole period. Again, particularly religious texts, scientific texts and handbooks make regular use of code-switching to indicate textual boundaries: examples (10) and (11) illustrate the use of Latin in titles and chapter headings or the beginnings and endings of texts. Example (12) is from a ME mystery play, where stage directions are often in Latin (cf. Diller 1997/8). In some cases, code-switching co-occurs with a shift to an embedded text, such as a prayer, a recipe, or a charm, as in the trilingual example (13), where the language changes several times.

(10) **AD DENTES. DE CAUSA DOLORUM DENTIUM. TO ÞAN TOÞE.**
Þes lacecraft ys to ðan menniscan toþan ðat grecas nemneþ **organum.** þt ys ... (MX/1 1150-1250, Handbook Medicine, Peri Didaxeon, 102)

(11) in recognysaunce of this gracyous benefyte of remyssyon we may lovyngly prayse God as I exhortyd you before, sayeng, **Laudate, Pueri, Dominum**, graunt us all, **Cryste Jhesus Splendor Patris, corona Innocencium. Amen. Explicit sermo ista**. (M4 1420-1500, Sermon, *In Die Innocencium*, 12-3)

(12) **Satanas incipit dicens**: For woo my witte es in a were ... (M4 1420-1500, Mystery Play, The York Plays, 64)

(13) I vndurstonde schal hele an hors for þe farcioun ful wel. A charme for þe same. **Dytez ceste charme par .iij. iors apres le solayl couchaunte sur le chyual uers le west turne primez pater noster hysmabet pater noster mechay pater noster amathanay pater noster Crux Christi amen pater noster. Cinke foyrz dirrs cest charme. par .iij. iours outre le chyual & par seux. iij. iours ne doit le chyual este en bon erre ne prouendre mag ne ewe currant passer mays selk fame manguse & garra.** ffor þe farcyn & for þe feloun a good charme. **In nomine patris & filij & spiritus sancti amen. Ie te coniure felon ou farcyn ou verme male suz d[a]uant par dieu omnipotent de ceel & de terre & de solial & de lune & de tutz creaturis & de sent autres & de sent abbes & de sent euesqes bien atturnes com de messes chauntere de nuit de noele & de la paylle so[?] dount deu fuit en-volupe si tu i es ne demurrez niemt si tu ne es ne entres poynt al nom du pere & fitz & saunt espyrit te coniure qe tu ne augz. Ceo ditz troi foitz outre le best & garra.** Or ellus take þe rede nettel. & þe popi rote. (M3 1350-1420, Handbook Medicine, A LME Treatise on Horses, 97-99)

4.3 Quotations

Code-switched quotations are frequent throughout the corpus especially in scientific treatises, handbooks, sermons, homilies, religious treatises and rules, but also in some educational treatises and travelogues. Examples are given in (1) to (3) above. Switched quotations can also be regarded as a subcategory of textual organisation, as code-switching occurs at a boundary between different levels of text. They are also related to the next category of switches, references, as both quotations and references can be interpreted as indications of intertextuality.

4.4 References

References are particularly common in ME scientific texts and sermons. As examples (14) to (16) show, they vary in specificity: some only contain a general reference to a text by its Latin title, whereas others refer to a specific *locus* in a text.

(14) And þay beeþ 8 in nombre, after Galien in **4ᵗᵒ De Vtilitate** and **6ᵗᵒ Terapeutice**, þat is to say, two longitudinales (i. longe synowes) (MX/4 1420-1500, Science Medicine, Guy de Chauliac, 57)

(15) þer was neuer man aʒeyn-seid hym into oure tyme, as Seynt Thomas writeþ, **prima parte Summe, questione 61, articulo 3ᵒ, in pede**? (M3/4 1420-1500, Sermon, Royal, 253)

(16) ther vnto we shall bynde hym by his owne reason. he sayth in the booke **de captiuitate babilonica** (E1 1500-1570, Sermon, John Fisher, P1,314)

4.5 Dates

Code-switched dates are especially frequent in historical writings, but they occur sporadically in many other text types, e.g. letters and various kinds of handbooks and scientific treatises.

(17) se mona aþystrode on þære nihte **Nonæ Aprilis** . & wæs **x iiii luna** .(O4 1050-1150, History, Chronicle MS E, R 1121.5)

(18) Writen at Cales the xvij day off Maii, **Anᵒ. ut supra**. Be your ffeythffull servaunt, Thomas Betson. (M4 1420-1500, Correspondence (private), Betson II 47)

4.6 Conventionalised chunks

Most text types contain sporadic instances of various kinds of conventionalised chunks, including religious phrases (example (19)), names of prayers or psalms (example (5) above), and formulaic expressions like *per annum* (example (20)) that border on borrowing.

(19) **In nomine Domini nostri Ihesu Christi** Ic Aelfred aldormon ond Werburg min gefera begetan ðas bec ... (O2 850-950, Document, Aureus, R 1)

(20) The first I may call *mixt Schooles*, where a structure is made, and an allowance given of ten, twenty, or thirty pounds **per annum** onely to one man to teach children (E3 1640-1710, Educational Treatise, Charles Hoole, S3, 213)

5. Conclusion

In this study we have examined code-switching in a long diachronic perspective in the multi-genre *Helsinki Corpus*. Considering that the *Helsinki Corpus* was compiled to represent the English language, code-switching in the texts is fairly frequent. There are in fact surprisingly few texts in the corpus with no instances of code-switching. The language of the switches is predominantly Latin, although other languages do appear. The frequency of switching declines somewhat in the EModE period, but the average length of switches remains constant.

When analysing switching with regard to the various textual parameters coded into the *Helsinki Corpus*, it became clear that the domain of texts was the most decisive factor. Any texts connected with religion or science seem to favour switching. In this respect, the results of our study are in line with studies by e.g. Wenzel (1994), Voigts (1996) and Pahta (2004a), which have shown that medieval texts in these domains are characterized by multilingualism. The prototypical text categories of the *Helsinki Corpus* which exhibit most switching are expository and religious instruction, and the text types where switching most frequently occurs are science, homily and sermon. The prevalence of switching in scripted language is again due to homilies and sermons. The high frequency of switching in ME texts for a non-professional audience is due to handbooks, which mostly deal with scientific matters.

The discourse functions attested in the corpus are fairly conventional, whereas free, creative use of multilingual resources is rare. This could be interpreted in terms of a lack of linguistic competence: the authors of these texts may not have been fluently multilingual. On the other hand, switching for example in religious contexts may not allow for free variation, since it deals with the accepted dogma of the church, and faithful repetition of the set formulations can be regarded as a distinctive feature of the domain. Similarly, the use of scientific terminology, as well as quotation of and reference to earlier authors, is a well established practice throughout the whole domain of science.

With this overall view of code-switching practices attested in English texts over a thousand years we hope to have provided other researchers with a baseline for comparisons. We intend to continue analysing the data collected for this study in more detail, focusing particularly on the microlevel of variation between individual texts.

References

Adams, J.N. 2003. *Bilingualism and the Latin language*. Cambridge: CUP.
Adams, J.N., Mark Janse and Simon Swain (eds.). 2002. *Bilingualism in ancient society: language contact and the written text*. Oxford: OUP.
Argenter, Joan A. 2001. "Code-switching and dialogism: verbal practices among Catalan Jews in the Middle Ages". *Language in Society* 30: 377-402.
Callahan, Laura. 2004. *Spanish/English codeswitching in a written corpus*. Amsterdam and Philadelphia: Benjamins.
Clyne, Michael. 2003. *Dynamics of language contact*. Cambridge: CUP.
Diller, Hans-Jürgen. 1997/8. "Code-switching in medieval English drama". *Comparative Drama* 31: 506-537.
Dossena, Marina. 2002. "*A strong Scots accent of the mind*: the pragmatic value of code-switching between English and Scots in private correspondence – a historical overview". *Linguistica e Filologia* 14: 103-125.
Graedler, Anne-Line. 1999. "Where English and Norwegian meet: codeswitching in written texts". In: Hasselgård, Hilde and Signe Oksefjell (eds.). *Out of corpora: studies in honour of Stig Johansson*. Amsterdam and Atlanta: Rodopi: 327-343.
Grattan, J.H.G. and Charles Singer. 1952 [1972]. *Anglo-Saxon magic and medicine, illustrated specially from the semi-pagan text 'Lacnunga'*. London: Richard West.
Helsinki Corpus of English Texts. 1991. Compiled at the Department of English, University of Helsinki. Available through ICAME: (http://helmer.hit.uib.no/english/icame-pro.htm) and the Oxford Text Archive (http://ota.ahds.ac.uk/).

Kytö, Merja (comp.). 1991 [1996]. *Manual to the diachronic part of The Helsinki Corpus of English Texts. Coding conventions and source texts*. 3rd ed. Helsinki: Department of English, University of Helsinki. Online: http://helmer.aksis.uib.no/icame/hc/index.htm.
Myers-Scotton, Carol. 2002. *Contact linguistics: bilingual encounters and grammatical outcomes*. Oxford: OUP.
Nurmi, Arja and Päivi Pahta. 2004. "Social stratification and patterns of code-switching in early English letters". *Multilingua* 23: 417-456.
Pahta, Päivi. 2003. "On structures of code-switching in medical texts from medieval England". *Neuphilologische Mitteilungen* 104/2: 197-210.
Pahta, Päivi. 2004a. "Code-switching in medieval medical writing". In: Taavitsainen, Irma and Päivi Pahta (eds.). *Medical and scientific writing in late medieval English*. Cambridge: CUP: 73-99.
Pahta, Päivi. 2004b. "*So seiþ idem comentator*: code-switching and organisation of knowledge in John Trevisa's translation of *De Proprietatibus Rerum*". In: Rodríguez Álvarez, Alicia and Francisco Alonso Almeida (eds.). *Voices on the past: studies in Old and Middle English language and literature*. La Coruña: Netbiblo: 35-48.
Pahta, Päivi. forthcoming. "On code-switching in Early Modern English medical texts".
Pahta, Päivi and Arja Nurmi. forthcoming. "*What we do cón amore*: code-switching in eighteenth-century personal letters". In: Bueno-Alonso, Jorge, Dolores Gonzales-Alvarez, Javier Perez-Guerra and Esperanza Rama-Martinez (eds.). *'Of varying language and opposing creed': new insights into Late Modern English*. Bern: Lang.
Rissanen, Matti, Merja Kytö and Minna Palander-Collin (eds.). 1993. *Early English in the computer age: explorations through the Helsinki Corpus*. Berlin: de Gruyter.
Rothwell, William. 1991. "The missing link in English etymology: Anglo French". *Medium Ævum* 60: 173-196.
Schendl, Herbert. 2000. "Linguistic aspects of code-switching in medieval English texts". In: Trotter, D.A. (ed.). *Multilingualism in Later Medieval Britain*. Cambridge: Brewer: 77-92.
Schendl, Herbert. 2001. "Code-switching in medieval English poetry". In: Kastovsky, Dieter and Arthur Mettinger (eds.). *Language contact in the history of English*. Frankfurt/M.: Lang: 305-335.
Schendl, Herbert. 2002. "Mixed-language texts as data and evidence in English historical linguistics". In: Minkova, Donka and Robert Stockwell (eds.). *Studies in the history of the English language: a millennial perspective*. Berlin: de Gruyter: 51-78.
Schendl, Herbert. 2004. "*Hec sunt prata to* wassingwellan: aspects of code-switching in Old English charters". *Vienna English Working Papers* 13/2: 52-68.

Sharp, Harriet. 2001. *English in spoken Swedish: a corpus study of two discourse domains*. Stockholm: Almqvist and Wiksells.
Trotter, D.A. (ed.). 2000. *Multilingualism in later medieval Britain*. Cambridge: Brewer.
Voigts, Linda Ehrsam. 1996. "What's the word? Bilingualism in late-medieval England". *Speculum* 71: 813-826.
Wenzel, Siegfried. 1994. *Macaronic sermons: bilingualism and preaching in late-medieval England*. Ann Arbor, Mich.: The University of Michigan Press.
Wright, Laura. 1994. "Early Modern London Business English". In: Kastovsky, Dieter (ed.). *Studies in Early Modern English*. Berlin: de Gruyter: 449-465.
Wright, Laura. 1998. "Mixed-language business writing: five hundred years of code-switching". In: Jahr, Ernst Håkon (ed.). *Language change: advances in historical sociolinguistics*. Berlin: de Gruyter: 99-118.

Tamás Eitler
Audience rules: interspeaker accommodation and intraspeaker syntactic variation in Late Middle English[1]

1. The role of interspeaker accommodation in intraspeaker variation and language change

In many cases the most obvious proves to be the least explored, and we often find areas in which much of what we seem to have accumulated a sufficient amount of knowledge has in fact remained *terra incognita*. With a view to gaining some new insights into the mechanism of variation and change through tackling the obvious, this paper deals with some audience-related communicative aspects of the variation between V2 and V3 word orders in the context of main clause non-operator fronting in the LME period. Intraspeaker variation is exemplified in (1) and (2) below, taken from John Capgrave. Whereas (1) shows the outgoing V2 order, (2) displays the incoming V3 pattern in the mid-15th century.

(1) To pore men gaf he þese goodys...
    (*The Life of Saint Gilbert*, 77.7)
    'He gave these goods to the poor...'

(2) Euery day sche offered for him at þe auter; euery day sche gaf elmesse. (*The Life of Saint Augustine*, 14.12)
    'Every day she offered for him sacrifice at the altar; every day she gave alms.'

To explain such trivial variation, we must look beyond the stock answers and investigate the causes rooted in communication itself. Accordingly, a major communicative aspect directly deriving from an interactional situation is the influence of the target audience. It will be claimed that it is accommodation to this audience that accounts for

---

[1] Let me thank the two anonymous reviewers for their very detailed and useful comments, which made it possible to improve the paper considerably. Naturally, all remaining errors are my own.

intraspeaker variation when the variable grammar in different works of the same author cannot be explained by other influences like copying, text type, translational interference, and medium. In some cases both text type and target audience can equally well explain the different variational character of texts by the same author. However, it will be pointed out that text types and the texts themselves can be regarded as mere projections of the audience, whose language in turn is socially defined.

As the present study deals with written texts, indirect communication is the focus of our investigation. Accordingly, one can adopt the identity-projection model of accommodation, which holds that adjustment occurs on the basis of the communicator's mental representation of the linguistic behaviour of absent target audiences rather than on the basis of ambient usage frequencies typical of present audiences (Auer and Hinskens 2005:337-338). The frameworks which capture such adjustment processes are called Communication Accommodation Theory (henceforth CAT) and Audience Design.

Linguistic accommodation between interlocutors both in the short and the long term can modify the linguistic evidence available to the learners. Based on numerous experiments, the social-psychological model of CAT holds that interlocutors can converge or diverge linguistically (Giles and Coupland 1991; Giles et al. 1991). Accommodation must not, however, be seen as mere imitation, and in a broader sense it rather means adjustment to the situation itself. In accordance with this, under the newer versions of CAT it can be sufficient to approximate to the interlocutor's features at a rate that does not match the perceived rate of frequency.

Short-term accommodation can be defined as adjustment at the level of discrete, particular conversational interactions. This, however, can lead to long-term accommodation at the level of the individual through the cumulative effect of countless acts of short-term linguistic adjustments pointing to the same direction. By contrast, long-term accommodation can be defined as semi-permanent changes in an individual's habitual speech after a period of contact with interlocutors using different varieties (Kerswill 2002:680, citing

Trudgill 1986:11-38). These long-term individual changes, counting as the modified linguistic input, are acquired by the next generation of speakers, who will come up with usage frequencies appearing to be the default, i.e. unaccommodated, grammar for the even newer generations. Meanwhile, however, these grammars can also undergo long-term individual accommodation and thus usage frequencies can shift further naturally. As a cumulative consequence of such long-term individual adjustment, accommodation becomes observable at the level of the population in the form of change. It must be seen, however, that short-term accommodation can also lead directly to gradual change in other speakers as even transitional individual frequency shifts can temporarily serve as input to a number of ambient learners, who continuously calculate usage frequencies of the target grammar, and who do not ignore any material in the input (cf. Clark and Roberts 1993).

Under the behavioural frequency model of accommodation, interlocutors calculate each other's usage frequencies for given variants so that they can converge on or adjust away from these frequencies. An essential element of this model is that frequency of direct interaction is instrumental in short-term accommodation becoming long term, the prerequisite of language change (Auer and Hinskens 2005:336-338). Studies supporting the identity-projection model show that speakers accommodate as they wish to identify with a reference group, which represents some type of social prestige for the speaker. Auer and Hinskens add that it is necessary that the converging speakers have some knowledge of the language of the reference group although neither frequency of contact nor direct contact is essential for accommodation.

Adjustment is understood to take place in direct, face-to-face communication. In line with the aforementioned influence of non-present audiences, accommodation, however, is claimed to occur also in indirect communication, when the audience is not present. It can be claimed that identity-projection may have a more important role in indirect than in direct communication, where the actual frequencies of the audience can be calculated with more precision. The present study deals with texts that represent acts of indirect communication resulting in short-term shifts in usage frequencies calculated on percentages associated with audiences. On the basis of the identity-projection model, one can even regard intraspeaker variation due to text type as a form of accommodation to different linguistic images associated with text type conventions. The audience effect, however, is still there: different text types and the texts themselves eventually cater for different audiences (cf. section 3).

Rooted in CAT, the Audience Design model was advanced and reworked by Bell (1984; 2001) to explain the exact nature of audience influence. Under this model, intraspeaker style shifts respond to audience members whom the individual contacts. Importantly, however, this response is not precise, and Bell (1984:158) thinks that speakers only try to approach the usage frequencies. This imperfect response justifies the introduction of speaker agency into the newer versions of the model: according to this, speakers are claimed to initiate shifts which do not exactly respond to the linguistic composition of the actual audiences.

Audience Design contributes considerably to the understanding of accommodation processes, which is also evident in that besides the nature of matching, the degree of variation and the relative influence of the audience have been examined, and axioms have been advanced based on a number of sociolinguistic surveys. A case in point is that topic-related and setting-related effects are claimed to be derivative of audience-related effects (Bell 1984:180). For example, when individuals seem to shift styles topicwise, this shift is according to addressees who are associated with the given topics and settings. This generalisation can be captured in the implicational scale in (3) below:

(3) register variation according to audience[2] > register variation according to topic and setting

---

[2] For convenience, in the present study the term 'audience' is used for addressees; in the more recent models of Audience Design, however, audience can consist not only of addressees but also of auditors, overhearers and eavesdroppers. The implicational scale is modelled on the one used by Nevalainen and Raumolin-Brunberg (2003: 191; 200).

In the present study variation according to topic and setting are regarded to constitute text type variation as text types themselves largely depend on the choice of topic and setting. Therefore the scale in (3) can be substituted with the one in (4):

(4) register variation according to audience > register variation according to text type

Bell provides a further generalisation which predicts that the degree of register variation will be smaller than that of social variation (Bell 1984:151; 2001:145). This axiom was tested in historical sociolinguistic investigations. On the basis of the findings for the supralocalising features in ME and EModE personal correspondence, Nevalainen and Raumolin-Brunberg (2003:200) generalise that the degree of register variation according to addressee is smaller than that of social variation. This can be shown as (5):

(5) social variation > register variation according to audience

This means that audience effects are derivative of social effects: ultimately, the language of an audience is always socially defined. By scrutinising social variation further, Nevalainen and Raumolin-Brunberg (2003:200) advance that the extent of regional variation exceeds that of gender variation, as illustrated in (6):

(6) regional variation > gender variation

The aforementioned hierarchical implications can be represented in a somewhat simplified form in (7) below:

(7) social effects (regional effects > gender effects) > audience effects > text type effects

Importantly, this implicational scale also predicts that it is the dialect and sociolect of the audiences that will define the language of the text types used by the given author. Thus, intraspeaker variation, as evidenced in the different variational character in a given author's texts, may be ultimately traced back to the distributional frequency of the dialect and sociolect features of the target audiences. In the following two sections, the prediction of the implicational scale in (7) will be verified through a case study from the LME period.

2. Accommodation in John Capgrave

The four prose works of John Capgrave investigated in the present study provide an excellent basis for testing the extent of the influence of various factors in the adjustment process. This is mainly because of two characteristics of these texts. First, Capgrave's English prose oeuvre represents three text types: following Bækken's (2002) terminology, the *Sermon* (1452) can be regarded as 'religious prose', the *Abbreuiacion of Cronicles* (1464; henceforth *Chronicle*) can be classified as 'history', whereas *The Life of Saint Augustine* (shortly before 1451; henceforth *Augustine*) and *The Life of Saint Gilbert* (1451; henceforth *Gilbert*) are in between these two categories. Second, all of these works are holographs. As can be seen in Table 1, usage frequencies are different in the four texts.[3]

Table 1. Frequencies of V2 and V3 in John Capgrave's prose works

Texts	nominal subject				pronominal subject			
	V2	Rate of V2	V3	Rate of V3	V2	Rate of V2	V3	Rate of V3
Sermon	4	100%	0	0%	10	91%	1	9%
Augustine	48	67%	24	33%	85	61%	54	39%
Gilbert	51	67%	25	33%	84	56%	66	44%
Chronicle	503	54%	426	46%	107	48%	117	52%

The *Sermon* has a systematic CP-V2 syntax, as evidenced in the behaviour of the pronominal subjects, which invert with the tensed verb at a rate of 91 per cent whereas V2 with nominal subjects is completely systematic. *Augustine* and *Gilbert* show a considerable erosion of inversion both with nominal and pronominal subjects. V2 is stronger in the case of nominal subjects, where two thirds of the clauses show inversion. A larger degree of erosion can be seen in the case of clauses with pronominal subjects. This means that besides a still relatively strong CP-V2 grammar, these two texts show a

---

[3] The full text versions of these works were examined. In the *Sermon* the small number of four nominal subject occurrences cannot provide statistically reliable results. However, the CP-V2 syntax of this text can be diagnosed on the basis of the presence of inversion with pronominal subjects (see Eitler 2006).

considerable intrusion of V3. Further erosion can be seen in the *Chronicle*, in which V2 is the majority variant in clauses with nominal subjects, and pronominal subjects trigger V2 in slightly less than half of the clauses. Here again one can witness the competition of the CP-V2 and V3 variants.

Among the possible text type-related factors explaining this divergent intraspeaker behaviour medium and style may seem the most plausible.[4] Let us first investigate the difference between the *Sermon* and the *Chronicle*. Since sermons are as a rule spoken and thus may tend to be more informal than most written texts, they could be expected to have a high rate of the innovative V3 variant. Even if a sermon is written down after it has been preached, which was the case with Capgrave's *Sermon*, the spoken features can be claimed to be preserved to some extent. In the same way, since chronicles as a rule represent a written tradition and hence also may tend to be somewhat more formal, they could be expected to have a high rate of the conservative V2 variant. These expectations, however, are not borne out by the data. While it can be seen that the rate of V2 is fairly high in the *Chronicle*, it is almost the default choice in the *Sermon*. Therefore one has to consider two other possible factors underlying the divergent syntactic behaviour of these two texts. The first of these is the possible difference in the time of composition, the second is the language of the target audience of the texts. Since presumably the 12-year time gap between the *Sermon* and the *Chronicle* could not have witnessed a drop of 46 per cent (with nominal subjects) and 43 per cent (with pronominal subjects) in usage frequency, one is left with the possible influence of the audience.

Before investigating this audience-related factor, let us first discuss whether the aforementioned arguments still hold for the variation in Capgrave's texts when *Augustine* and *Gilbert*, too, are considered. As regards medium and style, both *Gilbert* and *Augustine* represent the conservative written tradition of saints' lives, which means that features characteristic of formal style can be expected to be dominant. As in the present case V2 is the conservative variant, the rate of V2

---

[4] This paragraph is based on Eitler (2005:97-98).

could be expected to be high. Again, these expectations are not borne out by the data. While the rate of V2 is rather high in these two works, it is even higher in the *Sermon*. It can be noted at the same time that the rate of V2 in these two texts lies between that in the *Sermon* and the *Chronicle*. As regards the time dimension, *Gilbert* was composed in 1451, and *Augustine* was written shortly before 1451 (Munro 2001:vii). This means that in the mid-15th century, Capgrave could produce both a text with systematic CP-V2 syntax and three others with a mixed grammar in which CP-V2 and V3 variants were in competition. There is a clear tendency from the CP-V2 towards the V3 syntax, but the differences in usage frequency in such chronologically close texts cannot be accounted for with the arguments provided so far.

What if the text type-related, yet derived factors used in the previous argumentation are substituted with differences in the text type itself? If one considers Bækken's statement that the text type 'history' is more innovative whereas 'religious prose' is more conservative (2002:28), one can expect that (contrary to the conservative written tradition to which it belongs) the *Chronicle* represents an innovative text type, while *Sermon* represents a conservative one. Accordingly, *Augustine* and *Gilbert* can be claimed to have an intermediate position in that they stand in between innovative and conservative text types. They both have extensive narrative parts, which may make them similar to the linguistically more innovative text type of 'history'. At the same time they are still religious in their topic area, which may make them linguistically similar to conservative religious texts. A compromise can be reached by modifying Bækken's classification and categorising *Augustine* and *Gilbert* as 'religious history'. Their intermediate text type character may then account for their intermediate syntactic behaviour. Nevertheless, even if one accepts the text type difference as the underlying cause behind the variation in Capgrave's works, one has to reckon with a rather unlikely patterning for the influence of medium and style. This is evident e.g. in the *Sermon*, which represents the spoken vernacular but is more conservative than e.g. the *Chronicle*, which stands in a more conservative written literary tradition but is more innovative in its word order. Also, a further complication is provided by *Augustine* and *Gilbert*, which seem to be relatively innovative but are more distant from the vernacular East Anglian CP-V2. In the following it will be shown that these apparent contradictions can be resolved by introducing the dimension of linguistic accommodation.

As explained in section 1 above, accommodation characterises both direct and indirect communication. In indirect communication adjustment occurs even when the usage frequencies of the reference group cannot be calculated from ambient frequencies. The *Sermon* was originally preached to a local religious community in Cambridge, which means that besides the projected frequencies, Capgrave could rely on first-hand linguistic evidence to calculate the audience's usage frequencies and thus could accommodate to his audience more precisely (cf. Eitler 2005:98). In the case of the three purely written works of Capgrave, however, one can claim that the writer had to rely on projected usage frequencies of the relatively remote target audiences. In the *Chronicle*, targeting a nationwide audience, Capgrave could opt for more widespread forms understandable in larger areas. Besides the emerging standard itself, a candidate type of a language having these forms can be the neutral regional standard (cf. Eitler 2005:98). As by the time of the composition of the *Chronicle* V3 had gained acceptance in the standard and in many dialect areas (for a detailed discussion, cf. Eitler 2006), it can be assumed that the neutral regional standard understandable *inter alia* in wider East Anglian and Central Midlands areas must have had a lower rate of the conservative variant V2. It may be exactly this lower rate that is found in the *Chronicle*.

The composition of the audience may explain the intermediate word order character of *Gilbert* and *Augustine* as well. The former work was written for the nuns at the Sempringham monastery in Southern Lincolnshire, and the latter one was commissioned by a noblewoman of unknown, though probably East Midlands residence. Building on sociolinguistic evidence (e.g. Labov 1990:213-215 and 2001:274, 292) that women tend to use a higher rate of high prestige standard variants and innovations than men, it may be claimed that

Gilbert and *Augustine* have a larger share of the innovative V3 syntax besides the conservative CP-V2 probably because they target female audiences.[5] Here, however, caution must be exercised. Nevalainen and Raumolin-Brunberg refer to evidence which shows that in the late medieval and early modern periods women favoured and promoted vernacular forms (2003:116-117). Besides the southbound diffusion of *-s*, female advantage is found in the spread of other forms originating in the vernacular (Nevalainen and Raumolin-Brunberg 2003:131). Since V3 was also spreading from the North, and since it is favoured by less formal text types (Eitler 2006:210) as well as by Bækken's (1998) innovative text type categories, it can be argued that in the LME period, the innovative vernacular V3 word order variant was presumably spreading from below the level of consciousness. Thus it is possible that women used this variant to a larger extent than men. In accordance with this, the intermediate position of these two texts between the *Sermon* and the *Chronicle* can be due to Capgrave's accommodation to female audiences having an innovative V3 syntax mixed with their dialectal CP-V2 syntax. Although female audiences seem to trigger the somewhat different usage frequencies, it must be seen that Capgrave's adjustment to the sociolect of the target audience is eventually dialectally defined. The features that are accommodated to are ultimately dialectal because the gendered audiences themselves are regionally defined (in that they could not but use a version of a conservative local dialect with CP-V2 diluted with a delocalised regional or national standard variety with V3) in the first place. This complies with the relative order in the implicational scale in (7).

---

[5] At present I can only tentatively suggest the influence of female audiences using a higher percentage of V3, the variant which was selected into the emerging standard. V3 seems to have been preferred by two well-educated East Midland/East Anglian women in the first half of the 15th century: in the *Book of Margery Kempe* (c1438) we find 87% V3 with pronominal subjects and 83% V3 with nominal subjects; in Julian of Norwich (c1450/c1400) we find 79% V3 with pronominal subjects and 69% with nominal subjects. This is in contrast with the male writers of the same region: e.g. as late as 1495 we find 51% V3 with nominal subjects and 72% V3 with pronominal subjects in Richard Fitzjames' *Sermo de Lune* (Haeberli 2002: Table 5).

In summary, it can be claimed that in Capgrave both direct and indirect accommodation to the target audience can underlie the effect of the text type. This tentative explanation can be equalled by the introduction of the intermediate text type 'religious history'. Also, medium can play a minor role in intraspeaker variation (see above), its influence being smaller than that of variation due to audience. As Capgrave's works were written roughly within two decades, chronological difference may not have any considerable influence on usage frequencies either. Table 2 shows the possible factors behind the examined intraspeaker variation, which are cross-tabulated against the word order differences in Capgrave's works.

Table 2. Possible factors behind intraspeaker variation as evidenced in John Capgrave

texts	translation	medium	chronological difference	text type	scribal interference	audience
Sermon – Chronicle	+	–	–	+	–	+
Sermon – Augustine	–	+	–	+	–	+
Sermon – Gilbert	+	+	–	+	–	+
Chronicle – Augustine	+*	–	–	+	–	+
Augustine – Gilbert	no difference in variational character					
Chronicle – Gilbert	–	–	–	+	–	+

*The issue that *Augustine* is a translation is still a moot point (cf. note 6 and Munro 2001:viif.).

The works with different variational character are contrasted pairwise in each line, whereas the columns show which factors may play a role in the different variational character of the two texts in question. It can be seen that text type and audience perform equally well in explaining the intraspeaker variation in Capgrave, an aspect which is examined briefly in the following section.[6]

---

[6] Unfortunately, in Capgrave there are no texts that differ in one variable only. If we do not opt for their intermediate text type status and categorise *Gilbert* and

3. Texts and text types as projections of audiences?

The fact that text type and audience can both explain the different variational character may in fact shed light on the connection between these two factors. Even if text types seem to explain intraspeaker variation equally well, the effects of the text types themselves can be argued to be ultimately due to linguistic accommodation to the audience. This idea is supported by the observation that different text types target different audiences. Texts written for one particular audience type can be claimed to represent text type conventions which have canonised styles and language. Thus when a new text is produced, it needs to be accepted into the relevant convention as the aim of the writer is to succeed in making his point understood by his audience. This audience is regarded by the author as the default audience of the text. As such, the linguistic behaviour of this audience need not be directly observed by the writer: as is typical of indirect communication, it is sufficient if the author has some mental representation of the linguistic behaviour of the audience (see section 1). Therefore when he conforms to the text type convention, he at the same time conforms to the linguistic convention of the given text type, which in turn is determined by the audience represented in a projected way in his mind. At first sight this influence of the target audience may seem rather indirect. However, the adjustment process can also be interpreted in a more direct way: ultimately, text types can equal audiences. Accordingly, the linguistic characteristics of the text type can be actually the linguistic characteristics of the audience associated with the text type. As a further dimension to this generic association one can add a specific one, according to which individual texts

---

Augustine as East Midlands religious prose and regard the *Sermon* as East Midlands rather than East Anglian, these three works may be claimed to differ in the audience variable only. Consequently, the innovative nature of the two saints' lives can be more straightforwardly linked to the presence of adjustment to female audiences. Regarding interference from translation as a variable does not invalidate the above claim as there is no significant difference in the word order character of the allegedly non-translated *Augustine* and the translated *Gilbert* (Munro 2001:vii f.; see also note to Table 2).

themselves can equal audiences. Accordingly, the linguistic characteristics of individual texts can be in fact the linguistic characteristics of the audiences associated with those texts. In the strict sense, this view renders both entire text types and individual texts no more than projections of the audience. The hierarchical implications shown in (7) are consistent with this tentative claim.

4. Conclusion

Intraspeaker syntactic variation in Late Middle English may have been characterised by interspeaker accommodation in the form of adjustment to various audiences. The analysis of John Capgrave's word order syntax has provided two major insights. First, accommodation to socially defined target audiences can be argued to be one of the strongest factors to influence intraspeaker variation, whereas text type influence can be claimed to be derivable from audience effects. This complies with a reinterpreted and slightly modified version of Bell's Style Axiom, according to which the scope of social variation exceeds that of register variation according to the audience, while the scope of the latter exceeds that of text type variation. Second, the present findings indicate intraspeaker competition between a local and a delocalised word order syntax type. This is entirely compatible with the observation of McIntosh *et al.* (1986:1.47), according to which co-existence of two distinct types of written language was possible within a single LME community. The findings for word order syntax may prove even more convincing if we add that according to McIntosh *et al.*, such dichotomy is especially visible in Norfolk (Capgrave's home county), where the language of writings for local use differed markedly from the language of texts intended for a wider public.

References

Auer, Peter and Frans Hinskens. 2005. "The role of interpersonal accommodation in a theory of language change". In: Auer, Peter, Frans Hinskens and Paul Kerswill (eds.). *Dialect change: the convergence and divergence of dialects in contemporary societies*. Cambridge: CUP: 335-357.

Bækken, Bjørg. 2002. "Word order in different text types in Early Modern English". *Studia Neophilologica* 74: 15-29.
Bell, Allan. 1984. "Language style as audience design". *Language in Society* 13: 145-204.
Bell, Allan. 2001. "Back in style: reworking audience design". In: Eckert, Penelope and John R. Rickford (eds.). *Style and sociolinguistic variation.* Cambridge: CUP: 139-169.
Clark, Robin and Ian Roberts. 1993. "A computational model of language learning and language change". *Linguistic Inquiry* 24: 83-149.
Eitler, Tamás. 2005. "Some dialectal, sociolectal and communicative aspects of word order variation and change in Late Middle English". In: Fortescue, Michael, Eva Skafte Jensen, Jens Erik Mogensen and Lene Schøsler (eds.). *Selected papers from the 16th International Conference on Historical Linguistics, Copenhagen, 11–15 August 2003.* Amsterdam: Benjamins: 87-101.
Eitler, Tamás. 2006. "Some sociolectal, dialectal and communicative aspects of word order variation and change in Late Middle English". Unpublished Ph.D. dissertation. Budapest: ELTE SEAS.
Giles, Howard and Nikolas Coupland. 1991. *Language: contexts and consequences.* Milton Keynes: Open University Press.
Giles, Howard, Nikolas Coupland and Justine Coupland. 1991. "Accommodation theory: communication, context, and consequence". In: Giles, Howard, Justine Coupland and Nikolas Coupland (eds.). *Contexts of accommodation: developments in applied sociolinguistics.* Cambridge: CUP: 1-68.
Haeberli, Eric. 2002. "Observations on the loss of verb second in the history of English". In: Zwart, Cornelius Jan-Wouter and Werner Abraham (eds.). *Studies in comparative Germanic syntax.* Amsterdam: Benjamins: 245-272.
Kerswill, Paul. 2002. "Koineization and accommodation". In: Chambers, Jack K., Peter Trudgill and Natalie Schilling-Estes (eds.). *The handbook of language variation and change.* Oxford: Blackwell: 669-702.
Labov, William. 1990. "The intersection of sex and social class in the course of linguistic change". *Language Variation and Change* 2: 205-254.
Labov, William. 2001. *Principles of linguistic change. Volume 2: Social factors.* Oxford: Blackwell.
Lucas, Peter J. (ed.). 1983. *John Capgrave's Abbreuiacion of Cronicles. (= Early English Text Society, Original Series 285).* Oxford: OUP.
McIntosh, Angus, Michael L. Samuels and Michael Benskin. 1986. *A linguistic atlas of Late Mediaeval English. Vol. 1.* Aberdeen: Aberdeen University Press.
Munro, John (ed.). 2001. *John Capgrave's Lives of St Augustine and St Gilbert of Sempringham, and a Sermon. (= Early English Text Society, Original Series 140).* Oxford: OUP.
Nevalainen, Terttu. 1996. "Gender difference". In: Nevalainen, Terttu and Helena Raumolin-Brunberg (eds.). *Sociolinguistics and language history: studies based on the Corpus of Early English Correspondence.* Amsterdam: Rodopi: 77-91.

Nevalainen, Terttu and Helena Raumolin-Brunberg. 2003. *Historical sociolinguistics: language change in Tudor and Stuart England*. London: Longman.
Trudgill, Peter. 1986. *Dialects in contact*. Oxford: Blackwell.

Index

A

Ablaut 1, 12-4
accommodation 221-35 *passim*
 - identity-projection model 222-4
agent noun 169, 174-6, 179-181, 184
 - construction 174-6, 179, 184
alternative suffixes 83
American English 47, 59
analogy 1, 7, 13
Anglo-French 66
Anglo-Norman Dictionary 65-7, 73
article, indefinite 37-40, 50, 52, 54, 55, 57
articulatory effort, economy 49
aspect 167, 172-4, 176, 177, 182-4
audience 221-235 *passim*
 - design 222, 224, 234
 - female a. 230-2

B

bifurcation 190, 197, 199
 - saddle-node b. 196, 197, 200
borrowing 211, 213, 216
British English 47, 51, 58, 59

C

Capgrave, John 221, 226-31, 233, 234
code-switching 203-20 *passim*
Communication Accommodation Theory 222
consonant cluster 38, 48
consonantal onsets 37-9
consonantal strength 42, 51, 56
consonanthood 56, 57
contact situation 181, 182
contextual predictability 48
coreference 152
CP-V2 (syntax) 226-30
cue 190-4, 199, 200
cue-based learner 190

D

Danish, Modern 144
demonstrative determiners 1
derivational gap 84, 85, 89, 91
deverbal classes 82, 96, 98
deverbatives 77, 78, 82, 88-90, 102
diachronic onomasiology 77, 82, 84, 100
dialectal differences 41
differential equation 194, 195, 200, 201
distal 1-2, 5-8, 13
-*dōm* 105-23
 - deadjectival derivatives 112, 113, 119

- denominal derivatives 111, 112, 118, 119
- de-pronominal derivatives 113
- deverbal derivatives 113, 119
- semantics of 110-3, 116-20
- status as a suffix 108-10, 114

Domesday Book 20, 21, 23-5, 30-2

dynamical system 190, 192, 194, 195, 199, 200, 201

E

/εu/ 52-5, 57
/eu/ 48, 52, 55
emotional emphasis 41
English Prose Drama 39, 58
expanded form 172, 173, 175-8, 181, 183, 186

F

Fiction
- *Early English Prose* 39, 57
- *Eighteenth-Century* 39, 57
- *Nineteenth-Century* 39, 58

fixed point(s) 194, 195, 197
Frankish 44
Französisches etymologisches Wörterbuch 65, 74
French 65-70, 205, 206, 208, 219
- Old French 44, 49
- Anglo-French 66

frequency 38, 48, 55-7
functional selection 2

G

German 64, 70-2
Germanic 38, 42, 45, 57
- languages 64, 70, 71
- (proto-) 125-45

glide formation 51
grammaticalisation 157-9, 161-4, 165-87 *passim*
Great Vowel Shift 30, 33
Greenberg, Joseph 126-8, 130, 132, 135, 140, 145
Grimm, Jacob 125, 145

H

/h/ 38, 40, 41, 43, 44, 47-51, 54-9
- initial, 'mute' 46, 57
- initial, pronounced 44, 46-8, 51
- unetymological /h/ 40

/hj/ 38, 48-51
Historical Thesaurus of Verbs and Deverbatives 89
hybrids 119

I

/iu/ 48, 49, 51, 52, 54, 55, 57
identity emphatic 161
intensifier 148, 155, 160-4

L

Late West Saxon 24, 25
Latin 52, 59, 204-6, 208, 214, 216-8

- Classical 44, 140
  - Late 41, 44
  - Medieval 44
learner
  - cue-based 190
  - memoryless 190, 198, 199
lengthening,
  - compensatory 19
  - homorganic 19, 26
  - ME open syllable 19
lexical diffusion 47
loans, loanwords
  - French 37, 52
  - Old French 19, 44, 49
  - Romance 38, 43, 44, 47, 49, 55, 57
locative construction 181
Luick, Karl 20, 25, 33

M

memoryless learner 190, 198, 199
merger
  - 'near' 54
  - phonemic 54
multilingual 203, 204, 208, 213, 217-9, 220
multilingualism 217, 219, 220

N

numeral 125-45
  - (cardinal) 125-45

O

Old French 44, 49
Old Norse 44, 142-4
onomatopoeia 9
OOZE 63, 64
OPPOSE 67-9
OPPOSITION 68
origin of grammar 166, 167

P

phase portrait 194-7, 199
place-names 19, 20, 30-5
phonaesthesia 1, 9-12, 14
phonemic shift 19
phonemic merger 54
phonological integrity 55
phonological change 180
possession 147, 149-52, 157, 159, 161, 162, 164
prescriptive norms 47
principle of divergence 169
production-perception asymmetry 54
productivity 105, 106, 120-4
progressive 165, 172, 174-8, 183, 184, 186, 187
prothetic
  - /j/ 39
  - /w/ 39
(proto-)Germanic 125-45
proximal 1, 2, 5-8, 13

R

reanalysis 166, 170, 171, 174, 175, 179, 183-5
resyllabify 38, 55

S

settlement patterns 5
similarity
  - degrees of 92, 94, 96
  - temporal expansion 93, 97-101
similarity matrix 85
social stigma 41
sound change(s) 37-9, 55, 57, 59
stress reduction 20
stress 37, 41, 49, 51
  - reduced 20, 21, 23
string
  - of synonyms 79
  - of deverbatives 82, 88, 90
  - derivationally related s. 85
structuralism 167
Svenska Akademiens ordbok 64
syllable structure 38, 55, 59
syntax
  - CP-V2 226-30
  - V2 221, 226-9
  - V3 221, 225-30

T

temporal expansion
  similarity 93, 97-101
text type 222, 224-8, 230-4

textual parameters 204, 208, 212, 217
'tremulous hand' (Worcester) 25, 32
Trésor de la langue française 65

U

unidirectionality 168-70, 184, 185, 187

V

V2 (syntax) 221, 226-9
V3 (syntax) 221, 225-30
verbs and deverbatives 77, 78, 89, 90, 102
vernacular 228-30

W

word-formation 105-23

Y

/y/ 49, 52, 55

Studies in English Medieval Language and Literature

Edited by Jacek Fisiak

Vol. 1 Dieter Kastovsky / Arthur Mettinger (eds.): Language Contact in the History of English. 2nd, revised edition. 2003.

Vol. 2 Studies in English Historical Linguistics and Philology. A Festschrift for Akio Oizumi. Edited by Jacek Fisiak. 2002.

Vol. 3 Liliana Sikorska: *In a Manner Morall Playe*: Social Ideologies in English Moralities and Interludes (1350-1517). 2002.

Vol. 4 Peter J. Lucas / Angela M. Lucas (eds.): Middle English from Tongue to Text. Selected Papers from the Third International Conference on Middle English: Language and Text, held at Dublin, Ireland, 1-4 July 1999. 2002.

Vol. 5 Chaucer and the Challenges of Medievalism. Studies in Honor of H. A. Kelly. Edited by Donka Minkova and Theresa Tinkle. 2003.

Vol. 6 Hanna Rutkowska: Graphemics and Morphosyntax in the *Cely Letters* (1472-88). 2003.

Vol. 7 The *Ancrene Wisse*. A Four-Manuscript Parallel Text. Preface and Parts 1-4. Edited by Tadao Kubouchi and Keiko Ikegami with John Scahill, Shoko Ono, Harumi Tanabe, Yoshiko Ota, Ayako Kobayashi and Koichi Nakamura. 2003.

Vol. 8 Joanna Bugaj: Middle Scots Inflectional System in the South-west of Scotland. 2004.

Vol. 9 Rafal Boryslawski: The Old English Riddles and the Riddlic Elements of Old English Poetry. 2004.

Vol. 10 Nikolaus Ritt / Herbert Schendl (eds.): Rethinking Middle English. Linguistic and Literary Approaches. 2005.

Vol. 11 The *Ancrene Wisse*. A Four-Manuscript Parallel Text. Parts 5–8 with Wordlists. Edited by Tadao Kubouchi and Keiko Ikegami with John Scahill, Shoko Ono, Harumi Tanabe, Yoshiko Ota, Ayako Kobayashi, Koichi Nakamura. 2005.

Vol. 12 Text and Language in Medieval English Prose. A Festschrift for Tadao Kubouchi. Edited by Akio Oizumi, Jacek Fisiak and John Scahill. 2005.

Vol. 13 Michiko Ogura (ed.): Textual and Contextual Studies in Medieval English. Towards the Reunion of Linguistics and Philology. 2006.

Vol. 14 Keiko Hamaguchi: Non-European Women in Chaucer. A Postcolonial Study. 2006.

Vol. 15 Ursula Schaefer (ed.): The Beginnings of Standardization. Language and Culture in Fourteenth-Century England. 2006.

Vol. 16 Nikolaus Ritt / Herbert Schendl / Christiane Dalton-Puffer / Dieter Kastovsky (eds): Medieval English and its Heritage. Structure, Meaning and Mechanisms of Change. 2006.

www.peterlang.de

Nikolaus Ritt / Herbert Schendl (eds.)

Rethinking Middle English

Linguistic and Literary Approaches

Frankfurt am Main, Berlin, Bern, Bruxelles, New York, Oxford, Wien, 2005.
XI, 339 pp., num. tab. and graf.
Studies in English Medieval Language and Literature.
Edited by Jacek Fisiak. Vol. 10
ISBN 3-631-52032-8 / US-ISBN 0-8204-6550-X · pb. € 56.50*

This volume presents Middle English studies as a modern discipline which unites linguistics, literature, philology, the history of ideas, textual studies including recent developments in the study of text types and genres, as well as the sociohistorical perspective. This large variety of both traditional and new approaches is mirrored in the four main parts of the book, starting with texts and text types, and moving on to vocabulary, syntax and morphology, and finally phonology and orthography. Aspects of language contact as well as corpus linguistic studies are also addressed in a number of contributions. Authors are leading experts in their fields, and come from the United States, South Africa, and all parts of Europe.

Contents: Text types, texts, and text explication · Words: meaning, use, and context · Syntax and morphology · Phonology and orthography

Frankfurt am Main · Berlin · Bern · Bruxelles · New York · Oxford · Wien
Distribution: Verlag Peter Lang AG
Moosstr. 1, CH-2542 Pieterlen
Telefax 00 41 (0) 32 / 376 17 27

*The €-price includes German tax rate
Prices are subject to change without notice
Homepage http://www.peterlang.de